THE AGE OF PERICLES

County Council

D1785225

Libraries, books and more . . .

2 6 MAY 2011		

Please return/renew this item by the last due date.
Library items may be renewed by phone on
030 33 33 1234 (24 hours) or via our website
www.cumbria.gov.uk/libraries

Cumbria Libraries
CLIC
Interactive Catalogue

Ask for a CLIC password

1875

TO

The Society of Dilettanti

(ANN. SOC. CENT. QUAD. SEC.)

AND

TO THEIR TREASURER AND SECRETARY

THE RIGHT HON. SIR EDWARD RYAN

THIS HISTORY

OF THE MOST FLOURISHING PERIOD OF

THE ARTS OF GREECE

IS INSCRIBED

(IN THE TWENTY-FIRST YEAR OF HIS OWN MEMBERSHIP)

BY

WILLIAM WATKISS LLOYD

PREFACE.

THE story of the period that intervened between the Persian and the Peloponnesian wars had been so far neglected when Thucydides commenced his history of the latter, as to elicit an observation that the records of its incidents and the determination of their sequence were alike incomplete. He supplied in consequence a connecting summary, the section known to the ancients as the Pentecontaeteris or Pentecontaëtia, from the number of years embraced, such as appeared sufficient for his own purpose; compared however with our present rational requirements, it is, as might be expected, jejune and unsatisfactory. The history of the arts, which is for us one of the main interests of the period, escapes his notice entirely; and yet at this particular time a work of art was apt to have the significance of a political incident, as its purport and vicissitudes had no unfrequent bearing on political feeling. The life of the people during this happier and more tranquil period, was as much engrossed by poetry and the arts as by politics; of the two interests, at present so distinct, each is found among Greeks reacting on the other, and it is often difficult to determine which is predominant. Notices dispersed and incidental doubtless, are fortunately recoverable from other sources, that go some way to supply what did not fall within the plan of the historian; it is in the belief that these have not hitherto had full justice done to them as illustrations of the progressive Hellenic story, that

b 2

attention is invited to yet another English presentation of the history of Hellas.

Again, as even Thucydides somewhat deviates in his summary, brief as it is, from his declared intention to adhere to chronological sequence, the moderns have for the most part carried the deviation further, and declining to deal with what hints of order of time are salient, to say nothing of others that if obscure are discoverable and are ever the more valuable as more scanty, have been content to supplement political narrative a little at random by chapters that group and classify rather than arrange historically the characteristics of the age.

My own endeavours have been directed to make the most, but ever under control of sober consideration, of every help available to determine the order of incidents, and to disentangle confusion that was indifferent to biographers intent exclusively on the illustration of character, to compilers who were more concerned to be comprehensive than critical, to theorists who cared more for general philosophy than its particular development, to say nothing of writers only on the look-out for opportunities to be smart in the first place and in the next picturesque. That the very varied evidence that comes under consideration renders necessary an occasional and even a frequent shifting of point of view, is an inconvenience which must be accepted if we would survey with an approach to comprehensiveness the contrasted yet ever importantly connected movements of human activity, as they proceed contemporaneously over a very extended field; nor is it amiss that the student should be thrown upon some experience which will only be irksome at first, in combining contrasted observations; only so indeed may we acquire the instructive apprehension of the life Hellenic, in all the multifariousness of interests that was consistent with its unrivalled concentration of power.

Into every history and all history conjecture enters of

necessity very largely indeed, and even when testimonies and materials are most abundant, the writer who deals with them has a sufficient burden of responsibility; an attempt to evade it will only condemn him to overload his pages with discussions and rejoinders, to conclude nothing and vex his readers by leaving them the very work—happy if not further confused—which they justly look to him to set well in advance. Even this, however, is perhaps more tolerable than the tyranny of a quiet dogmatism, which silently tightens every knot while assuming to untie it, or the facile scepticism that cuts all indiscriminately and destroys the web at once, by disallowing the 'historical character' of every incident of which the record can by any possibility, however remote, involve an element of error.

It would be strange indeed if the materials of ancient history could be relied on more positively than has been justified in such cases as the Waterloo campaign and the diplomatic and military incidents of the Crimean war; and an admission of not mere liability to error, but of general uncertainty in history, must be taken once for all as standing in lieu of constantly intercalated hesitations. The utmost positiveness of the writer's expressions will then be understood to mark in any case only his appreciation of highest probability, and any less positive tones must be estimated relatively to this primary intimation. If appropriate graduations of conviction have been marked as recognisably as it is hoped, the writer may claim to be credited conditionally with having regulated them with reference to comparisons and enquiries which he often spares to set down in tedious detail,—whether or not he is so happy as to gain confidence further for a portion of that sagacity which it should be the great aim of one who is bound to estimate human motives, faculties and dispositions, to acquire.

Here, as elsewhere, the reader is entitled to full liberty of judgment; to the same that he is driven upon perforce when he has to arbitrate betweeen the representations of Cromwell by Carlyle and by Pope, not to say Hutchinson and Ludlow; of Henry VIII, as reported by Froude, or by Cavendish and Shakespeare; of the character and designs of Julius Caesar, as seen by Cicero, or as conceived by Mommsen; the utmost the author can claim of him is that in questioning a decision he will not be too hastily credulous of his own.

To return to Thucydides: the same liability that he knew and repudiated of a history of the past to be written with less consideration for either past or future than for a bearing on present politics, has been and is a besetting liability of Greek history still; in a certain qualified sense the liability must be admitted, for it cannot be escaped from. Some of the strongest light that falls on ancient history, is ever reflected for us from modern contemporary politics, and modern eyes are of necessity attracted to these most highly illuminated spots. It is however the opprobrium of the historian if he regards such accidental lights alone, and worse if he is so misled as to accept as realities the colours which may be thrown by them, but are only due to the passions and the prejudices of the day.

CONTENTS.

CHAPTER III.

Mardonius in Bœotia and Attica.—Spirit and temper of Athenians and Spartans.

B.C. 479, Spring; Ol. 75. 1, 2.

CHAPTER IV.

The patriotic army in Bœotia.—The death of Masistius.—Persian preparations for final conquest.

B.C. 479, September; Ol. 75. 2.

CHAPTER V (VI).

The decisive battle of Plataea.—The death of Mardonius.

B.C. 479, September; Ol. 75. 2.

CHAPTER VII.

The spoils of Plataea.—The glory of Pausanias.

B.C. 479, Autumn; Ol. 75. 2.

THE AGE OF PERICLES.

B. C. 480–461.

INTRODUCTORY.

THE subject-matter of the ensuing history is comprised in the fifty years that intervene between the repulse of the invasion of Greece by Xerxes and the outbreak of the Peloponnesian War — the interval therefore between the closing events of the history of Herodotus and the opening of that of Thucydides. A certain overlap is admitted at either end for the sake of more distinctly marking the connection with the two great continuous histories.

The political events that occupied these years, though anything but unimportant, were yet, even in antiquity, not made the subject of any special narrative, the more momentous struggles and wars of the adjacent periods withdrawing attention from them. The quarrels that occurred within this period and led to open conflicts were, though all under a main drifting influence, short and disconnected; and it may therefore be considered as, on the whole, an oasis of peace in the midst of surrounding devastation and disorder.

But it was within this period that all the germs were deposited which sprang into such rank vitality afterwards. The predominance of Athens was then advancing to consolidation, and already giving signs of that vigour which was to be shown in conflict with the animosities and discontents among which it was growing up, and the growth of which, however latent, was an historical event as important as their manifestation in virulent activity, or even more so.

The most salient manifestation of human activity however within that period was the marvellous attainment to unrivalled perfection of the most refined arts and culture of civilised life,—the acme of the plastic, poetic, and generally intellectual arts, and the securing of the conditions of continued progress to the abstract sciences and speculative philosophy.

A material exponent of this full bloom of the best faculties of man is the single building of the temple of Athene— the Parthenon; the description of this and all its adjuncts, together with the actual remains, attest that sculpture and architecture then reached a perfection that has never been rivalled since, even singly, not to say conjointly, in respect of touching the utmost point of which either is susceptible. The consent of antiquity adjudged the palm to Pheidias above all other sculptors, and sufficient fragments of his works are preserved to happily attest the truth and value of such an assignment. If all evidence of the characteristics of the age were lost but these memorials, they would be sufficient to indicate a pitch of civilised refinement that has never since been surpassed; which may have been more or less partial and exclusive, but which to have been reached at all, especially in the midst of a democracy, is sufficient to preclude despair for the capabilities and progressive hopes of humanity.

And, as if grouped around this central symbol, we have no insufficient portraitures of the statesmen who prepared for and perfected such achievements—of Aristides, Themistocles, Ephialtes, Cimon, Pericles; we have lively delineations of the Athenians themselves—the demus—so highly and energetically endowed, whatever the defects, the miserable follies, the shameful faults with which the entire people, as if representative of the character of so many an individual man of genius, was at the same time chargeable.

We have then, preserved most happily, a body of literature —invaluable, however relatively small a salvage from a wreck of incomparable abundance—which gives us the still living words that rung in the ears of those generations, to amuse or to elevate, for encouragement or rebuke. Eupolis and Cratinus are lost, but Aristophanes remains to tell us, and to exemplify to us also, the best and the worst of the times. The last echoes of lyric poetry, dying out in the remoter odes of Pindar, are renewed in the choruses of the theatre; and, while other inferior dramatists still live only in renown, though not inconsiderable renown, the great triad of tragic dramatists—Aeschylus, Sophocles, and Euri-pides—are not unworthily, however scantily, represented in their extant tragedies.

To Athens in this age, as to a centre, was attracted all that profound reflection had been maturing throughout Hellas, and her claim to be the host of the best foreign wits was approved by her constant production among her own citizens of the crowning intelligence. The crude, inaccurate, or sophisticated speculations of Ionia and Italy found their correction here; and already the genius of Socrates was abroad, which was to mould for all time the acutest and noblest exercise of human thought.

The rapidity with which human faculties at this period pushed forward into bloom is as remarkable as the perfection which they attained. Accordingly, as is usual in such cases, the characteristics of the anterior time are by no means utterly obliterated in the new. We must accustom ourselves to regard the sculptures of Aegina and of the Parthenon as possibly contemporary works—even as Perugino not merely preceded and taught but survived Rafael—for the contrast is scarcely so great as between the almost childlike playfulness and devoutness of Herodotus, and the tone of his contemporary,

the sedate and statesmanlike Thucydides. Herodotus is in
many respects more near to the people than Thucydides, in
his fondness for the picturesque, which disinclines him to
reject a fabulous story too expressive of his purpose to be
put very strictly to the test, and in his willingness to wander
somewhat far afield to obtain it; but he is at the same
time distinguished by a larger and more general geographical and chronological scope, and seems to belong to a
period when Greece was still only in course of assuming its
absolute and separate individuality. His history collects the
scattered rays of historic interest which, when it concludes,
are for a period to be restricted within Hellenic limits, and
ultimately brought to a focus at Athens.

If we are to understand the period which we are about to
consider in detail, we must first take a somewhat wider
preliminary survey. This could only be done with completeness by the aid of histories equally detailed for the antecedent
periods; but it may, as indeed it must, suffice here to give
an introductory sketch of the more remotely anterior incidents,—so far as these will not offer themselves more readily
for recapitulation afterwards,—and those from which our
narrative actually starts.

Even more necessary is it to adduce some notice of the
previous developments of Greek genius, as demonstrating the
native endowments of the race; of what had been already
achieved and long in familiar possession, and of what early
promise the achievements of this period were the maturity.
Surprising and brilliant as our period is, it is but one in
succession to several others in many respects still more
surprising; and conspicuous as Athens now appears, the city
does but come forward as continuing a line of glories to which
she had heretofore scarcely contributed, and during the course
of which she was lost in a crowd, or all but nameless.

The Homeric epos—the Iliad and Odyssey conjoined—
stands at the very commencement of Greek monumental

records, and is not only the greatest of all Greek, but, it must be said, the greatest of all works of art whatever. There are two questions of date concerned with it, and both lie far back in indefinite centuries, beyond the commencement of even plausible history. The question of the date of the poetry is one, and that of the time when the state of Greece most nearly corresponded to the general aspect given by the poems, is another. That such a general correspondence did once exist, and even in respect of confederacies more or less comprehensive warring against the north-eastern districts of Asia Minor, I do not doubt, though I cannot pause to argue it at length; that the poem was reduced to the form in which we now have it by the genius of one man—a single Homer being conceivable, but scarcely a multitude—I doubt as little; but the question remains still as to what stores of scattered materials, more or less extensive, may not have been prepared to his hand; nay, whether the latest poet may not have been under the same obligations, or something like them, that Berni or Dryden owed to Boiardo or Chaucer, or that Goethe owed to the epic fable of the middle ages.

As the work has been so happily handed down to us, it is unrivalled in expressiveness of language and rhythm, and in beauty of versification; a perfect model of construction; unsurpassed in natural description by sea and land; while in personal portraiture, in variety and distinctness of characterisation, in the definition of sentiment and all the shades and colours of moral good and evil, Homer may have a rival in Shakespear, but in Shakespear alone. In this poem we have all the conditions anticipated in epithet or description, of the perfection of plastic and imaginative art; and finally, a mastery of the problem of raising all natural incidents and characteristic human endowments to a height of more than experienced idealisation, without ever withdrawing the action from our closest and liveliest sympathies.

The mere language by which all this is preserved has itself the characteristics of a work of consummate art. For anything that has yet been discovered, we may consider the proximate roots of the Greek of Homer to be as near the origin of language as any others, though doubtless still very remote. If we were to give in to the exclusive influence arrogated to so-called phonetic corruption and decay in changing and modelling language as applicable to ancient Greek, we should indeed forfeit the most valuable lesson of etymology. Originally the urgent need of language was to express—to express feeling as well as thought—and it is for expression that it is ever struggling. Between the varieties due to the eagerness of those muscular sensations which are incident to the production of sounds, and the visible facial movements by which they are accompanied, and with which they are connected in the mind of the listener, there is large opportunity for indirect intimation, and direct mimesis by sound, of physical accidents, changes, and actions. Man possesses organs formed as specifically for speech, as others are for grasping or locomotion, and there is no mystery in the multiplication and appropriation of these signs for the sake of convenience; while analogy and metaphor insensibly transfer these material signs to mental and moral experiences; thus, in time, 'understanding' is applied to 'intellect' as readily as to the leg of a chair; 'sweet' becomes a common epithet for a ripe fruit, a feminine smile, and the disposition which inspires the smile. No doubt dialectic change is influenced by special powers of producing certain combinations of sound, but phonetic change can only be properly called corruption or decay when it clings to the positively disagreeable, or destroys expressiveness. Even with the most uncultured, the struggle to express governs the direction and degree of change; and such forms as 'squirrel' or 'queer' are no casual results of mere disintegration, but, like 'thunder' and other words of the same nature, have

been gradually modified and fixed at last in virtue of this
constant aim and influence; poetry would have expired
long ago if language had not chiefly grown out of and
by mimetic expressiveness. The degree of elegance with
which this expressiveness is finally attained is the measure
of the natural refinement and taste of the people among
whom it has grown up. The same influence may be traced
in the rejection of various forms for the sake of avoiding
discords in combinations of frequent recurrence, or in coarse
and careless disregard of them. Extrusion of clumsiness,
that is, the rejection of unnecessary syllables and cumbrous
combinations, is above all, and in the first place, characteristic
of the Greek language. Beyond this, what grace, elegance,
and euphony were attained, as the language proceeded, not
through corruption and decay, but through healthy and
vigorous growth, must be studied in other pages; but it
is important to bear the fact in mind here.

With regard to the political condition of Greece as exhibited
in the poems, its relations to grand exterior empires is much
the same as we find it at the dawn of history. It is in
contact occasionally, and no more, with Phoenicia, Egypt,
and northern tribes; enough so to make the transfer of arts
and the course of mercantile exchange familiar probabilities,
but not to induce important hostile collisions. Within the
limits of European Greece, the divisions of states are almost
identical with the lines of boundaries during the war with
Xerxes,—lines determined by the physical character of the
mountain-traversed land, and further by the susceptibility of
the people for tribal influences and attachment to distinct
local centres. Still there is the same sense of unity of race,
and sympathy in language, customs, maxims, religion, among
these independent communities, as in later times; and they
are exhibited, also, as having a capacity for joint action
under one predominant state, just as when they adhered · to
the hegemony, or leadership of Sparta or Athens; and the

great moral of the whole is, that if ever Greece was to be
ruined, it would be by her incapacity to take to heart and
profit by the poet's lesson of necessity for concord in confederation as a condition of national safety.

But there are two great differences between the Greece of
Homer and that of the opening of regular and authentic
history. The Homeric states are not in a single instance
republican, whatever the indications of a vigorous public
opinion which has to be managed, cajoled, or even sometimes cowed; they are all under the sway of kings, and
kings who claim by divine right, and indeed, for the most
part, by divine descent, a title which dates beyond the memory
of man. The germ of the later development is there—especially of that republican condition which admitted the predominant influence of the Eupatrid—but at present it gives
only feeble and occasional signs of vitality.

Another great distinction is that the leading tribe which
now gives general title to the nation is Achaian, whereas,
when history opens in full light, Achaian has sunk or receded
into the title of a very secondary district, or even into a third
rank; the nation at large calls itself Hellenic, and its leading
subdivisions, comprising groups of states not especially associated in Homeric times, are Aeolians, Ionians, and Dorians.
Dorian Sparta is now the most powerful, and asserts somewhat of the comprehensive control of the regal Agamemnon,
though in every respect the most distinct and abnormal in
habits and institutions, and in rudest contrast to the luxurious home of Menelaus and Helen. The identity of the
race at large, however, is certified not less by language
than by the continuance of all earlier characteristics; energy
by land and sea; admiration of beauty in all things, especially in what is susceptible of most beauty, the human
form and character; enthusiasm for lofty ideals, however
often unrealised in practice; the love of poetry, of art, of
athletic exercises; the assertion of free action and free

speech; a sense of the dignity and power of the race, especially as contrasted with the enervated or slavish tribes to the east of the Aegean.

The social contrast, therefore, is as great as between the sculpture of the gate of Mycenae and that of the Aeginetan pediments; as great, and as certainly marking an intermediate period of active revolutions, with movements and collisions of tribes and populations.

And if such changes took place after the Homeric epoch, surely we are entitled to ask, whether the like, and even yet more violent, did not probably take place before? The poetry, for good poetic reasons, makes no mention of any forcible origin of the Achaian power in Southern Greece; but traditions, the more trustworthy because independent of each other, told how the Achaians had descended from Thessaly and original seats at Phthiotis which continued to retain the name of Achaia. Thus is explained how it was that the chief hero of the Achaian epic is Achilles, who belongs to these original seats, and not the more powerful Agamemnon of the later seats, and who, moreover, was traditionally of foreign lineage.

Tradition, borne out again by corroborations which it is idle to extenuate, told further how, after the period of Achaian domination in Southern Greece, and the collision with Asia in the Troad, a great movement of tribes was urged southward upon Peloponnesus, which displaced or subdued the former occupants, and gradually established the system of tribal distribution as represented in history. A significant threat in the Iliad, of the subversion of Mycenae, Argos, and Sparta, has been fairly held to intimate that the poet lived after, or during the course of, these revolutions; the conjecture may be confirmed by a similar hint to a future reign of descendants of Aeneas in the Troad.

It must have been in the course and as a consequence of these convulsions—whose evidence is absolute, however ob-

scure their dates and details—that the distinction of Dorians
and Ionians took definite form. Of this more must be said
hereafter; at present we have to note that it constitutes
a main feature in a further contrast between this later
epoch and the earlier Homeric.

The epos exhibits the coast of Asia Minor as uncolonised
by Greeks, except for some occasional connection, as in Lycia;
but we now find it fringed with Greek cities, active, powerful, populous, and grouped in marked agreement with relationship. There is an Asiatic Aeolis, Ionia, and Doris.

The Aeolian cities—earliest and oldest—are settled about
the islands and districts that were the reputed seats of the
Achaian warfare of Homer. The poetic war is not waged
for territory, but for plunder; not for established settlement,
but in retaliation for something like piracy: but here nevertheless it must be observed, that the poet seems to carry back
to the earlier period of his subject the conditions of his own
time; the Achaians, from their mountainous peninsula, are
made to fight habitually in chariots, a mode of warfare only
suitable for the extensive plains of Lydia or about the coast;
and that women are among the most valued spoil, seems a
glaring transference from the later time, when, according
to other notices, the immigrants systematically arrived as
warriors alone, and trusted to their arms to gain the wives
with whom they commenced a new race in a new country.

Tradition, then, is borne out by manifest facts in establish-
ing that the Achaian domination was superseded by violent
changes in the seats of Greek tribes, due to the so-called
return of the Heracleid dynasty to assert ancestral claims in
Peloponnesus, and that thereafter ensued a long period of
active colonisation both east and west.

Particular chronology here must always be disputable; let
it be enough to state a conviction, founded on the tenacious
adherence of the Greeks to certain ceremonious forms in
founding colonies and their heroic estimate of the honour of

leading such enterprises, that there is no reason to set down all traditional names, and even dates, as 'unhistoric.' The return of the Heracleids was currently dated in a year 1066 B.C., precisely at the distance anterior to our epoch that the Norman Conquest, to which it is in many respects a parallel, occurred after it. Three centuries lie between it and 776 B.C., the epoch of the first Olympiad, when Coroebus was a victor; of whom, it is true, we know nothing else, in a period that is equally unknown. And yet the commencement of that reckoning was itself an important historical fact. It marks generally, and must mark, the attachment to celebrations which became so expressive of the sympathetic self-consciousness of the Hellenic race. The Olympic truce was an occasion of suspended enmities, of meetings in joyful amity; the olive crown, the coveted prize, was taken from the tree which can only arrive at profitable fruit-bearing through years exempt from devastation, and hence was the accepted symbol of peace, as it also provided the oil that gave vigour in noble games; and all comparisons point to this date as one from which the settlement of Hellas became recognised as permanent.

In these intervening centuries lay the plantation of the numerous colonies, which attained to such prosperity, that they themselves became mother-cities and planted colonies far and wide again, at cited dates posterior to 776 B.C., and probably in many instances authentic.

To the century 800–700 B.C. is referred, with every assurance of correctness, the origin of a vast mass of heroic poetry, the work of what were known as the Cyclic poets, which was extant through the classic ages. It was in the style of the Homeric epos, and some long poems were even ascribed very currently to the same poet. Others of the poems were attached to names of other poets; some were anonymous. Regarded as a whole, they gained their title of Cyclic from completing, when taken together, with more or less inter-

ference of subjects, a poetical account of all events from the
creation, or even before it, down to the death of Ulysses.
At this point mythological story closed, and the blank that
then intervenes before a more simply pragmatical story re-
commences with the return of the Heracleids, is strong
evidence of a new spirit having supervened·on national
thought at a period that followed this crowning revolution.
Mythology does not take its subject very near to the time of
the mythologist; History is shy of an immediate attachment
to a series of events with which its own are incongruous, and
a break is inevitable.

Dionysius of [1] Halicarnassus fixes the date of Arctinus, the
author of the Aethiopis, one of these poems, and the most
ancient poet, as he believed, of whose historical existence distinct trace could be recognised, as 775 B.C. But the general
period alone is of consequence, and it is limited and certified by the unquestionable fact that this poetry was the production of a period anterior to that of the Iambic poets, who
can be far more accurately dated.

Distinct authentic history, we have said, only begins two
centuries after the assigned date of Arctinus, with the usurpation of Peisistratus, or at most the legislation of Solon, 594 B.C.;
but the preceding century, which followed the age of the
Cyclic poetry, was most brilliant and fertile of Greek genius,
and bequeathed productions that were the admiration and
delight of the best ages of antiquity, and down to the very
establishment of Christianity.

The poems of this period, lyric, iambic, elegiac, melic,
were full of personal and passionate allusions, and re-
sponsive hints, that would certify at least their order of
succession. Archilochus of Paros dates as early as 708 B.C.
The consent of antiquity adjudged him a fame only second to
that of Homer; the earliest of the lyric poets, he is credited
with exhaustless fertility in invention of new metrical com-

[1] i. 68.

binations : this style of poetry, imbued with the passions of the moment, so different from the genius of epic poetry, had thus a definite historic as well as poetic value; it is not too much to say that the personality of Archilochus was as salient in his works as that of Horace or Ben Jonson ; and in various degrees the case was the same with all his successors—with Simonides of Amorgos, Tyrtaeus especially, Anacreon, Alcman, Arion, Alcaeus and Sappho, Erinna and Stesichorus, until Mimnermus, lastly, comes into direct relation with Solon.

The cultivation of music was pursued not less enthusiastically during this age, but here we are of necessity at greater disadvantage in forming a judgment, though we cannot hesitate to accept the ancient renown as well deserved, and do homage to the antecedents of the odes of Pindar and the choruses of the dramatic poets, both comic and tragic.

Thus it is that beyond the limits of the broad light of Herodotus a sort of historical twilight extends, and even as it settles into darkness we see reflected in the sky the splendours of works that unhappily have all but perished ; we gather faint echoes of music and song from a succession of singers as gifted as those who made the glory of the age of Pericles, and still more numerous in their succession. Pushed back certainly by this unbroken series to the very commencement of the Olympiads, was the age which had transmitted the vast mass of Cyclic poetry, afterwards to be subjected to the criticism of Aristotle, but only to be found wanting as compared with the unequalled art of the Homeric epos, descending from a still more remote and obscurer Beyond. Even in a summary so largely comprehensive we omit the important class of hymns both poetic and properly sacred, and the peculiar compositions of the Hesiodic cycle.

Such was the wealthy heritage of literary art and beauty

which Hellas had long enjoyed before the age of Peisistratus, barely a century before the birth of Herodotus, when at last the obscurity clears away from the historic field, and we can follow with confidence a series of connected events and the actions of identifiable characters. It is certain that the plastic arts and architecture had already made advances scarcely less important; technical processes had been mastered, the principle of constant and ever-renewed reference to nature had been combined with the aspiration to correct the individual model by 'an idea within the mind,' by study persevering and yet so sensitive that it caught exactly the moment to resign itself to the free guidance of imagination. It must remain doubtful whether any of the statuary of this period could hold its ground in comparison with the Pheidian period in the same sense in which works of Archilochus or Sappho took equal rank with Sophocles, but at least the preliminary conditions of the later development were mastered. The case was certainly the same in architecture; the vast temple of Samos, and the earlier Parthenon, had already decided all the leading members of the style, and the remains, archaic as they are, of the temple at Corinth, evince that the application of proportion to building, the counterpoint of architecture, had already become matter of theoretic study, of which the marvellous results were to be fully manifest later on.

Government also, in its best sense, as the systematic conciliation of Force and Order with individual freedom, had made corresponding advances, when all the accumulated preparations for human culture were threatened by Asiatic despotism. The age of divinely-descended and authorised kings had been succeeded, after years of compromise or convulsion, by constitutional order, oligarchical doubtless in most cases, but still tempered, destined to yield in its turn, however, to an age of Tyrants; but with the fall of the sons of Peisistratus at Athens the last traces of this latter period also had passed away. The vigorous constitution of Sparta had retained the form of royalty with much outward ceremony, but under severe control; and the dominant oligarchs had taken care to secure the power of their fellows throughout the length and breadth of Hellas, by suppressing all the tyrannies one after [1] another. The last of their achievements in this way was the expulsion from Athens of the son of Peisistratus, who took refuge in Persia, and there exerted himself, only too effectually, to bring the scourge of Oriental invasion upon his native land. Tyranny at Athens, however, was only superseded by another force scarcely less repugnant to Sparta. The spirit of democracy, native here, was inimical alike to oligarch and to tyrant; and with hands free, and aided by a remarkable manifestation of individual genius, it made the next great chapter of Hellenic story— a conflict of democracy with Oriental despotism in the first place, but with Hellenic, and especially Spartan, oligarchy immediately and constantly thereafter.

The same date marks the power of Peisistratus at Athens and the accession of the Median Cyrus; and the extraordinary development of Persian power absorbed, in its movement westward, the recently consolidated Lydian kingdom,— together with all the Hellenic cities on the sea-board, which after centuries of independence had only just succumbed to Lydia when they were transferred to a still more powerful master,—and under his son Cambyses subjugated the primaeval civilisation of Egypt. The growth of this great power proceeded even still more formidably when it was wielded by the organising energy of Darius Hystaspes, about thirty years after the conquest of Lydia. Darius in person led armies into Europe as far as the Danube, his lieutenants Mardonius and Megabazus secured permanent hold on many parts of Macedonia and Thrace, and an

---

[1] Herod. v. 92.

attempt was máde (501 B.C.) as far to the west, and as near to Athens and Sparta, as the island of Naxos.

The time was now at last once more at hand when the comparative mettle of Greek and Oriental, Western and Eastern tribes; which had met in such unequal conflict in the Homeric epos, was to be tried in mortal combat for life or death to liberty, and to civilised and progressive culture.

Ionia rose in revolt against the Persian, Sparta withheld the solicited aid, but Athens was roused by the peril of cities which owned her as their metropolis; even her effort, however, was but single and spasmodic, and she withdrew entirely, after giving mortal affront by assisting the insurgents in the burning of Sardis.

Within ten years she found herself exposed to a retaliatory attack upon her own ground. The valour of the unassisted Athenians, and the conduct of their general Miltiades, inflicted on the host of Datis and Artaphernes on the field of Marathon a defeat which brought that expedition to a disgraceful end. The Spartans arrived too late for the battle, and afterwards, with characteristic sluggishness, left the more acute and alert Athenians to anticipate and prepare for a renewal of the conflict. For three years Asia was stirred from end to end by a single resistless mandate to prepare for the subjugation of this little group of independent communities, while Xerxes, in the pride of youthful sway, and heir to his father's animosity, prepared to make the progress of triumph and revenge in person.

At Athens at least the impending danger was not unprepared for; though that it was not so even here was due chiefly to the foresight and energetic genius of one man— Themistocles. He read the lesson of the past, that the salvation of the Athenians, if not of Athens, must, under a renewed attack, depend on their possession of ships, and that the severest stroke which could be dealt against an invader, however he arrived, would be the annihilation of his fleet.

On this occasion at least the Spartans set one grand example, which was probably due to the personal spirit of their king Leonidas. The embattled nations of the Persians crossed the Hellespont and wound round through Thessaly, embarrassed only by their own encumbering numbers, to encounter opposition at the first spot under the circumstances even moderately defensible, the pass of Thermopylae. There is no need to recount the circumstances of the conflict; but whatever may be thought of the strategic insight of the Spartan, there is no reason to condemn the exploit as heroism thrown away; from the result of it Sparta may have learnt to be cautious in committing . her fortunes to entire sacrifice on a point of honour; but the approval at home of the steadfastness of the three hundred, the proof they gave before they were destroyed of the efficiency of Hellenic against Persian arms, and the moral impression created upon the Persians themselves, were not without most important influence upon the later conflicts.

In the meantime Themistocles was labouring to keep the ships of the various Greek states together, and to unite them in well-concerted action, by persuasion, self-control, and bribery. He inflicted severe losses on the hostile navy as they advanced towards the shores of Attica, and was happily seconded by the elements. He then carried the resolution for the general evacuation, not only of Attica, but of Athens itself, transported the entire population to the islands and opposite peninsulas, and watched with vigilant anxiety for the opportunity to strike his long-expected blow.

The confederate fleet was mustered in the Saronic Gulf about the island of Salamis, as the Persians rendezvoused in the roadstead of Phaleron; while Xerxes had already occupied Athens and Attica, and might at any time move forward upon the Peloponnesus. In such a confined position the smaller fleet had everything to hope from an engagement, but the Greek commanders of the Peloponnesian states had neither the confidence of Themistocles, nor—trusting in the blockade of the Isthmus—did they conceive that their stake was equally emperìlled.

The rest is, for our present purpose, soon and briefly told. Themistocles sent a private message to the Persian king, which was too like many another communication from Greek traitors to be suspected, and which determined him to commence the attack at once. While the allied commanders were still proposing immediate departure and separation, they found that retreat was already cut off, that the enemy were advancing, and that the only alternative—accepted then for the most part with unhesitating courage—was to fight at once.

Such were the circumstances that brought on the battle, and, with the battle, the victory, of Salamis.

CHAPTER I.

WHEN night closed upon the scene of the battle of
Salamis, the victorious Greeks were unaware of the full
extent and value of their success; the enormous land army
of Xerxes was, they knew, entirely uninjured, except by the
loss of a trifling detachment cut off by Aristides on the islet
Psyttaleia, and of some leading officers who had taken part
in the sea-fight; and even at sea the ships that had never
been engaged at all, or had escaped with little damage
to the station at Phalerum, were so numerous that the
allied commanders fully anticipated a renewed attack. The
moral victory, however, proved to have been more decisive
than the material—itself not unimportant. It was not
so much that the troops and mariners of the invader
were seriously demoralised, as that Xerxes himself had
looked on in surprise and agitation at all the incidents
of the conflict. Even if the loss of his brother and the
slaughter of his personal friends before his eyes might not
have affected the nerves of the Great King to the degree
described by Aeschylus (Pers. 474), he could not but observe at what disadvantage his forces, for all their superior
numbers,—fighting bravely as they might in the consciousness of his immediate presence,—had contended with
the patriotic enthusiasm, the order and skill of their opponents. It might indeed seem that with power at his

c 2

command which was still so preponderant, he could well
afford to strike another blow even at equal cost, a blow
which must have fallen with decisive disastrousness on the
smaller force of the Greeks. But the stanchness of his
Phoenician and Cilician forces was thoroughly discredited
by their behaviour in the battle; the Ionians could not
be trusted at a turn of fortune, and the better troops
whom he had embarked, having no opportunity for their
valour in a form of contest unknown to them, were
simply thrown away. The superiority of the Greeks on
their own element was too manifest and too serious for
the repetition of a venture that might jeopardize his own
personal safety; by one more such battle his fleet might
be utterly disorganised and dispersed, and then the enemy,
established in full command of the sea and the straits,
could cut off his retreat from Europe, and even interpose
an obstacle to his return beyond, by inciting a general
Ionian insurrection. It was not because his private resolve
was not fixed at once, that his immediate commands implied
a purpose to remain and prosecute the enterprise without
intermission; preparation was to be made for another sea-
fight, and a project that had been mooted and perhaps
commenced before the [1] battle, a familiar and favourite
Oriental expedient, was again spoken of; Phoenician transport vessels were to be fastened together to form a bulwark
and floating pier, and a causeway was to be completed from
the mainland to the island of Salamis, the refuge of the
Athenian families and the storeplace of their property.

A show of consultation was then made with Mardonius,
son of Gobryas, the most eager instigator of the expedition,
and separately with the Carian Queen Artemisia, who had
already commanded the confidence of the King by the frank
independence of her counsel no less than by its wisdom.

---

[1] Ctesias; and Strabo, ix. 573.

Both were forward to minister the desired advice. Mardonius especially had motives of his own for pressing what he might easily divine was the only recommendation that would be listened to; he had little inclination to be responsible at home for the entire and disastrous failure of his policy—a failure which in truth it was as yet premature to admit. The prospect of being left with a brilliant independent command, in the conduct of which he was not unnaturally or unfairly still sanguine of success, was tempting; the more speedy and alarmed the flight of Xerxes the larger the proportion of the army that he would be both disposed and obliged to leave behind as an obstacle between himself and the possible pursuit of the Greeks. As for Artemisia, she had distinguished herself by remarkable bravery in the battle; and even without insisting on the feminine liability to excessive reaction after displays of unfeminine vigour, we need not hesitate to infer that she was well content to be now dismissed in honour. The Great King consigned to her charge some of his illegitimate offspring, and she loosed at once for Ephesus, where it was said that primaeval Amazons had founded the great temple for the goddess from whom this modern Amazon derived her name.

The speeches which Herodotus assigns to the two counsellors are excellent examples of his apt dramatic invention, and curiously display how thoroughly a republican Greek of his time could enter into the spirit of an absolute monarchy. Xerxes is flattered and capable of being flattered by the suggestion of an option, although the necessity for his flight is a foregone conclusion, since both to his own conviction, and to that of his advisers, an alternative of any kind is out of the question. To soothe or seem to soothe his pride, the losses that have been incurred are made light of when set against the glorious and literal fulfilment of the purpose of the expedition; Athenian insolence and sacrilege at Sard had found its threatened retribution in the capture of Athens and the smoking ruins of its most sacred temples; losses, of whatever magnitude, that might ensue to the avenging army, are treated as of little consequence in comparison with the all-important safety of the King; Artemisia, with something different from the abasement of sycophancy, in all the sympathetic candour of royalty in secluded conference with royalty, adverts to the possible destruction of Mardonius and his host as comparatively of little consequence.

Among the ostensible reasons for the departure of the King were some which told with equal cogency against the further prosecution of the war; and these were made the most of, especially by Artabazus son of Pharnaces, who had opposed it from the very beginning. Mardonius however carried his purpose by skilfully connecting it with conditions of self-complacent comfort for the disheartened Xerxes, and with the propriety and security of his speedy return.

Accordingly, at daybreak of apparently the day but one after the [1]battle, the Persian army indeed was still seen across the gulf in its place on land, but the Greeks discovered that the hostile fleet had vanished from the harbour and roadstead of Phalerum. Its destination and the full significance of the move were at once divined. It had in fact started during the night, and though dispersed for a time off Cape Zoster, where jutting rocks—so it was afterwards believed—were mistaken in the darkness for Greek ships, had reassembled and was already in full course northwards to secure the Hellespont. The Greek fleet put off in pursuit with the utmost alacrity, and proceeded as far as the island of Andros, where the sea-line was open northwards, but as the chase was still not in sight, the commanders paused to consider their further movements.

---

[1] Herod. viii. 107.

The Athenian crews in all the elation of success were exasperated at the escape, and eager to go on, even against the opinion of the allies, and even by themselves. Themistocles was not likely to be less confident, or less eager to make the most of the superiority of the fleet which he had himself created; and, as something more than their mouthpiece, he was urgent in the same direction. He pressed with all his influence for continuing the pursuit of the fugitive navy, the annihilation of which was certainly important, and in its present state of dispersion and demoralisation presumably easy; and he held out the prospect of intercepting the retreat of Xerxes and the land army by breaking the much-talked-of bridge across the Hellespont, and so remaining in command of the channel. The apparently more astute policy of declining to offer an impediment to the flight of a formidable enemy is assigned to the Spartan Eurybiades, though Plutarch, writing with Herodotus before · him, prefers some other authority in ascribing it to Aristides. To a Spartan at that time the mere remoteness of such an expedition, and that by sea, would in itself be a sufficient objection, even though not reinforced by the national maxim which discouraged prolonged pursuit after a victory, or by more refined considerations. The majority of the allies fell in easily with the resolution to give no hindrance to the evacuation of Europe by an army which, as they prematurely flattered themselves, was as ready to retire as the fleet had been, but which, if obliged to remain, must be driven, by the necessity of obtaining subsistence, to perilous activity, and had still sufficient force in reserve to overawe or subdue all the cities and tribes of Hellas one after another. 'With the command of the sea lost, retire he must, and it were best to allow him to do so now, and continue the contest afterwards on his ground instead of on our own. Plausible as the project of crushing Asia in Europe might sound, the King at the head of such an army would, if driven to extremity, rouse himself, and would not be content a second time merely to look on, sitting in state under a gold umbrella.'

Themistocles, constrained if not convinced, gave an example of loyal deference to the alliance by bringing over his reluctant countrymen. He quoted to them the proverbial danger of provoking desperate men, hinted that as the disaster of Xerxes was a manifestation of the angry grudge of the gods at his impious over-confidence, so it would be well for the Athenians—and he touched here one of the most sensitive of their superstitions—to avoid giving like perilous and presumptuous affront by assuming to be invincible; it was also urgent to attend to families, houses were to be rebuilt and resettled, the harvest of next year at least to be secured—the present being lost—by getting seed into the ground, and after all spring would come round, and then would be the time to deal with the Hellespont and Ionia.

But in fact the retreat of the Persian army was not yet declared; and it was not certain that Attica might not continue to be occupied as a base of further operations. It was not many days however after the battle of Salamis before this immediate apprehension found relief; the confined and closed-in Attica was not a district for such a host to remain in now that failure of supplies and support by sea had put further advance out of the question; and its departure by the same route that it came, in the direction of [1] Boeotia, revived in the Greeks the illusive hope of speedy and final deliverance.

Xerxes himself, had he even been inclined to linger, might have been hastened away by a secret message that reached him from the Athenian commander. Themistocles, overruled in his plan to cut off the retreat, fell back on the next best policy to hasten it. With some reliance it would seem on the simplicity of the barbarian, he sent to him again

[1] Herod. viii. 113.

the same Sicinnus who had before carried the treacherous warning that precipitated a naval engagement just in time for the salvation of the Greeks. The instrument was no doubt well chosen, as his dexterous service was richly rewarded afterwards, when Themistocles made the former pedagogue of his children a well-endowed citizen of the resettled and repeopled Thespiae. The liberation moreover at the same time of a captured royal eunuch, Arnaces, was a personal favour to the King, and supplied an independent witness of the sincerity of the message and the reality of the peril with which he had doubtless been sedulously impressed. A boat's crew of faithful adherents, who might be fully relied on to keep the secret of the mission, even under torture, conveyed the agent to the shore of Attica. The communication which he bore was to the effect that Themistocles, the Athenian commander, out of desire to be serviceable to the King, had succeeded in restraining the Greeks from their eagerness to pursue his fleet and cut the bridge of the Hellespont, and that he could now draw off in perfect security. We may assume that this tranquillizing assurance was qualified by some intimation of the precarious nature of the restraint which Themistocles could exercise, and would thus be calculated rather to enhance the apprehension of the King. The Persian was only too well accustomed to receive very valuable aid from Greek treachery, but had not learnt to suspect still further treachery beneath.

So far therefore, Athenians and allies, Spartans and Persians, believed alike that they had reason to applaud Themistocles, who, himself a serviceable friend, had too lively a sense of the advantages which he and his country might derive from enthusiastic and powerful friends, to neglect to provide them beforehand, or to use or abuse them prematurely. That he may have designed to confirm the previous confidence of the Great King in his sympathy, for future as well as present use, as it did indeed afterwards stand him

in good stead, is probable enough; but his caution in rendering his country this service only implies that he knew
how his countrymen, if it came to their knowledge, might
misunderstand or misrepresent it; that the establishment
of a personal claim was his sole or his main object, it were
absurd to suppose.

In a cruise with his victorious fleet among the islands,
Themistocles now commenced a system of requisitions, independent, not merely of the participation, but even of the
knowledge of the commanders of the allies, and, as Herodotus implies, very considerably also for his private advantage.
No time was lost therefore in giving notice of the lofty
pretensions of maritime Athens; his demands were made
in the name of Athens, and Athens alone; and whether
simply on the ground of fitting contribution to the common
cause, or as penalty for aid rendered to the Mede by the cities
or by individual citizens, and for the delivery at his summons,
by almost all, of earth and water, as tokens of submission—
those demands were backed by threats which his authority
and the force at his command made in most cases immediately effectual. The Andrians were curtly informed by his
messenger, that the Athenians had with them two potent
divinities, Persuasion and Compulsion, and that on the terms
of one or the other they must needs pay. The Andrians,
however, felt themselves secure enough within their walls
to retort that these goddesses, serviceable as they were,
would avail nothing against a pair not less unserviceable,
Poverty and Inability—impersonations already coupled in
the poetry of Alcaeus as [1] sisters—and that pay they would
not. The island was beset by the fleet, and the demonstration at least brought in considerable sums from other
quarters, from Paros and Euboea certainly, and, as Herodotus believed, from elsewhere. The Parians thus bought
themselves off, but the Carystians of Euboea were less

---

[1] Stobaeus, xcvii. 17 ; Bergk, 90.

fortunate, and, by what misarrangement does not appear, incurred devastation of their territory all the same, when the fleet, relinquishing the attempt against Andros, was on its return to Salamis.

It is perfectly consistent with what is known of The-mistocles that his own fortune was increased by the proceeds of these exactions; it would be less than justice to assume that no larger share of the benefit accrued to the service of the state, of which the necessities consequent on cost of war, on devastation and expatriation, must have been most urgent. It was quite in his way, as he had shown before the battle of [1]Artemisium, to take bribes with the left hand for patriotic services with the right.

Re-assembled at Salamis, the first care of the Greeks was to select three of the captured Phoenician vessels for dedica-tion to the gods, to whom by vicinity or special appeal their victory was peculiarly ascribed. One was dedicated at the Isthmus,—presumably to Poseidon,—and was seen there by Herodotus; another to Athene, on the promontory of Sunium; and a third to Ajax,—but this not at Aegina, whence the Aeacid had been summoned to aid,—but at Salamis, closer to the scene of victory, and the town from which the hero had led twelve ships against Troy, and there 'stationed them,' according to the line suspected of being interpolated for a political intent, 'alongside the Athenians.'

The divine share of the spoil was then distributed; from the prime of it the Greeks dedicated at Delphi a statue of [2]Apollo, twelve cubits high, holding the prow of a ship. It stands, says Herodotus, with a particularity that marks the already crowded state of the precinct, near the golden Alexander of Macedon. This Delphic statue was probably of bronze, like the Zeus at Olympia, which Pausanias men-tions in the same passage as another dedication—of which we shall hear more—from the Medica.

---

[1] Herod. viii. 4. [2] Pausan. x. 14. 3.

The silver-footed throne from which Xerxes had watched the battle on the height above the shore was catalogued among the treasures of the Athenian acropolis under [1]Pericles, but probably was spoil of a later conflict.

Meanwhile, whatever sanguine hopes might have been formed that the retirement of the invaders implied their final departure, were speedily undeceived, and the news of the halt of the main body was promptly followed by that of renewed preparations to complete the subjugation of the Greeks.

There is no appearance that the Persian hold even on Boeotia was relaxed, and a pause which was made by the King in Thessaly, and his departure northwards shortly afterwards with a strong escort, would not be known much sooner than the sure signs that the principal danger was still impending over Hellas, 'like the stone of [2]Tantalus.'

It was during this halt, if we are to believe Herodotus, as I doubt not that we may, that an application was made to Xerxes which, strange as it sounds to modern ears, would not have been recorded had it seemed so extravagant to a Greek of the time; and that is not more strange than many of the old world notions that are perfectly authenticated as then still lingering, especially at Sparta. A herald of the Spartans presented himself at Larissa, and formally demanded of the Great King satisfaction for the slaughter of their King Leonidas, 'slain by Medes while defending Hellas.' Xerxes not unnaturally laughed, and at first made no reply; then presently, pointing to Mardonius, who was standing by him, he said, 'Here is the man, Mardonius, who shall render them satisfaction of such kind as is fitting.' The herald accepted the answer, and returned to report it. He had been despatched in haste in obedience to a Delphic oracle, which was afterwards believed to have enjoined acquiescence in whatever reply the application provoked, and was credited with anticipating an

----

[1] Schol. Thuc. ii. 13.   [2] Pindar, *Isth.* vii. 11.

involuntary and significant presage of the defeat and death of Mardonius at Plataea.

The ample powers committed to Mardonius might reasonably make him confident of ultimate success in the enterprise of which, in the face of ardent opposition, he had originally been the chief adviser. He was allowed to retain all the best troops, consisting for the most part of Persians and Medes in equal numbers—the latter, however, of inferior account; he retained all the Sakae, Bactrians, and Indians, both horse and foot, and picked men from all the other tribes, including Aethiopians and Egyptians whom he had withdrawn at Phalerum from the fighting armament of the Phoenician [1] galleys. The Persian Immortals all remained with him, though their commander Hydarnes declined to quit the King. Of the retained army as many as 60,000 men were to be detached to accompany Xerxes until he was safe in Asia, and then rejoin. This important body was under command of Artabazus son of Pharnaces, previously named as a leader of the Parthians and Chorasmians, who would fain have made the withdrawal from Southern Hellas definitive and total, and was now submitting only perforce and most reluctantly to the superior influence of Mardonius. The later consequences of this disagreement, combined with his military influence, which would of necessity be confirmed by so important an independent command, were momentous.

The resumption of operations southwards was necessarily deferred until the ensuing spring; by that time the troops that conducted Xerxes could return, and Thessaly meanwhile, where the Aleuad Thorax of Larissa was still zealous for the expedition that he had done so much to invite, and the nearer district of [2] Macedonia, afforded undisturbed winter quarters, and the best opportunity of providing subsistence for a renewed campaign.

---

[1] Herod. ix. 31.   [2] Id. viii. 126.

CHAPTER II.

THE RETREAT OF XERXES.—ARTABAZUS IN THRACE.—
THEMISTOCLES AT SPARTA.

480 B.C.; Ol. 75. 1.

XERXES, we are told, reached the Hellespont in five and forty days, and as the term is manifestly mentioned to emphasise his precipitate haste, it seems that we must reckon it from Attica and the day of Salamis. The date of this can only be fixed generally as in the autumn, but the retreat appears to have been late enough in the year for at least some of the fugitives to suffer considerably by the incipient, perhaps premature, inclemency of the Thracian winter.

On arriving at Siris in Paeonia, Xerxes found that the sacred chariot, which he had deposited there on his way south, was not again forthcoming. The historian, finding, as usual with him, a Greek name for a foreign divinity, calls it the chariot of Zeus; he notes [1] elsewhere that the Zeus of the Persians was the general circle of the heavens. It was never ascended by man, but in the pomp of the army was drawn vacant before the King by eight white Nisaean horses and preceded by ten others. Doubtless it is to be regarded as properly the chariot of the sun; and this sacred character explains its disappearance in this particular locality as due to something beyond common sacrilegious rapine. The traces of a native solar and planetary worship are peculiarly persistent in this region, and among them this very symbol of a chariot with white horses is at home.

[1] Herod. i. 131.

In Homer the Paeonians, of a somewhat more western seat on the Axius, appear under the leadership of Asteropaeus and Pyraechmes, significant names when we read in independent authorities that the Paeonians worshipped the sun, of which their symbol was a small disk on a high [1] rod.

If there could be any doubt as to the original source of the legend of the chariot and white horses of Thracian Rhesus, son of Eïon,—Eïon at the mouth of the Strymon,—it should be dispelled by Nestor's comparison of the steeds, as Diomed and Ulysses are bringing them in through the night, to the solar [2] beams. The Magians of the expedition of Xerxes, by sacrificing white horses to the Strymon, had recognised the genius and traditions of the [3] locality.

The Thracians gave the sun the name or the epithet Zeuxippus, and it is as ' lovers of horses ' that the Thracians of the Tereus of Sophocles invoke the ' holy radiance of the sun.'

Thracians were now in any case in surreptitious possession of the Persian sacred chariot and its white horses, stolen from their custody, as the Paeonians professed, by the remoter tribes about the sources of the Strymon, but purposely transferred to them according to the belief of Herodotus.

The persistence of local characteristics seems curiously illustrated by an anecdote of barbarism that the historian next details—the blinding by a Thracian king of his disobedient sons. We are checked in an inclination to disallow it as a mere reflection from the mythical atrocities of Thracian Phineus, by remembering how unnatural cruelty of the like type repeats itself afterwards, as if ineradicably native to the region, in the chambers of Byzantine emperors.

Xerxes, then, reached the Straits with extraordinary speed, and it may be, as regards his immediate escort, with comparative immunity ; but the route was marked by the falling-out of the stragglers and the sick, whom it was a mere formality

[1] Max. Tyr. *Diss.* viii. c. 8.   [2] *Iliad*, x. 547.
[3] Herod. vii. 113.

to command the exhausted cities on the line of march to tend
and nourish. It fared necessarily still worse with the vast
crowds that had been mustered originally in a spirit of
barbaric display of power, and that Mardonius neither cared
to retain nor to provide for—the least effective, the least
healthy, with whatever supernumeraries and camp followers
could only remain as an encumbrance. The sufferings of these
had commenced even before Thessaly was attained. The difficulty of feeding the effective force and of filling its magazines
for the prospective campaign was relieved by abandoning the
ineffective to what chances they had of providing for themselves unaided against such competitors for failing food and
forage.

Herodotus tells how, when all stores were exhausted, the
growing crops were snatched from the ground, and the
famished hordes were at length driven to devour grass
and the bark and leaves of trees without distinction, culti-
vated or wild, 'and they left nothing;' the work of famine
being followed up, as ever in such cases, by dysentery and
pestilence.

Not poetry itself can heighten the horrors of such a
retreat. Imagination indeed, drawing from its own resources, is even more likely to match the truth than are
the prosaic details gathered by an historian. According to
Aeschylus, scarcity of water was already fatal in Boeotia,
and even insufficiency of clothing during inclement and un-
sheltered nights, no doubt especially with the tribes coming
from such climates as that of India, and even others. Still
more fatal were the combined effects of hunger and thirst in
Thessaly, and even more deadly pestilence as they went on.
By the time Thrace was reached, at least by some lagging
portion of the wretched fugitives, the nights were cold
enough to cover the Strymon, or possibly some other river
eastward of [1] Pangaeus, with ice strong enough to bear—an

---

[1] Aesch. *Persae.*

assistance for the moment; but the very sun-god of the locality seemed in league against the unhappy train upon the way so treacherously shortened. Those who passed early were saved ; but, as day advanced, 'the bright circle of the sun, ablaze with beams, warmed the ford with fire, and split it in the midst—happiest then he who was first to perish.' Of those left behind, and who had to make a long circuit through Thrace, few ever reached their native land. Hasty and uncontrolled indulgence in more abundant food as soon as it was obtainable, and—it is especially noticed—substitution of other drink for water, caused large fatality even after Asia was regained.

Another story, in itself improbable enough, was current, that Xerxes embarked for Asia in a Phoenician ship at Eïon on the Strymon; it was told apparently for the sake of an illustration, one out of several of the kind, of the cruel and irrational punctilios of the court of an Asiatic despot. The ship, so went the tale, was endangered by a storm, overladen as it was with Persians of high rank. The ship-master, appealed to by the alarmed Xerxes, declared that the only hope of escape was to lighten it of passengers. The Persians were at once advertised by the King of the opportunity for their services, and at once making their parting prostrations, they one after another, as if still with observance of due precedence, leaped into the sea. The first act of Xerxes upon landing in safety was to reward the ship-master for saving the royal life, and the next to have his head struck off for causing the destruction of so many Persians. The conditions of giving wise advice to a tyrant here are essentially the same as are illustrated in the subject of the Council of Darius on the Naples vase. The counsellor there stands on the golden plinth which he will receive as reward for his advice—with, however, a scourging for his presumption in offering [1] it. Herodotus discredits the story,

[1] Aelian and Ctesias.

D

on the ground that the Phoenician rowers would have been sacrificed in preference ; and so leaves us to debate whether he could have overlooked the enhanced peril of a storm-tossed galley when reft of oarsmen, or what escape he could imagine from it. A more reasonable objection, provided in his reference to the local tradition of the Abderites, that Xerxes passed through their city on his return, only invalidates the statement of his port of embarkation. The further tradition of Abdera, that it was there that the King first loosened zone after quitting Athens, may be taken as expressing at least the state of discomposure in which he arrived. The fleet which had retired, or rather escaped, from Salamis and the Saronic Gulf, duly reached the Hellespont, where it was the more needed as the bridge had already been carried away by storms, and there aided the transit of the King and some inconsiderable bodies of troops and stragglers. It then retired for the winter to the coast of Asia Minor—most of the ships to Cumae, the rest to the harbour of Samos, where the Samian Theomestor, son of Androdamas, in requital of good service done at Salamis, was established by the Persian in the authority of Tyrant—that is, under such circumstances, of Satrap.

Artabazus, having so far accomplished his task and seen the King in safety, turned his face, however unwillingly, again westward, along with his large force, to rejoin Mardonius and the main army. On his way he halted at the Chalcidic peninsula, on the eastern side of the Thermaic gulf. From thence he could move south in time for operations in spring, and could meanwhile more conveniently obtain subsistence for his forces; he had there also the opportunity to repress in the interval some examples of defection which, if neglected, might spread, and compromise communications of which he best knew the precariousness, and was well disposed to forbode the coming need.

Potidaea, on the isthmus of the fertile peninsula of Pallene, was already in declared, and Olynthus, in less secure position, suspected as on the verge of revolt. The latter town was occupied by Bottiaeans, who had been driven eastward from the Thermaic gulf by Macedonian encroachment, and as a lately Hellenised, or at best semi-Hellenic [1] tribe, and perhaps from the circumstances of their settlement, seem to have been out of sympathy with their immediate neighbours. Olynthus was in consequence attacked by Artabazus, and on its capture the inhabitants were carried out into an adjacent marsh and there massacred, as a measure preparatory to the delivery of the town into the keeping of Critobulus of Torone, on the adjacent Sithonian peninsula, and to the introduction of a Chalcidic population. In this manner, says Herodotus, Olynthus—which was destined to a conspicuous place in later history—became, like its neighbours, Chalcidic.

With Potidaea the Persians had far different fortune. This city—which also we shall soon hear of again—was a Corinthian colony, and named from the god Poseidon, who, in colony as in metropolis, could look down from his temple upon a sea on either hand. The towns within the peninsula contributed to the defence of Potidaea, which, by its position as a bar to the Isthmus, was the bulwark of their own immunity. But the severity of the treatment of Olynthus, while it nerved resistance generally, was calculated to make some timid traitors. In the course of the siege a citizen was struck in the shoulder by an arrow, and the bystanders who hastened to his assistance found that the shaft was laden with a missive, which had been intended for traitorous hands. It was at once taken to the generals, who were thus put on their guard against a clandestine correspondence carried on by Timoxeinus, commander of their Scionaean allies, which might otherwise have had serious consequences. The warning had its value, though, for some unexplained politic tenderness to Scione, the matter was hushed up. At last, after three

---

[1] Plut. *Theseus*, 6; *Graec. Q.* 35 : Strabo, vi. 3 ; ii. 6.

months of urgent but vain siege, an unusually low ebb of the sea appeared to furnish Artabazus with an opportunity of turning the defences and penetrating into Pallene by land. Two out of five divisions intended for the service had passed through the shoal water, and the others were on their way, when the sea returned in flood of a volume which natives said was of the very rarest occurrence. Those who were unable to swim perished at once, the remainder fell by the hands of the besieged, who sallied upon them in boats. The Potidaeans naturally recognised a special interposition of their god to avenge the desecration of his temple and statue by the Persians in the suburbs; 'and so saying,' adds Herodotus, 'to my mind they say well.' Upon this failure Artabazus drew off, and marched in due time with the survivors of his forces to join Mardonius in Thessaly.

Meanwhile the confederate Greeks had been occupied in the partition of the spoils, and, which was a far more delicate matter, the honours, of their victory. In the division of the spoil the Aristeia were assigned to the Aeginetans as a nation, the Athenians obtaining only the second place; of Aeginetan individuals, Polycritus was placed first, of Athenians, Eumenes and Ameinias (of the deme Pallene according to [1] Herodotus, of Decelea according to Plutarch), whom Diodorus affirms to have been a brother of Aeschylus. The poet in the [2] Persae marks the exploit of Ameinias in commencing the battle with noteworthy emphasis; his suppression of the name cannot be taken as an argument either way. For this pre-eminence of Aegina the Delphic oracle afterwards demanded a special acknowledgment, which was rendered by the island in the form of a dedicated bronze mast with three golden stars, symbolical perhaps of Apollo, Artemis, and Latona, though with equal probability of Dionysus, Apollo, and Artemis. The animus

[1] Herod. viii. 84.   [2] 415-417.

of the inspirers of the oracle—to confer divine sanction on
a questionable adjudication—is less equivocal. A further
illustration of Delphic partisanship occurred in the rejection
of a dedication of Median spoils offered by Themistocles on
his own account.

The precedence assigned in such a manner to Aegina
above its ancient rival, and of late threatening and encroaching enemy, Athens, could not but tend to strengthen
and revive the acerbity of a party feeling to which the Athenians afterwards take credit to themselves for being [1]superior.
The Spartans, whose influence was also predominant at Delphi,
might naturally be inclined towards Aeginetans as fellow-
Dorians, rather than to Ionian Athens; but to indulge such
feelings now, and under such relative circumstances, was to
take sides in a quarrel that had been nobly set aside in a
moment of common peril, and which it would have been well
to consider as extinguished for ever. Themistocles had been
earnest before the war in urging his countrymen to establish
a decided naval predominance over Aegina, with ulterior views
that were not less alarming because undefined; and he had
made the most of every pretext, and some fair ones had not
been wanting, to impute to the commercial islanders a disposition to Medism; Aeginetan citizens had certainly struggled
nobly to purge their country of the charge, but, as there was
a serious slight implied to Athens in subordinating her services to those of Aegina, so the selection for the personal prize
of valour of precisely that Aeginetan who in the midst of the
fight had upbraided Themistocles as a false [2]accuser, was not
likely to soften the sentiments of the powerful Athenian
towards his country.

Themistocles was to experience another rebuff, when the
Greeks, after the division of the spoil, sailed to the Isthmus
solemnly to adjudge the prize to him who had deserved best,

---

[1] Thuc. i. 74. [2] Herod. viii. 92.

not in the recent battle, but in the war at large. There
on the altar of Poseidon the assembled generals of the confederate states deposited votes for the first and second in
desert. Examination of the ballots showed that each voter
had received one, presumably his own, for the first prize; as
none had the requisite majority, the ballot for this was void,
and with it, apparently as a consequence, that for the second,
which by a large majority was due to Themistocles. And so
the congress separated. Themistocles, however, immediately
on its breaking up, proceeded direct to Sparta, and there, by
a strangely sudden revulsion, of which we look in vain for
an explanation, received compensation for the slight inflicted
by the general congress, in honours such as Sparta had never
before conferred on a [1] foreigner.

The most indulgent conclusion to draw from this vehement
demonstration would seem to be, either that the sentiments
of Sparta, however declared, had not told upon votes when
delivered by secret ballot, or that the result of it was in fact
arranged on account of the difficulty of bringing into comparison the claims of Themistocles and Eurybiades, and in
order to avoid preferring either before the other. At Sparta
the same difficulty did not exist; there, at home and among
his own countrymen, Eurybiades had the first and rightful
claim to the olive crown which he was the first to receive
from them; a like crown was then assigned to Themistocles;
and so exceptional was such an honour from Sparta to a
stranger, that no derogation was implied in his receiving it
after their own countryman. That it was distinctly assigned
in recognition of sagacity and dexterous management might
enhance its value to him, and would carry no offence to the
Spartan.

But, making all allowance for a truly enthusiastic and
generous recognition of the services of Themistocles, some-

---

[1] Thuc. i. 74.

thing still remains to be accounted for by the ordinary laws of unusual and extravagant gratitude, when we read that he received at his departure the handsomest chariot Sparta could provide, and, after abundant eulogiums, was conducted to the frontiers—an honour entirely without precedent—by the chosen troop of three hundred mounted Spartans. It had, in fact, become apparent by this time that the liberation of Greece was not completed by the victory of Salamis. The fleet of Athens, not to say the talent of her general, could ill be spared if the conflict, the gravity of which had now been brought home, was to go on ; and the influence of Themistocles with his countrymen,—unless his sympathies, irritated like theirs by the invidious precedence voted to Aegina, were soothed and conciliated to Greece by the glory he loved,—might be diverted to a project which, already significantly mooted, had probably found some serious reception, namely, the entire withdrawal of the fleet, and the transference of the population of Attica, dispossessed and insulted as it now was, to new seats in Italy.

At a less critical time serious danger might have been incurred among jealous fellow-citizens by Athenians, who could harbour permanent resentment against the appearance of very moderate assumption even in Miltiades. As it was, the cavil that was one day to ruin him came from an insignificant quarter, and was lightly thrown aside with his ever prompt facility of sharp retort. Timodemus, of the deme Aphidnae, gained little by his carping sneer,—that it was on account of Athens, and not of himself, that he had been so honoured in Lacedaemon. 'Exactly so,' was the reply ; 'and had I belonged to the islet Belbinis I should have had as little respect from the Spartans as you and men like you command, Athenian though you [1]are.' Certain however it is that the name of Themistocles does for a time somewhat unexpectedly lapse

---

[1] Herod. viii. 125.

from the story; though the fact that Xanthippus, father of Pericles, next appears in command of the fleet may be simply due to the Athenian rule of succession in command, and not in itself be any confirmation of the statement of Diodorus, which may only express an inference, that Themistocles was superseded through popular discontent at these personal glories.

CHAPTER III.

B.C. 479, Spring; Ol. 75. 1.

THE approach of spring, says Herodotus, and the presence
of Mardonius in Thessaly, roused the Greeks to renewed
activity. The mustering of their land force was a matter of
time; but 110 ships were assembled early at Aegina under
the Spartan Heracleid king Leotychides, as General Commander and Admiral—Xanthippus, son of Ariphron, being
Commander of the Athenians. The first incident here was
the arrival of envoys from Ionia, eager to concert an immediate attempt for its liberation. The envoys themselves were
men who had planned to revolutionize Chios by the assassination of Strattis, who had been established there as tyrant by
the Persians since the time of the expedition of Darius to the
[1] Danube. Foiled by the treachery of an associate, the conspirators escaped and made straight for Sparta, and now came
on to the fleet to urge an instant movement on Ionia. One
of their number, says the historian, was Herodotus, the son
of Basileïdes, who is evidently distinguished in this way from
the rest for some particular reason. It is plausibly conjectured
that he was a relative of the writer, his namesake; it may
be said, perhaps as plausibly, that from him may have come
direct the pettish complaint and sarcasm that it was with
great difficulty they could induce the fleet to advance even

---

[1] Herod. iv. 138.

as far as Delos, 'for everything beyond was alarming to the Hellenes, who, unacquainted with the localities, fancied that all were crowded with hostile forces; and as to Samos, the station of the Persian fleet, conceived it to be as distant as the Pillars of Hercules. So that it came to this: the barbarians were too much out of heart to sail further westward than Samos, and the Hellenes would not move at the solicitation of the Chians further eastward than Delos, and fear occupied the interval between them.' In every word we catch the tones of the desperate and disappointed exile. The imputation attaches principally to the Spartan as Admiral, and, thus read, glances fairly at the home-keeping habits of the Lacedaemonians, and their systematic aversion—so strange to the maritime Ionians—to enterprises beyond the sea. The wild projects of Aristagoras might not unreasonably be dismissed by Spartans upon mere statement of their geographical [1]scope, but even the Mitylenians, though much later, and more moderate in their request, have to apologise, in soliciting their aid, for the remoteness of [2] Lesbos.

This is one of the occasions when Herodotus seems to speak of the Dorians as the Hellenes distinctively, and so far in consistency with his explicit theory, that that term as commonly applied comprised a number of tribes, which had only become secondarily hellenised by constant intercourse or subjugation, and included even the Athenians—who were in truth principally a contrasted Pelasgian stock, and others far less cognate than they.

There was now, however, sufficient reason why both the Athenian and Spartan commanders should be content not to proceed beyond an intermediate position of guard and observation, and to consider a movement upon Ionia premature. No success in this quarter could affect the impending conflict between the land forces, which must needs be decided on

[1] Herod. v. 50.   [2] Thuc. iii. 13.

Grecian soil. The mere weakening of the fleet, even in a successful conflict, would be disastrous, and might leave the coasts of Peloponnesus exposed to a descent. The Persian fleet seemed inclined to keep quiet at present, and nothing better could be desired. The enemy were, in fact, concentrated at Samos with 300 ships, including some Ionians; the fighting crews of most were Persians and Medes, and so, to judge by their names, were the commanders also—Mardontes son of Bagaius, Artayntes son of Artachaeus, and his relative Ithamitres. On their part they were chiefly concerned to overawe Ionia, were quite indisposed to risk another collision by moving westward, having indeed received neither summons nor command to do so, and only discussed plans and projects while they waited with impatience for news of the more hopeful action of Mardonius.

In the council of Mardonius there was a mixture of native Greek and Persian elements less divided in interests than in opinions and predilections, as to the policy that would best promote them.

Mardonius himself, as we have seen, was perfectly out of sympathy with Artabazus, the next most important Persian in the expedition, and leaned in preference on the Theban or Thessalian oligarchs, who, however they might differ as to the mode of prosecuting the war, were at least as eager for success as himself, and had a knowledge of the country and of the characteristics of his opponents, to which, since he had learned to distinguish and respect them, he found himself under obligation to defer. But he did so still with some impatience and some wavering. His own desire was for instant, dashing, brilliant action. He had all the barbarian confidence in masses,—he was proud of his position at the head of an army splendidly equipped, which, numerous as it [1] was, and recently increased by levies from Thrace,

---

[1] Diod. xi. 38.

Macedonia, and the Medising cities, comprised selections. of all arms from an immensely larger number. He had as yet witnessed no fair defeat of the veterans of his own race, and had sincerely represented his own conviction when he assured Xerxes that Salamis was lost by landsmen being set to cope on the sea with sailors, and by the cowardice of a mob of Phoenicians, Egyptians, Syrians, and Cilicians. The Thebans, on the other hand, had serious mistrust of even the best of the Orientals as opposed to the Greek hoplite, and had seen enough to judge well the material of which each was made. Preponderant as the numbers of the Persians therefore might be in any case, they knew that the fewer their opponents the better; they would deem no delay tedious that might serve to divide them, and had their own opinions how this was to be done : they especially urged Mardonius to be lavish in bribes to the men in power in the several states ; he would in this way break Hellas asunder, be in possession of all their counsels without trouble, and easily subdue the obstinate by aid of the factious. To this party of councillors we may also trace the politic skill with which the machinery of oracles and prophecies was set in motion to act upon the general Greek mind, and indeed with a certain degree of effect to control and hamper Mardonius himself. So the Pisistratids had, in the first instance, made use of the prophetic reputation of the soothsayer Onomacritus to decide Xerxes for the expedition, and had found the man not the less fit for their purposes because in earlier days he had been expelled by Hipparchus from Athens as a detected forger,—a fraudulent interpolator of the oracles of Musaeus, which he was professing to arrange. The Athenians were of all the Greeks peculiarly apt to be worked upon by superstition presented in this form,—their orators continued to appeal in all gravity to the prejudice, even while it was a standing joke upon the comic stage,—and it was upon the Athenians that the first attempts were to be made towards breaking up the

confederation. The Theban oracles of Ismenian Apollo and of
Amphiaraus were consulted, the first by the medium of priests,
interpreters of sacrifices, the latter through dreams invited by
sleep upon skins of victims within the sacred precincts. At
the temple of Ptoan Apollo, on lake Copäis, three citizens were
chosen to accompany the Carian agent of the Persian into the
fane and write down the response; it was a tale of the Thebans which proves at any rate a sense of mystification in the
transactions, that the oracle was delivered in a language un-
intelligible to them, and that the Carian, snatching the tablet
from their hands, wrote it hastily down, and carried it off
to Thessaly. Trophonius was consulted in his cave, even as
he was by the traveller Pausanias long after the Christian
aera,—and the Phocian oracle at Abae. Herodotus never
heard the particular enquiries or responses, and he says
nothing in this place of an application to Delphi ; but
at a fitting time Mardonius had a Delphic oracle also to
propound, couched in terms which, but that the instincts
of impostors have ever the same source of inspiration, might
have been imitated by an astrologer of Louis the Eleventh.

The reception of oracles from such sources was followed
naturally by the initiation of intrigues in the spirit of the
Medising Greeks. Money, destined for the hands of men
in power in the various cities, found its way into the [1] Peloponnesus; but there is no positive evidence that it was
to be credited with any of the dilatoriness which caused
so much difficulty later, but might be due to other familiar
causes. Against the Argives alone, who had all along refused
to give aid to Hellas against the Mede,—being jealous of
Sparta on much the same grounds as the Thebans of Athens,
—is there any charge of directly abetting the later attempt of
the invader. Even they only send information of but little
value, although certainly in terms which imply that they had

---

[1] Diod. xi. 28.

engaged, and no doubt had been paid for engaging, to do much more.

The temptations which were held out to the Athenians to desert the cause were more substantial and important; and to men who were incapable of understanding the enthusiasm of free nationality and honour, might well seem to promise a result. Attica had been ravaged once, and renewed invasion threatened the loss of a second, probably in any case but scanty, harvest, and the country was now again exposed to the first attack of overwhelming forces, and might expect to remain the cross-road and intermediate fighting-ground of all the [1] armies. The heartburnings caused by the votes at Salamis and the Isthmus could not be unknown northwards, any more than the high hand and ambitious pretensions of the city, which were not only unchecked, but even still further excited, by recent events. Some hints of covert intimations to Xerxes from Greek commanders may have helped to make the project seem more practicable. And a good price might well be offered and even paid,—though that might be optional afterwards,—if Athens could be drawn to make common cause with Persia; for, even if the Isthmus could be forced, it would manifestly be perilous to occupy Peloponnesus with no command of the sea to secure supplies or retreat by any other route. It was indeed too late to revert to the rejected counsel of Demaratus and threaten Sparta from the sea with a detachment of the Persian fleet, but an Athenian alliance would restore the lost opportunity. Communication was therefore opened through Alexander, King of Macedon, who was known to be recognised by the Athenians as their proxenus, or national host and guest. He was trusted by Mardonius from his intimate Persian connections, which read like the presage of some later Macedonian history; his sister Gygaia had married a Persian noble named Bonbares, and her

---

[1] Herod. viii. 140.

son Amyntas was established by the King as lord of Alabanda
in Phrygia; but true to the policy of double-dealing which
was the enduring characteristic of his dynasty, it was by his
warning of Persian movements that Themistocles had been
enabled to withdraw in time from the too advanced position
that he had taken up at the opening of the war, on the
northern frontier of Thessaly.

The message was delivered to the Athenians, probably by
way of flattery, as coming direct from Xerxes. Mardonius
had been commanded to pass over all former injuries,—the
rankling Sardis no less than Salamis,—and, on condition of
an alliance with him, was commissioned to restore their territory, with any addition they might desire, and their independence; and, furthermore, to re-erect all sacred structures
that he had burnt. The offer 'of freedom with no fraud or
deception' was of course backed by formidable statements of
Persian power, and, with rather less judgment, by emphasis
on the distinction of the Athenians being selected by the
Great King from the rest of the Greeks, for condonation of
offences and a proposal of friendship. The news of this communication caused the greatest alarm at Sparta, especially
in connection with the currency of a prophecy, which Herodotus says they called to mind, but which was probably
promulgated for the nonce, to the effect that Medes and
Athenians in alliance were destined to expel the Spartans
and all other Dorians from Peloponnesus. The Athenians
could not be unwilling to foster the panic by a temporary
suspense, if only to stimulate the Lacedaemonians to more
decided engagements than they had yet seemed disposed
to commit themselves to or to entertain. It is difficult to
suppose that the true scope of the crisis was not now
appreciated by the most influential men among them, but
their national maxim, to decline sustained efforts at a distance
from their frontiers, was notorious; and their inveterate
reticence, which could not but favour apprehensions of infirmity

of purpose, if not of faithlessness, was most exasperating to the Athenians,—even had they no reason to suspect that there still existed a jealousy of Athens, and an unwillingness to give her premature, or too hearty, support. But, for once, the urgency of the situation made the Spartan appeal distinct enough, and even oblivious for a moment, of the narrower affectations of Laconic brevity. 'Desertion of the cause of Hellas,' they represented, 'by those who had, by their own action and for ends of their own, provoked the invasion, would neither be just nor decorous; that servitude should be brought upon Hellas by the Athenians of all others, who had from the earliest days been champions of liberty, was intolerable. That they suffered by peculiar exposure in the contest was lamented by the Lacedaemonians and their allies, who would gladly contribute to the support of their families so long as the war should continue. Alexander was himself a tyrant, and, as the natural accomplice of a tyrant, had softened down the message of Mardonius, whose terms as delivered to others were imperious and insulting in the last degree: but the Athenians, if indeed in their right senses, — Alexander had begun with "how can you be so mad?"— would know that neither faith nor truth are to be found in the barbarians, and would accede to no such proposals.'

Thus far the Spartans, who characteristically did not spend a word upon the ultimate chances of success in the noble resistance they recommended, though they may have given offence by assuming the attraction of Persian gold for Athens under the pinch of her present destitution. In the same spirit the Athenians replied to Alexander that the numerical superiority of the Persian forces was known to them before, and in any case had nothing whatever to do with the matter in question,—their resolution to fight in defence of their liberty to the very last. With an image which glanced not only at the sun-worship of Persia, but at the tradition of the kingly rise of Alexander's own [1] family, he was commissioned to reply to Mardonius—' So long as the sun travels by the same path in which it is now moving, the Athenians will never come to accord with Xerxes, but will perseveringly resist him, putting trust for allies in the gods and the heroes, whose temples and images he has irreverently [2] burnt.

Alexander himself was warned, friend and well-wisher as the Athenians would willingly retain him, to come no more on such an unworthy and ignoble errand. It were handsome at least to think that such an expostulation, and the example of a resolution so contrasted with that of the Thessalians,— who had frankly announced that unless supported in bearing the brunt of the Persian approach, they should as a matter of course make terms with him for themselves, and had actually done [3] so,—may possibly have roused or strengthened the more generous though latent sympathies of the Macedonian, who claimed Hellenic and even Heracleidan descent, and have had influence on the circumstances under which he reappears in history.

To the decree which embodied this reply, and which was framed by Aristides, there was appended an instruction to the priests—most probably the Eleusinian, reputed descendants of Kerux and Eumolpus—to denounce curses against whosoever should make truce with the Medes or desert the Hellenic confederacy.

The reply to the Lacedaemonians was in as lofty a tone. It was excusable in the enemy, who knew no better, to believe that everything was purchaseable by money; but Lacedaemonians were justly to be quarrelled with for being capable of assuming, at sight of the present penury of the Athenians, that their resolution was likely to be decided by a promise of aid towards subsistence, rather than by their sense of duty

---

[1] Herod. viii. 137.   [2] Ib. viii. 143.   [3] Ib. vii. 172.

towards the gods of their profaned sanctuaries, and by their
Hellenic sympathies of common blood and language, of sacred
institutions and sacrifices, of conformity in moral principles.
'Know then now, if it has been unknown to you hitherto,
that never, so long as one Athenian survives, will we come to
terms with Xerxes. We acknowledge your good intentions
towards us with respect to maintaining our families in the
event of our homes being destroyed ; and so far your kindness has its full effect. For ourselves, we will get on as best
we may, and will not burden you. That which is really
urgent now is that you should send forward your army with
the utmost promptitude. The barbarian, upon learning the
failure of his envoy, will forthwith be upon us. Now therefore is the time, before he enters Attica, to advance with your
aid, and oppose him in Boeotia.' This the Lacedaemonians
engaged to do with a readiness that proved how great had
been their anxiety.

The terms of these Athenian replies might well, under
the circumstances, seem to savour of extravagance, did we
not know how well the brave words were acted up to
when the storm again broke. And if we consider what was
the ensuing history of liberated Athens, we shall recognise
from how worthy and profound a self-consciousness her enun-
ciations proceeded. Attica was now flourishing, with an
abundant population—a population that contained the men
who had conquered at Marathon and Salamis, and the fathers
of those who were to realise the best glories of the age of
Pericles. Past achievements and future resources were poten-
tially concentrated at a crisis when barbarism was threatening
all the results and all the germs of the noblest development
of humanity in its last refuge in the southernmost peninsulas
of Greece. A single generation had seen the glories of Ionia
brought to a bloody and stupefying catastrophe, and the
homes of the best Arts and the best Literature—both how
glorious !—which Hellas had up to this time originated on

her coasts and amidst her islands, ravaged by a vulgar,
tawdry, brutalised military power. The free speech of free
men in assembly and agora was proscribed, and for the independent bearings of equals, who only admitted reverence for
legal authority, for honourable age, or for moral excellence,
was substituted companionship in degrading prostrations
before the satraps of a king. The Greeks, then, were not resisting overwhelming power out of a blind obstinacy which
but for the turn of a chance or two would have been fatal,
and which no trust in such unhopeful chance could make
wise; they were not the unconscious guardians of a deposit
whose full value they did not appreciate. The last possibility
of saving Hellas was in their hands, and it was no mere
egotism on their part that made them regard this as identified with the saving of mankind, and therefore to be vindicated at any cost, at any risk,—vindicated in trust on the
gods even when no possibility of success was discernible,—for
was not death under any circumstances preferable to any life
that could continue after the obliteration from the world of
all the distinctive excellences of the life Hellenic?

The tone in which the Athenians had responded to the
envoys from Sparta intimated no disposition on their part to
withdraw from those pretensions to influence which had already
excited jealousy, and were in consequence scarcely calculated
to assist the endeavours of any partisans of Athens there who
might be anxious to hurry forward assistance. The positive
terms, again, of the defiance which was returned to Mardonius
by Alexander, had so far committed them, that apprehension
of their making terms was in a great degree set at rest.
Under these circumstances a Spartan politician might be
easily reconciled to the re-occupation of Attica, where after
all there was not much left to save; the pride of the Athenians, as he would think, might be a little reduced with no
general disadvantage; their fleet would remain as serviceable
to the cause as ever, and secure the coasts of Peloponnesus,

while no more favourable conditions could be desired for a
conflict with the Persian, than resistance to his numbers at
the narrow neck of the Isthmus, which was now fortified,
and the entanglement of his cavalry—his most formidable
arm—among the passes and declivities of the mountains
to the south. The entrenchment and fortification of. the
Isthmus had been commenced, upon the news of the death
and defeat of Leonidas, immediately after the Olympic and
Carneian festivals were [1] over. Every state of Peloponnesus
then lent aid to the work, except the Argives and Achaeans,
of whom Herodotus says that they 'kept neutral, or, to
speak frankly, by their very neutrality Medised.' The Sci-
ronian road, which was always difficult, was destroyed or
obstructed, and across the Isthmus a wall was completed of
stones, bricks, timber, and gabions, combined more or less
effectually and regularly, and by labour that went on without
intermission night and day. Nothing but the stratagem of
Themistocles, by which he succeeded in bringing on the sea-
fight against the intentions of the Peloponnesians, had prevented them, when they heard that this safeguard was so near
completion and the Persian land-force advancing upon it,
from breaking up from the Saronic gulf and leaving Aegina,
Megara, and the refugees at Salamis to their own resources—
or rather to what seemed their certain fate. After the naval
victory, and still more after the retirement of the Persians
from Athens, the work had slackened, and the Spartan regent
Cleombrotus, who superintended it, found sufficient cause for
alarm in an eclipse of the sun, that occurred as he was sacrificing, to make him withdraw home with his forces and leave
it at last unfinished. The work had therefore to be renewed
in the spring, and was still in progress when the envoys to
Athens were labouring to countervail the proposals of Alexander, and to its state of incompleteness at that time the

---

[1] Herod. viii. 71.

historian ascribes the great anxiety as to their reception. But it is difficult to suppose, as he intimates, that even the blindest Spartan could think that the defection of Athens to Persia would be of little consequence if once the fortification of the Isthmus were complete. The transfer of naval power and command of the sea would still have been as damaging as ever to the defenders of the Peloponnesus; if they were less eager to keep, or even to make, promises of sending their forces forward into Attica, it was sufficient that the promises already made had had their desired effect, and that they regarded the breach of the negotiations with Persia as irreparable. Subsequent events give us no right to suppose that Sparta was neglecting in the meantime the equipment of her own military power, or that she was less resolved than Athens to resist the invader, on her own part and on her own ground at least, to the last man.

The report which the Macedonian carried back to Thessaly had its anticipated effect, and the Persian army was at once set in motion upon Attica. Mardonius had proposed to commence operations in the spring, but it was [1] about the middle of July when he reached Athens, ten months after its occupation by Xerxes. Considerable time had been consumed in the negotiations, and even afterwards, when he arrived at Thebes, the temporising policy of that state embarrassed him more than ever. The leaders of the oligarchical party there in power were with the Persians heart and soul, and prepared even to sacrifice the independence of their country in order to secure themselves in that irresponsible supremacy allowed by Persia to faithful tributary princes,—whether tyrants or satraps,—though they knew that such a position, obnoxious as it was to their fellow-citizens, was still more so to their Athenian and Lacedaemonian neighbours, who would therefore be always ready to subvert it. The sincerity

[1] Ol. 75. 2 = B.C. 479.

of their counsel could not be doubted, and their voice
was still to corrupt and to divide the Greeks, who when
firmly united were invincible; and, in the meantime, to advance as far as Boeotia, of all places most suited for the
encampment of such an army, and there await a victory
that would come about without even a battle. Their arguments told in some degree, but could not in the end restrain
the Persian from moving on into Attica. Xerxes was still at
Sardis, and Mardonius was impatient to despatch to him the
news that he was again in possession of the hated Athens;
and he could not rest until a system of pre-arranged beacons
had transmitted, from island to island across the Aegean,
the announcement which was to vindicate the assurance of
complete success which he had given to the Great King.

There is little doubt that Aeschylus had this train of
beacons in mind, and purposely recalled it to the Athenians,
in his grand description of such a flight of fire in the 'Agamemnon.' The circumstances of time and space, which are
reasonable enough in this historical instance, have to be
strained not a little for the ten years' expectancy of Clytem-
nestra, and the provision of a series of telegraphic stations
from Troy by the line of Athos.

The Athenians had only quitted their city and country
at the last moment, trusting that in spite of deferments
and delays the Peloponnesian army would yet arrive according to engagements, and spare them a second migration; but
the enemy was presently as near as Boeotia, and no more
time was to be lost; without further delay they again moved
their families, with all their property that could be hastily
transferred, to Salamis and Troezene; and in pursuance
of a psephism of Aristides, Cimon Xanthippus and Myronides, accompanied also by representatives of [1] Megara and
Plataea, were despatched to Sparta, with fresh protest-

[1] Herod. ix. 10.

ations and [1] complaints. That Xanthippus, who was now
commander of the fleet, should have been spared for this
mission, is not so much improbable as suggestive of
the consideration that it was on the movements and destination of this fleet that the interest of the Spartans
turned. The immediate excuse for delay given to the com-
missioners was the sacred obligation to attend to the celebration of the Hyacinthia; the customs of the nation, rigid
and narrow, and adapted only for a limited range of relations, would in ordinary cases have caused this to be received
as a consistent if not reasonable apology. But the Lacedaemonians, who had appealed, so glibly for them, to what
was just and becoming, were now reminded of their broken
promises; they were reproached with the same insincerity
which they had imputed to the barbarian bidder for alliance,
in having only promised in order to gain time for completing the wall at the Isthmus, which was just fitted with
its battlements. However, let them now, though late, send
on their army, and, if not in Boeotia, fight the enemy at
least in the Thriasian plain, otherwise the Athenians on
their part too would have to look out for a 'shelter' (τινὰ
ἀλεωρὴν); an enigmatical allusion to the Isthmian wall,
made somewhat in their own laconic way, and to be interpreted by them in their own fashion.

When Mardonius had reached Athens, and was again
within a march or two of the difficult Isthmus, he thought
it worth while to make one more attempt to detach the
Athenians. We cannot wonder that the persistency professed by them should appear to him inconceivable; his
agents of corruption had made some reports, true or false,
of success,—another and that a third year of fields without a harvest was in prospect for them,—perhaps the
permanent hostile occupation of the country,—and lastly,

---

[1] Plut. *Aristid.* 10.

the support which their selfish allies had notoriously promised, and which, from the circumstances of their return, they had certainly counted on, had failed them, and failing, had left them without confidence thereafter. Accordingly, he ostentatiously refrained from doing further damage to the country, and re-opened, or endeavoured to re-open, negotiations with Athens by despatching to the Council of the Athenians at Salamis a new envoy, one Murychides of the Hellespont. This was news that of itself would fly through the Peloponnesus like wildfire, and there is no reason to suppose that the Athenians were less averse now than before to the policy of holding over an audience or a decision until the contingencies of the incident had told with full effect at Sparta. For ten successive days the Athenian envoys there had been put off, till they were wrought to the height of impatience. It was known that the fortification in the meantime was being strengthened, and it was natural to apprehend that the ephors would, at a convenient moment, put forward some pretext for breaking off their engagement. A final audience was therefore now demanded by the envoys before quitting to report at home the failure of the mission; they were, in fact, in possession of the renewed proposals of the Persian to treat, and were prepared to declare, as a final argument, that further delay must lead inevitably to their acceptance, and thence to joint action against Sparta. The ephors listened calmly to the taunt that they were occupied with the Hyacinthia, and trifling, not to say amusing themselves, while their ally was in extremity, and then announced, with the by no means superfluous guarantee of an oath, that their force was already despatched against the ' strangers,' and must by that time—in the early morning—be already well forward beyond the frontiers. The news of the reopened negotiation —so it was believed—had wrought this change over-night. If a certain Chileus of Tegea, who was credited with having

had most influence after Themistocles in originally uniting
Hellas against the [1] Mede, and was, of all foreigners, in the
highest credit with the Lacedaemonians, really contributed to
their decision now, it must have been by the expression of
his belief that there was imminent danger of the negotiation
resulting in an alliance.   That the consequence of this must
be ' to throw open wide portals into Peloponnesus, however
strongly the Isthmus might be barred,' the ephors did not
require to be told.

The large force which was despatched so suddenly must
necessarily have been under preparation for emergencies all
along, with the secrecy that was an established maxim of
Spartan policy; and this is adverted to by Pericles later
as a contrast to the fearless publicity of Athenian politics.
It consisted of 5,000 Spartiats, each attended by seven
Helots (5,000 + 35,000 = 40,000 men).   Cleombrotus had
died soon after his withdrawal from the Isthmus, and
the splendid command devolved, with most important historical consequences, on his son Pausanias, as regent in
the place of his cousin Pleistarchus, son of Leonidas, who
was still a minor.   He chose as his own second in command, Euryanax son of Dorieus, of the same royal house.
This army—by far the largest that we ever read of as
sent forth by Sparta—was complemented by 5,000 more
heavy-armed Lacedaemonians, or perioeci (citizens of other
Lacedaemonian towns than Sparta), and with them started
the well-satisfied envoys from Salamis, in all haste to overtake the first columns.   An untoward but natural consequence of the reserve, if not hesitation, of Sparta, was the
lateness in the field of some of the other Peloponnesian
contingents.

The negotiations at Salamis, which there was now no
further motive or even means for protracting, concluded

---

[1] Plut. *Them.* 6.

with a tragic incident. The Hellespontian Murychides was dismissed unharmed after delivering his message to the Council, but when Lycides, a member of it, whether influenced or not by Persian gold, proposed that the offer of the Persian should be submitted to the popular assembly, indignation rose instantly to its height among his assessors, and out of doors also as soon as the occasion was known. Lycides was set upon and stoned to death; the tumult presently roused the Athenian women, and in contagious excitement they rushed to his dwelling and stoned to death his family also—both wife and children.

It is probable that this fury had in part a religious origin, and that Lycides had brought himself and his family within the bitter and comprehensive terms of the curse that had been solemnly denounced against favourers of the Mede.

CHAPTER IV.

B.C. 479, September; Ol. 75. 2.

THE Lacedaemonians made halt at the Isthmus, where
they were joined by forces from other states of Peloponnesus. Here terms and resolutions were adopted in a Hellenic congress, as well for the concentration of troops and
supplies from various quarters both without and within the
Isthmus, as for the purpose of encouraging—or, let us rather
say, giving expression to—a spirit of common enthusiasm
and mutual reliance. The usual promises were made to the
gods in the event and expectation of victory; their assistance was claimed with confidence against the profaners of
their desolated sanctuaries—assistance which should be fitly
acknowledged and recompensed, though the ruins were to
remain in ashes for all time as memorials of barbarian
sacrilege. The terms of an oath that was to be a bond of
present and future unity ran thus :—' I will not regard
life as of any value in comparison with liberty ; I will not
desert my leaders either living or dead ; I will procure
burial for whoever of the allies may fall in battle ; and
when the barbarian is overcome I will not afterwards subvert any city that has taken part in the struggle against
him.'

The last clause is significant of the apprehensions that
were haunting some of the weaker and more exposed members

of the Hellenic community in presence of the growing ambition of stronger powers. The Argives, unconciliated by
this guarantee, held entirely aloof, avowedly on the ground
that their population had been too seriously reduced by their
defeat in a recent conflict with Sparta for them to risk the
loss of more blood at present, especially as such loss would
only leave them at the mercy of the protagonist whom they
were invited to strengthen; a further unavowed motive lay in
the fact that the strength of Sparta was the main obstacle to ·
certain ambitious projects of their own. That the Athenians
had very distinct views of encroachment was notorious, and
this notoriety had been ominously emphasised by the offer
of Mardonius to help them to whatever additional territory
they wished to acquire. Thus the threatened states of
Mycenae and Aegina had forebodings that were too well
justified in the event, and naturally claimed and clung to
the guarantee of a solemn sanction, the concession of which
at this crisis was probably due to the prevailing spirit of
high-wrought patriotic enthusiasm, as much as to any suggestion of policy.

As soon as the omens were favourable, and the requisite
arrangements and musters complete, the Peloponnesian force
was at last really set in motion to cross the Isthmus and
the Megarid. By this time Mardonius had determined to
evacuate Attica, after being kept in suspense by the Athenians till the very last [1] moment. A swift messenger from
the Argives now brought him the advice, perhaps not much
earlier than the bootless return of Murychides, that the
Lacedaemonians would certainly appear forthwith beyond
the Isthmus; so that any wild hopes of effective obstruction
that they might have encouraged the barbarian to expect
on their part, had to be renounced, and it remained for him
to take his own measures.

---

[1] Herod. ix. 13.

The unfitness of Attica for the action and evolutions of cavalry, and, ravaged as it had been, for furnishing supplies, as well as the difficulties of a retreat by a large force, in case of a reverse, through the northern passes, determined him to withdraw at once to the more open plains and accessible resources of Boeotia and the neighbourhood of the strong and friendly city of Thebes. His last days in Attica were spent in destroying whatever could be destroyed and had hitherto been politicly spared, and in throwing down, so far as time allowed, whatever still remained standing of the walls and temples of the city. The Boeotarchs, his zealous quartermasters, furnished him with guides for the eastern route by Decelea and Sphendale, across Parnes to Tanagra—a considerable circuit, but affording any more easy passes, and avoiding any risk of molestation from the Isthmus to which the western might be exposed. He was already on the road, when a report that a body of not more than 1000 Lacedaemonians had advanced to Megara tempted him to check his march and make an attempt to snatch a victory, however trifling, before he retired. Turning back his army, he despatched a cavalry force in advance, which rapidly overran the Megarid without encountering opposition; and this was the furthest point of Europe towards the setting-sun that a Persian invader ever reached. One of his detachments, however, became entangled among the mountains and was cut [1] off; and upon this check, and receipt of more formidable accounts of the muster at the Isthmus, he turned once more, and finally resumed the route to Decelea.

The dedication of a bronze statue to Artemis Soteira was in later days ascribed by the Megarians to the occasion of this incident, which, as it came to be related, wanted not mythic embellishment. It was, they said, by device of Artemis that night overtook the retiring Persians, who first

---

[1] Paus. i. 40. § 2.

lost their way among the mountains, and then, when they discharged arrows to test the proximity of an enemy, were so far beguiled by the echoes of the rock, which they mistook for groans, that they exhausted their quivers and fell an easy prey at daybreak to the Megarian hoplites.

Mardonius remained at Tanagra only a night, and the next day turned westward and reached Scolus on Theban territory, about forty stadia—four miles and a half—down the Asopus on the road between Thebes and [1] Plataea. The Lacedae-monians on their part advanced to the Thriasian plain as far as Eleusis, and then made halt. The sacrifices were again to be scanned for a suggestion to proceed; and, as at the Isthmus they had waited for the other Peloponnesians, who 'affected the better things,' to make an effort, in spite of the shortness of the notice, not to be behindhand in the field, so here also time was to be allowed for further pre-paration, and for a junction with an important reinforce-ment of the Athenians, who were to cross from Salamis, under command of Aristides, son of Lysimachus, elected [2] *autocrator*, and thus independent of the association of col-leagues which had hampered Miltiades. Then at last the combined army started direct for Boeotia. It crossed Mount Cithaeron by the western passes and emerged above Erythrae. The Persian host was full in view, encamped on the plain between the line of the Asopus, here flowing eastward and parallel to the main ridge of Cithaeron, and Erythrae and Hysiae on the higher ground opposite to the verge of the Plataean territory. In the rear of this position and beyond the Asopus a vast enclosure had been formed and strengthened by a timber palisade, for which all trees within reach were felled indiscriminately—necessity, says Herodotus, compelling disregard of the friendliness of the country. The enclosure, though over a mile square (ten

---

[1] Paus. ix. 4. § 3.   [2] Plut. *Aristid.* 11.

stadia), was not intended for occupation by the army unless
in the event of aught falling out untowardly in the expected
battle; in the meantime it was a repository of the vast necessary stores, as well as of the general baggage and appliances
that were always required by Persian luxury even in the
midst of a campaign.

In this position the Persian army received a lagging reinforcement of 1000 Phocian hoplites, under command of
Harmocydes, a citizen of marked reputation. The Medism
of the Phocians was most reluctant, but less so, Herodotus
thought, from Hellenic sympathy than out of hatred to the
Thessalians; and it was only under compulsion of their neighbourhood to Thessaly and Thebes that this dilatory aid was
rendered at all. They had not joined early enough to take
part in the invasion of Attica, and were the more mistrusted
from the direct hostility of a part of their population. These
had taken refuge in considerable numbers on Mount Parnassus, and found a place of security for themselves and their
property at Tithora, a steeply-scarped rocky position from
whence they had seriously harassed the Persians and their
[1] confederates.

Mardonius sent orders to the new arrival to take up a
position on the open plain, and then a scene ensued of which
Herodotus did not pretend to know the exact explanation.
A sudden suspicion—a φήμη or unaccountable sympathetic
impression—ran through all the Greek allies, including the
Phocians themselves, that mischief was intended towards them.
Harmocydes apprehended the ill offices of the Thessalians as
much as the anger of the Persian, and called on his company
to show their mettle by selling their lives dearly. His appeal
was scarcely made when a cloud of horsemen were upon them,
charged close up to them, now wheeled round and now sur-
rounded them, ever with threatening weapons, though only

---

[1] Herod. viii. 32 ; Plut. *Vit. Sullae,* 14 ; Paus. x. 32.

one or two darts may have been, as if accidentally, discharged. The intention probably was not so much to provoke attack as to cause alarm, and then, when the expected dispersion and flight began, to slaughter the fugitives. The Phocians however coolly stood to their arms, closed their ranks to the utmost, and faced to every threatened attack; and Mardonius was fain to turn the matter off with a compliment to the courage which he said had been impugned, but which, so tested, commanded his absolute confidence.

It was during these days that an incident occurred which, as recorded by Herodotus, has all the interest of an autobiographical notice: it brings home to us how near he himself was in time to the events his history had reached, and to authentic information respecting them; and by its implications adds great value to his general testimony as to the present crisis of the Persian expedition. A magnificent entertainment was provided in Thebes for the Persians and their Hellenic allies by Attaginus son of Phrynon, who together with Timegenidas was in control of the whole power and policy of the state. Mardonius and fifty of the most distinguished Persians were invited to meet fifty Thebans at dinner, where the two nations were not only arranged alternately but in pairs—a Theban and a Persian sharing a single couch between them. The dinner over, wine circulated according to universal Greek rather than earlier Persian manners; and it was then that a Persian who conversed in Greek opened his mind to the guest with whom he was associated. This was a certain Thersander, a man of much note at Orchomenus, and Herodotus received the particulars from Thersander himself, who assured him that he had given the same account to others at the time, before the catastrophe that was so painfully apprehended arrived. Having assured himself by an enquiry that his companion was not an actual Theban, and possibly of something more, ' With you, now,' said the Persian, ' as my partner at meat

and in libation, I would fain leave remembrance of what is
my conviction; that you may be forewarned on your own
account, and take counsel for the best. You see these Persians
feasting here; you saw the army that we left encamped down
by the river; let a short time have gone by and of all these
men you will behold but some few survivors.' The words were
spoken with the sincerity attested by abundant tears. The
Greek in surprise suggested (and we must assume that some
grounds were indicated for his conviction) that surely in this
case it was incumbent to communicate with Mardonius and
those of the Persians who were in credit with him. ' Stranger,'
was the reply, ' what God has determined shall be, man is
incompetent to avert; for none will give attention to any,
however credible their statements. Of all that I tell you
abundance of our Persians are conscious; but we go on
fettered by necessity; and the bitterest pang of all it is for
man to see and know what circumstances demand and yet
to be destitute of power.'

These are words of which the full import will only be
recognised by one who has been near enough to head-quarters
to see interests of great importance with which his own are
inextricably involved, going to rack and ruin through the
obstinate self-conceit and blind jealousy of managers alike
unassailable by their position and insensible to truth whether
bluntly demonstrated, or adroitly suggested. Whether the
dejected Persian was an adherent of the unhopeful and discontented Artabazus, or dreaded how Mardonius might
be hampered by his half-hearted support, it matters little;
more probably he had discovered that the organisation
and order requisite for so vast an army were wanting,
and that the supreme direction lay where decisive action
might be precipitated at any moment by the worst
advisers, the excitement of a moment, blind refusal to
modify a judgment once announced, or to accept information, much less a conclusion, from a subordinate though

F

sagacious associate. As we read the account of the final conflict, the elements of danger seem so rife on the other side within the Hellenic councils, that we can scarcely conceive the case to have been worse in the Persian. The difference lay in the fact that there was a germ of healthy vigour underneath the dissensions and heart-burnings of the Greeks, which counteracted great mischiefs, and assured a survival of their cause through embarrassments that would be fatal to their enemies.

The Persian commander had made no attempt to dispute or harass the passage of the mountains ; his expectation and hope was, to be attacked, or to have opportunity of attacking, in the position he had taken up in the plain, where his excellent cavalry, Persian and Thessalian—an arm of which the Greeks were entirely destitute—would operate with most effect ; the rugged and contracted passes being trusted to complete the confusion when the troops were flying in disorder. As the Greek forces emerged from the passes and took up their position along the higher slopes of Cithaeron, in the direction of Erythrae, eastward of the roads that ran direct to Thebes, they were out of reach of the enemy's cavalry. But there was scarcity of water from the first, and afterwards, as the rendezvous was completed, they were so far cramped for room, from the proximity of the enemy, that some detachments—the Megarians especially—had to occupy ground that was considerably exposed. Upon the Megarians accordingly Mardonius, after waiting in vain for the descent of the general army, gave orders for an attack by the entire division of cavalry, of which a large proportion at least were bowmen, under the command of Masistius, one of the most important of the Persians. This was executed by the wheeling of successive squadrons on the same system that was to be employed long after, with historic results, on the plains of Parthia ; and had so much effect, that the Megarians, while still maintaining their ground courageously, sent word to the generals that unless relieved they must break line and retire. An epigram collected among those of Simonides celebrates this resistance without the qualification. That the authority of the general-in-chief of the allied Greeks was limited, appears from the fact that Pausanias left it to their option who among them should undertake this duty; and Herodotus puts it unreservedly to the credit of the Athenians that they were the first to volunteer to the front. But the Athenians had in fact profited by their experience at Marathon to adjust their equipments in some degree to the special requirements of conflict with the Median archers. At Marathon they had been forced to rush to the attack—heavy-armed as they were—with no protection from skirmishers, either bowmen or cavalry, whereas we now find them provided with a force of bowmen whose special duty was to co-operate with hoplites; [1] Ctesias even states that they had been procured by Aristides and Themistocles from Crete. In the present case they accompanied three hundred select hoplites under the command of Olympiodorus, son of Lampon. The contest still continued for some time after their arrival, the Persian horsemen constantly careering past, and as they discharged their weapons adding taunts of womanishness, to provoke, if possible, an advance. At last, in the return of one charge, the Nisaean horse of Masistius was pierced in the flank by a happy arrow, and rearing in frantic pain, shook off its splendidly-accoutred rider. The Athenians were upon him instantly, the horse, golden-bitted and superbly caparisoned, was captured, and Masistius himself, though saved for a time by the accurate completeness of his armour—a mailed shirt of golden scales hid below his purple vest—which disappointed the strokes of his assailants, was at length killed as he lay prostrate, by a weapon which pierced him through his eye. In the speed and confusion of the wheeling horsemen this catastrophe was unobserved

[1] *ap. Phot.*

until the troop, drawing up at a distance to re-form, found themselves without a leader. As soon as the loss was known the word was given, and the entire force at once came on, no longer in detachments but in mass, resolved at least to rescue the body.

It was now the turn of the Athenians, as they saw the coming shock, to send for assistance, and, till it arrived, they had to sustain, and did sustain, a desperate conflict. Though compelled to retire from the dead body, they did not allow it to be secured by the enemy, before the arrival of the rein-forcements obliged the latter to retire in their turn and leave it with more of their numbers in the hands of the Greeks. At the distance of two stadia they again drew up, but were soon seen, after a short consultation, returning to their camp.

The elation of the Greeks at this success was boundless. It was much to have sustained unflinchingly the detached onsets of this redoubted cavalry, but how much more to have repulsed it in a body! The enthusiasm rose to its height when the corpse of Masistius was placed upon a cart and carried through the army, where all as it passed quitted their ranks to behold it, and gazed at it with the peculiar gratification of Greeks. It was well worth seeing, says Herodotus, so large it was and so beautiful. And soon a clamour from the Persian camps revealed how severe a blow was admitted in the death of Masistius, a man second only to Mardonius in the estimation of the Persians them-selves as well as of the Great King. The barbarians, in a frenzy of grief, were cutting off not only their own hair but even that of horses and beasts of burden, while 'the echo of their lamentations'—faintly represented to us by the prolonged wailings of the Persians of Aeschylus—'filled all [1] Boeotia.' The cries as they were re-echoed from the cliffs of Cithaeron confirmed the courage and enhanced the confidence of the defenders of their native land.

[1] Herod. ix. 24.

The elation of their own army and the dismay of the enemy now enabled the Greek generals to effect a change of position, which had indeed become urgent; and a descent of their entire force was at once made without molestation from the Erythraean to the Plataic district, the lower level of which afforded freer space for encamping, and access to water. The line of march inclined to the north-west, across the spurs of Cithaeron, past Hysiae; and the army, in its divisions of tribes or nations, ultimately occupied a line of intermixed plain and low hillocks, extending—as is distinctly implied in the phrase of [1] Herodotus—from another branch of the river on the west to a copious fountain called Gargaphia, eastward.

The formal order of array was not assumed without interruption from a tribal claim to precedence, which was asserted and set aside in a manner premonitory of the dying out of some other more important traditions. The right wing in the Greek army was the post of honour—possibly from mere symbolical dignity as right, or because, as exposing the unshielded side of the hoplites to a flank attack, it was a post of more peculiar danger than the left and otherwise equally uncovered extremity. This was conceded as a matter of course to the Lacedaemonians, but the Tegeans contested the left wing with the Athenians, to whom it had been assigned. With a certain Arcadian hebetude they pleaded before the Lacedaemonians a title based on the slaying of Hyllus, a Heracleid ancestor of their kings in mythical times, and many not unsuccessful contests against the present arbiters later on. The Athenians replied that they had come out to fight and not to argue; but for themselves, if antiquity is to be considered, they might say that if the Tegeans killed Heracleids, their ancestors took arms victoriously in defence of them, besides other exploits which they mentioned, but did not insist on. 'Courage or cowardice in one age is no warrant for the next; what is

[1] Herod. ix. 31.

more to the purpose in approving our title, apart from these later achievements, is our single-handed victory at Marathon against this same enemy. No difficulty however shall arise on our part at such a time; place us where you please, Lacedaemonians, and opposed to whomsoever; in any post we shall do our very best; give the command and you will be at once obeyed.' A general shout from the Lacedaemonian ranks in favour of the Athenians—a transference to camp of the vote by acclamation customary at Sparta—was accepted as a decision, and so this question was decided in accordance with the first intentions of Pausanias. In completing his general dispositions, he placed the Lacedaemonian force which was under his direct command at the extreme right, and consoled the Tegeans by giving them the position immediately next in succession.

The original order of array of heavy- and light-armed together then follows according to this enumeration :—

	Hoplites.	Light-armed.
Lacedaemonians 10,000, of whom 5,000 were Spartiats, each	5,000	5,000
attended by 7 helots	5,000	35,000
Total from Sparta	10,000	40,000
Tegeans	1,500	1,500
Corinthians 5,000, with whom, by special permission of Pausanias, were 300 Potidaeans from their colony at Pallene	5,300	5,300
Arcadians of Orchomenus, 600 ; Sicyonians, 3,000	3,600	3,600
Epidaurians, 800 ; Troezenians, 1,000...................	1,800	1,800
Lepreans, 200 ; Mycenians and Tirynthians, 400	600	600
Phliasians, 1,000 ; Hermionians, 300	1,300	1,300
Total Peloponnesians	24,100	54,100
From Euboea—Eretrians and Styrians, 600 ; Chalcidians, 400	1,000	1,000
Ambracians, 500 ; Leucadians and Anactorians, 800......	1,300	1,300
Palians from Cephallene, 200 ; Aeginetans, 500	700	700
Megaraeans..	3,000	3,000
Plataeans...	600	600
Athenians...	8,000	8,000
Totals....	38,700	68,700

This catalogue of names is verified by that copied by Pausanias the traveller from the base of a dedicated statue at Olympia, which contains them all except the [1] Palians. The names of islands of the group of Cyclades—Ceos, Melos, Tenos, Naxos, Cythnos—included at Olympia may have been omitted in the history solely from the trifling numbers they could contribute. The omission, in the inscription, of Andros and Paros, the only other important islands of the group, agrees with the pressure applied to them in the history, for Medism. Of the force of hoplites, in full defensive armour, the best—the Athenians and Plataeans 8,600, and Lacedaemonians 10,000—do not together amount to a full half, but their entire forces, heavy and light, including the vast proportion of helots, make up more than half the army.

The entire array as given by Herodotus comprised of heavy-armed men, 38,700, to whom he adds the light-armed, 69,500, made up of 35,000 helots (7 to each Spartiat), and 34,500 for the rest of the Lacedaemonians and Greeks ('about one to each man'); giving a total number of combatants 108,200.

The light-armed, as given in his grand total, are 800 in excess of the reckoning of one to each hoplite, but the difference—as indeed the expression of the historian—only indicates a variation from a general proportion, which must have occurred in one direction or the other. A muster of the round number of 110,000 is completed by reckoning in 1,800 Thespian refugees from their burnt city, who were 'without arms,' that is, equipped irregularly.

As soon as the ceremonial mourning for the death of Masistius was concluded, Mardonius moved his forces westward, so as to confront the Greeks in their new position. A branch of the Asopus now separated the two armies; the stream at this season—late in summer—must have been

---

[1] Pausanias, v. 23.

fordable all along its course, as it is not taken into consideration as a serious military obstacle ; even in spring it could be easily crossed between Plataea and Thebes, unless when swollen by sudden heavy [1] rain. His own forces, like those of the Greeks, were now disposed with reference to an impending conflict. The Persians, whom he accounted his best soldiers, he opposed to the Greek left wing, and the best of them again, by instruction of the Thebans, to the Lacedaemonians ; the others to the Tegeans, whose array they were numerous enough to overlap, though drawn up in deep ranks. Assuming that the helots and light-armed soldiers throughout were in proximity to their respective nations, the Persians would be opposed to 50,000 Lacedaemonians and 3,000 Tegeans, or little under one half the numerical Greek force, though to less than a third of the heavy-armed. The Medes were next, opposed to 17,800 Corinthians, Arcadians, and Sicyonians ; the Bactrians were opposed to Epidaurians, Troezenians, Lepreans, Tirynthians, Mycenians, and Phliasians ; the Indians to the Hermionians, who from their Dryopian relationship were ranged, not with their neighbours of Troezene, but with Eretrians, Styrians, and Chalcidians from Euboea ; the Sakae opposed the Ambracians, Anactorians, Leucadians, Palians, and Aeginetans. The Bactrians, Indians, and Sakae—for the most part a miserably armed and undisciplined mob—had thus to match 13,400 men. Lastly, the strong force and approved quality of the Athenians, together with the Plataeans and Megaraeans—23,000 of all arms—were to be encountered by the Medising Greeks, the Boeotians, Locrians, Melians, Thessalians, and neighbouring tribes, and the 1000 Phocians ; and here also were the Macedonians. Other troops, whose places are not noted, were Phrygians, Thracians, Mysians, Paeonians and others, besides the Aethiopians and Egyptians, who had been withdrawn from the fleet. The total barbarian forces of Mardonius, at least at their original [2] muster, are numbered

---

[1] Thucyd. ii. 1–5.   [2] Herod. ix. 32 ; cf. viii. 113.

at 300,000 horse and foot. Of his Hellenic allies the number had never been taken, and was not known—at a guess it might be 50,000, exclusive of horsemen ; and for these figures Herodotus is responsible.

The most formidable superiority of the Persians however lay not in their numbers at large, but in the numbers and excellence of their cavalry, both of their zealous Thessalian supporters and of the Sakae and their own mounted bowmen —(*hippotoxatae*)—in many respects the equivalents of modern field-artillery. The Greeks, on the other hand, had the advantage of armoured as opposed to unarmoured men, with that corresponding superiority in offensive weapons which Aristagoras had urged on Cleomenes as an encouragement to the Greeks to strike for the conquest of Susa [1] itself,— in terms as ominously significant as the conviction put into the mouth of Xerxes, that the quarrel between Greece and Persia was to the death, and would only be concluded by the entire subjugation of Greece by Persia or of the Persian empire by [2] Greece. The short spear and bow of the Persian foot-soldier prevented his carrying a shield of any strength and magnitude, and the want of such defence was poorly supplied by *gerrha,* a kind of wicker hurdles covered with hides, and fixed into the ground by spikes as a fence before the line. With no body armour whatever, nor effective helmet, he was but a poor match at close quarters for the Greek, of sedulously strengthened and exercised frame, protected yet not encumbered by the shield and panoply of the hoplite, and still equal to wielding a stouter and longer spear. Any advantage that the Persian might hope for and even be encouraged in by his Theban allies, from the unity of a despotic command as opposed to a confederacy of commanders, mutually and not without reason jealous and distrustful of each other, was just now materially counteracted by the withdrawal of Xerxes,

[1] Herod. v. 49. [2] Ib. vii. 11.

and is at best always dependent on the co-existence with irresponsible power of military genius, or at least of a spirit that would repudiate reliance on the lash as the leading motive of concerted [1] energy.

As regards the Lacedaemonians, it was most true, as Demaratus warned [2] Xerxes, that freemen as they were, in one sense they were not free, for Law (ὁ νόμος) was to them a master who exacted obedience more implicit than was ever rendered to the Great King himself; obedient to this master in all respects, they were especially so in this, that they were under obligation when battle once was joined never to fly before any number of enemies, but standing their ground either to prevail or perish. For the rest, a still nobler self-consciousness was animating the Athenians,—the rivals of the Lacedaemonians by their achievements at Marathon, and especially at Salamis. With them individual genius was of more avail than rigour of technical discipline; and even among the minor states a spirit of enthusiastic emulation in patriotism went far to obliterate for the time the jealousies that were being nobly set aside by their leaders.

The two armies were now within easier reach of each other, and yet the collision was delayed. The Greeks were still receiving reinforcements and supplies, and had taken up ground where they were content to await an attack, but which they could not quit without seriously exposing themselves to the formidable flights of horsemen, especially about the banks and channel of the river should they attempt to cross it. The conclusions of the generals were duly reflected in the entrails of the sacrifices, which on either side were interpreted so as to promise success in repelling attack, but failure in case of commencing it. Such was the report made to the Hellenic generals on the second day after the army had taken up its new position. Their soothsayer was Tisamenus, son of Antiochus, an Iamid of Elis, and as such

[1] Herod. vii. 103. [2] Ib. vii. 102.

a member of a highly-reputed family of hereditary diviners; the origin of their ancestor and his art furnishes the mythical adornment of an ode of Pindar for a mule-car victory at Olympia gained by a relative of the clan some ten years after the present date. Tisamenus had been engaged by the Spartans for this war under circumstances calculated —we may probably say literally so—to raise confidence in him to the highest degree. They had made a concession— unparalleled since the mythical instance of Melampus, which it mimicked — of adopting him and his brother also — the latter on raised terms after their first hesitation—as a Spartan citizen; for it had been promised to him by the Delphic oracle that he should preside as diviner at five first-class victories, and of these not one was as yet accomplished. Tisamenus— so much for the consciousness of the prophetic faculty—had first interpreted the oracle as promising a victory in the pen- tathlon, but missed it through failure in the wrestling-match against Hieronymus the Andrian at Olympia. Pausanias saw the statue of the victor athlete there centuries after. The credit of the oracle was saved, apparently without damage to that of the merely instrumental diviner, by the alter- native reference to military victories. Herodotus catalogues its fulfilments in this sense, with a simplicity of faith that vindicates the prudence of the politicians who, what- ever their own faith,—and the survival of dread is not inconsistent with mistrust,—could not prudently forgo any influence either for encouragement or restraint. Aristides, according to Plutarch, had obtained a Pythian response which was inconveniently—or conveniently—equivocal. It might even have sanctioned a present retreat or renewed contest in Attica. As matters stood, means were afterwards found for reconciling it with a station near an ancient fane of Eleusinian goddesses, which, if not the best strategically, was at least unavoidable. Near such a fane, we learn from Herodotus, the battle raged at last, so that Plutarch appears to be in error in placing it in proximity to Hysiae, the earlier Athenian [1] station.

Like ceremonies with like result were proceeding in the Persian camp, where Mardonius chafed impatiently under the restraint they imposed upon him. His soothsayer, Hegesistratus, was also of Elis and of the Telliad branch of the Iamid clan; but to him no good fortune is ascribed. He had once escaped death at Spartiat hands by breaking from prison, where he had slipped bond by mutilating his foot; he was now by his own hatred and a heavy price engaged against the Spartans on the side of the Mede, but to little purpose, as he was doomed to be caught and put to death by them at last, when again as vainly exercising his function at Zacynthus.

The Medising Greeks had also their diviner, Hippomachus, a Leucadian, who naturally told the same tale as Hegesistratus, and as day drew on tediously after day, forbade joining battle, and so aided the temporising policy of the Thebans, who still urged upon the fretting Persian that corruption, if but sufficiently unsparing, and combined with delay, must infallibly break up the Greek confederacy.

Herodotus, though assuming throughout that in the Greek cities without distinction there were men in influential positions so susceptible of bribery as to make such a policy by far the most natural and promising, yet warns us not to disallow the existence of a healthy patriotism—which he asserts with enthusiasm—in the very communities most liable to be weakened and disabled by the selfish treachery of a class. It was not without some special encouragement that the Medising Greeks beyond the Asopus promised speedy fruits from such intrigues. Treachery had obtained some footing even in the Athenian camp, and, however serious in itself, would certainly be magnified by agents with the treasures of Persia at command. The head-quarters of the inchoate

---

[1] *Arist.* 12.

conspiracy were in a house at Plataea,—the haunt of discontented men, whose importance was originally based on
family and wealth, and was now reduced both by the
impoverishing ravages of the war, and by the emergence
of new men at the requirement of the country for the
service of more genuine personal endowments. Even the
democratic innovations of Cleisthenes were not likely to be
held irreversible, when the tone of the embattled combatants
by land and sea already threatened their extension. An
attempt at oligarchical if not tyrannous reaction was always
ready to arise amidst the difficulties of a Greek democracy;
it was only by promptitude that Athens had been saved from
such a crisis, when Miltiades was afield with her citizens at
Marathon. The leaven was still within the lump,—and every
Athenian politician knew it be there, and the apprehension
of it was never so justifiable, or so soon likely to be confirmed by events, as while it was being made a stock jest
against Demus by Aristophanes. The first step towards the
'dissolution of the demus' was to play into the hands of the
Persians, and it would be no matter of surprise if the Delphic
oracle, which seemed to counsel retreat to Eleusis, and which
Aristides could only with difficulty strain into an equivoca-
tion compatible with strategic requirements, were procured
by the bribes of Medising Athenians. The ears of statesmen
worthy of the name, like the eyes of physicians, are quick
for symptoms that ought to be expected. Aristides was on
the alert, but took measures rather to disperse the germs
of mischief than to attempt to extirpate radically what he
was well aware could never be absolutely destroyed; and
at the present conjuncture especially it was better thoroughly to overawe the discontented than to reveal to them
their own strength and thus drive them into more complete intercommunication, or to risk a panic by publishing
the existence of treachery at such a moment. He seized
eight only in the camp, brought two of these as the

most compromised—Aeschines of the deme of Lampriae, and Agesias an Acharnian — to immediate trial, and on being, perhaps purposely, rid of these by flight, had a pretext for moderate treatment of the rest. To the accessories—left in uncertainty whether they might or might not be known—he indicated the field of the coming battle as the true court in which it was open to them to clear themselves of all imputations. The secret of this policy appears to be the same as that of the tenderness of the Potidaeans to the traitors of Scione.

For eight days the two armies were thus confronted in inaction, when Timegenidas son of Herpys, the colleague of Attaginus at Thebes, suggested to Mardonius a stroke which inflicted serious loss and embarrassment on the Greeks. By their movement westward the latter had left· unguarded a road that led direct from Thebes to the same pass over Mount Cithaeron by which their chief supplies reached Plataea, along a branch road from the Pass of Three Heads as the Boeotians, or of Oak-heads as the Athenians called it. A body of horse despatched at night swooped upon a train of five hundred beasts of burden laden with provisions for the Greek camp; in a fierce onslaught they killed a number of the animals as well as the men conducting them, and carried off the remainder beyond the Asopus. Nor was the Greek army in the position it now occupied able to secure the passage for the future, and their supplies were in consequence blocked up in the [1]mountains.

Two days more were marked by no further hostilities than harassing annoyance to the Greeks from the enemy's horse, which, constantly incited but not much aided by the Thebans, skirmished to the right of their line in the direction of the pass. The barbarians also came down as far as the Asopus, and there annoyed the Greeks with missiles; but neither crossed the channel.

[1] Herod. ix. 39–50.

By the eleventh day the impatience of Mardonius under the restraint to which he had subjected himself by deference to the diviners of his Greek allies, and in a degree to Artabazus, who was among the few Persians whose authority was conferred by a personal hold on the Great King, became no longer endurable. Remonstrance served but to precipitate his resolution. The only effect of their delay had been that the Greek army had been growing stronger and stronger, and would continue to do so. The Persian army must act at once, before their vast superiority, which now assured to them the victory, was further impaired; they must not force Hegesistratus and his victims by continued pertinacity, but just leave them alone, and join battle, employing simply the old Persian forms. His resolution had only been confirmed by the plain-spoken objections of Artabazus, who, in terms that could not but be offensive, and intentionally so to a sanguine chief who saw victory before him, urged that the entire army should fall back at once and, relying on Theban fortifications, remain on the defensive; they would there be within easy reach of abundant stores and forage, the exhaustion of which in their advanced position must no doubt have weighed with Mardonius; they could resort to intrigue and bribery, as recommended by the Thebans, and wait tranquilly for a result that must come about without any battle of importance.

But against the absolute determination of the appointed head of the expedition—who was not only brother-in-law to Xerxes, as having married his sister [1] Artazostres, but also at once son-in-law and nephew, both by blood and marriage, of [2] Darius—nothing was to be said; a very short leading question silenced the patrons of the diviners. The Persian officers and Hellenic commanders were assembled; to the demand, Were they aware of any oracle predicting the destruction of the Persians in Greece, they could only

---

[1] Herod. vi. 43.　　　　[2] Ib. vii. 2 ; vii. 5.

say No, or be silent. 'Well then,' he resumed, 'I will tell you that such an oracle there is ; but it declares the catastrophe to be contingent on our sacking Delphi. This, forewarned, we have neither done nor attempted, and therefore let all who are friends to the Persians know that our victory over the Greeks is certain.'

Herodotus takes upon himself to say that he knew what oracle Mardonius had in mind, but that it was entirely misapplied by him—not an unusual accident with prophecies. He himself knew prophecies, both of Bacis and Musaeus, much more to the purpose, and quotes one which is certainly as explicit as could be desired—whenever it may have been composed.

The council, if it can be so called, broke up with a command to have all in readiness for action the next morning.

In the depth of that night a horseman from the Median camp rode over secretly to the Athenian outposts, and, obtaining an interview with the commanders, gave warning of what was to be expected on the morrow, that they might not be taken unawares. He added the encouraging information that the sacrifices were still adverse to the Persians, and that Mardonius, who had been long ago eager for battle, and had done all he could to get more favourable omens, was now going to fight, notwithstanding their adverseness, at break of day ; he counselled them to stand their ground even should the onset be deferred, as their enemies would run short of supplies within a few days at farthest. 'And should this war have the event that you desire, let some thought be taken of me and of my liberation, who—a Greek by descent—have run this risk from sympathy with general Greece ; I am Alexander of Macedon.'

This news was immediately communicated by the Athenian commanders to Pausanias at the other extremity of the line, and elicited a proposal to which the Athenians at once assented, professing indeed that only delicacy prevented their own suggestion of it at first as the most reasonable plan.

It was that the Athenians should change places with the Lacedaemonians—from the left wing to the right,—so as to be opposed to the Persians, of whose mode of fighting they had had experience at Marathon, while the Lacedaemonians would be opposed to familiar enemies—Boeotians and Thessalians. The readiness with which Pausanias, Spartan as he is, resigns the traditional post of honour is to his credit as a general, if in truth the change had a sound military motive. The explanation of this, though passed in silence by Herodotus, lies no doubt in the fact already noticed, of the large proportion of bowmen in the Athenian armament, adapting it peculiarly for resisting troops, especially cavalry, equipped with the same weapon. The surmounting or uptearing of such a fence as the Persians were wont to place before them was again manifestly a feat more easy for Athenians than for Lacedaemonians, whose drill, however perfect in itself, left them always at a loss before a fortification which compelled them to break line and rely on individual activity. That the Greeks—the Boeotian hoplites especially—whom they took in exchange as opponents were in any degree less formidable is not to be thought of, and indeed, if they had been, the consideration would certainly not have been entertained.

A greater difficulty lies in the relative numbers of the interchanged. The Athenians and Plataeans numbered only 8,600 against 10,000 Lacedaemonian hoplites; and, still more important, their light-armed were again only 8,600, while those of the Lacedaemonians were 40,000; and no doubt, if they moved at all, they moved in a body. The interchange therefore involved much more than an alteration of mere extremities; the extremities of the array constituted the bulk of it, and the Lacedaemonians by far the larger proportion. Their movement therefore would throw the Corinthians, Sicyonians, and Troezenians and their associates much more to the right, and bring them as well as the Athenians into contact with the Persians.

G

The change agreed upon was made at daybreak, but the Boeotians recognised their new antagonists and apprised Mardonius, who on his side again brought round the Persians to confront them. Pausanias, finding that the movement was observed, carried back the Spartiats—Aristides overcoming some reluctance among the Athenians to be marched and countermarched, as they said, like helots; and, Mardonius on his side countermanding the Persians, the original positions were maintained unaltered.

That there is no hint in Herodotus of an attempt of the enemy to use their numbers to outflank the Greeks is in favour of the fact stated in the otherwise wretched account of the battle by Diodorus, that the left wing was protected by high ground ; the deep formation of the Persians noticed by Herodotus may, however, have been according to customary tactics, and not from any necessity. Otherwise, as at Marathon, the chief Greek strength was stationed on the wings.

The pride of Mardonius interpreted this attempted change as due to fear on the part of the Spartans to encounter his vaunted Persians; he was at least surprised at movements apparently so inconsistent with notorious Spartan tenacity of position on the field of battle—the point of honour to which Leonidas had so lately approved his loyalty; and he took the opportunity to taunt them with renouncing a maxim, from their unreasoning reverence for which he would fain have profited. He is represented as having promised Xerxes an easy victory over tribes who in their quarrels amongst themselves had not the wit to employ their common language to settle disputes without fighting ; and who, when they fought, were too stupid to take advantage of opportunities or position, but had no other thought than to appoint a meeting in a fair field and fight it out precisely where the vanquished had no chance of escape and the victors must needs purchase victory at the very dearest price. Taunts had been before employed without effect to overcome

the disappointing appreciation by the Greeks of the comparative value of positions ; and he now despatched a herald
with a formal challenge in terms that might well wound
the feelings of Spartans of the ancient rigid school, already
bewildered by the frank manœuvring of their general. A
dead silence however was the only greeting which the Persian
herald received when he taunted the Lacedaemonians with
being false to their principles in deserting their post, with
flying from Persians, whom they set the Athenians to
encounter while they went themselves to combat the Persians' slaves; if they would vindicate their renown let
them come down, Spartans alone opposed to Persians alone,
in equal numbers, whether the victory as between the
armies were to be decided by the result, if so they pleased,
or the rest still left to fight it out afterwards.

Between marchings, countermarchings, and messages the
day had already worn on ; but when the herald returned with
the report that he had been left unnoticed after waiting a
considerable time, Mardonius was more than ever confirmed
in his belief that Greek valour had been over-estimated, and
elated at the prospect of a 'cool victory.' He at once delivered
his most effective force of mounted archery against the two
advanced wings of the Greeks, and then in flying clouds
against the intermediate bodies. The Athenians on the left
had been constantly harassed from the opposite side of the
Asopus, and were now driven back and excluded from further
access to the water of the river. The supply for the entire
army thus became dependent on the fount Gargaphia, near
the Lacedaemonian position ; and this also was cut off in the
progress of the contest by the enemy's horse, who succeeded
in choking it and rendering it unavailable—an occasion on
which we see the important service that might have been
rendered by the bowmen of the Athenians.

CHAPTER V.

THE position of the Greeks, already embarrassed by the blockade of their supplies in the defiles of the mountains, was thus made finally untenable. The generals assembled in council with Pausanias at the right wing, and it was determined that if the Persians, as was likely and as proved to be the case, deferred their general attack over the day, the entire line should be drawn back under cover of the night to the so-called Island, some ten stadia, or less than a mile and a half, distant from the fount Gargaphia, in front of the city of Plataea; this was ground lying between streams that flowed from Cithaeron for some distance about three stadia apart, till they united in one channel forming the Oëroe, that flowed westward to an inlet of the Corinthian gulf. On the usual principle of geographical personification, still too spontaneous to be distinguished from matter of fact, Oëroe was said by the natives not merely obliquely to have been, but to be the daughter of the more important eastward-flowing Asopus. Here there was abundance of water; and some degree of protection from the horse—which during the day had inflicted unceasing loss and worry—was afforded by interposed marshy [1] ground, and roughness or steepness of approach: moreover from such a station a full

---

[1] Sir Wm. Gell, *Itin. Gr.*

half of the force could be spared to effect the reopening of the communications through the passes.

Night fell, and at the appointed hour the numerous bodies of troops, from the Corinthians to the Megarians inclusive, who had been drawn up under their own leaders in the interval between the Lacedaemonians and the Athenians, commenced their march. In the loose coherence of the army, however, their destination was as much a matter of [1] agreement as of imperative command, and with a hurry which amounted to flight from the dreaded horse they retired almost double the appointed distance, not stopping till they reached the temple of Here, under the walls of Plataea, twenty stadia—some two miles and a half—from the fount Gargaphia. Here they took up a regular station. It is most probable that it was this portion of the army—the least homogeneous and proved—that was intended to march to the relief of the passes; but in any case the commanders, whether acting on their own discretion or carried away by their troops in spite of it, by retiring to such a distance ceased to be available as a reserve, and were disabled from supporting either one or the other of the wings in case of an attack during their convergence to a new position.

The centre having thus, according to agreement, moved off the ground first, Pausanias gave the word for the Lacedaemonians to follow; while the Athenians, whose route would be shorter and easier, awaited notice of their progress to move in concert with them. This notice was, however, both strangely and alarmingly delayed. The fact was, that when all the taxiarchs of Pausanias were prepared to march, there was one—Amompharetus, son of Poliathes, the lochagus of a troop (the troop of Pitana according to Herodotus, though Thucydides, with an emphasis not quite explained, denies that there was such a troop)—who positively refused to budge.

---

[1] Sir Wm. Gell, *Itin. Gr.* ix. 32.

He had executed the countermarches parallel to the enemy,
without making an open difficulty, though not without
scruples; but his old Spartan rigour had since been galled
by the insults of the Persian challenge, and he now declared
that he was 'not one to fly from the foreigners or be a party
to the disgrace of Sparta.' Pausanias and Euryanax exhausted themselves in endeavours to convince him of his
absurdity, but arguments and commands were alike vain.
The dilemma was perplexing, and even dreadful. To leave
the man behind with his troop was to leave them to annihilation. Such a loss in itself was serious, and moreover his
motive for such inopportune wrong-headedness was one that
appealed and might hereafter appeal seriously to Spartan
sympathies. It was the great merit of Pausanias that he
had learned a lesson from the splendid but wasteful self-
sacrifice of Leonidas, and was capable of subordinating
Spartan scrupulousness to the urgencies of new conditions.
But in this host beside the Asopus was the sole survivor
of the three hundred of Leonidas, still fretting under the
ignominy with which he was marked only because he had
not, like an associate who had the equal and sufficient
excuse of ophthalmia for absence, thrown his life uselessly
away. The achievements of Aristodemus in the battle that
then ensued would have entitled him to the prize of pre-
eminent valour, had they not been the frenzied deeds of a
man who was only desirous to die, and moreover had
quitted his place in the ranks to perform them. The
best part of a night might well be consumed in contending with feelings that could on such grounds exclude
Aristodemus from posthumous honours as a 'recreant.' In
the meantime the Athenians, hearing nothing of any commencement of movement by the Laconian camp, and bearing
in mind former disappointments in the execution of Laconian
engagements, became not only uneasy but seriously distrustful, and despatched a mounted messenger for instructions

and information. The quarrel had reached its height when he arrived, and as he stood by, Amompharetus was expressing his reply to the abuse of the generals by lifting a great rock with both hands, and declaring as he threw it at their feet, ' Thus I cast in my vote not to fly before the foreigners.'

Pausanias bade the messenger report the difficulty thus interposed by the obstinacy of a madman, and desired the Athenian generals to incline in their march towards their left, so as to co-operate more directly with the delayed Lacedaemonians. Time indeed was pressing, since it was absolutely imperative to move a body of fifty-three thousand men—Lacedaemonians and Tegeans, light and heavy armed —to some distance at least before daybreak. Pausanias therefore set them in motion ; but even then, unwilling to take all the risk of the possible obstinacy of the lochagus, he resolved to halt at an intermediate position, from which he could still help him if follow he would not,—directing the march meantime across a series of low hills towards the higher ground beyond, under the declivities of Cithaeron and inaccessible to the hostile cavalry. It was only as morning broke that the appearance of Amompharetus and his *lochus* enabled the march to continue as originally proposed. The movement of the entire force had at last convinced him that he was not to have his own way, and had brought him—still at deliberate pace —to move his men. But daybreak also revealed the Persian cavalry on the alert, and shewed that an immediate attack was to be expected while the ranks were still on ground exposed to their onset. Pausanias disposed his troops on the march in the best available order, and despatched a horseman to the still distant Athenian force to urge them to come up to his support as speedily as possible, or if this could not be done to send him their detachment of archers to oppose the cavalry, the entire force of which was coming down upon him. He was in fact overtaken by the nearer detachments, and in the absence of the bowmen, suffered considerably before he could reach a favourable position near a fane of the Eleusinian Demeter, at a place called Argiopis, on the stream Moloeis, ten stadia, or about a mile, from his starting-point. This is the distance assigned for the Island, and of this therefore, allowing still for some indirectness in the march, the Moloeis was probably one boundary, and so the verge at least had been attained of the desired position. That the Demetrion was intended to be included in this the oracle already quoted may be taken to prove. The excitement in the enemy's camp was by this time intense; the course of the Athenians from the flat ground by the Asopus led them behind a ridge of low hillocks, where they were altogether invisible from the Persian head-quarters. The vaunted and immoveable Spartans had also evacuated their position, and were already descried at a distance in full retreat for the passes, while the forces of the Greek centre were remoter still. The exultation and confidence that now hurried Mardonius into precipitate action cannot be better expressed than in the short speech assigned to him by Herodotus. He summoned Thorax of Larissa and his brothers Eurypylus and Thrasydeius, and in the presence of Artabazus pointed to the scene beyond the Asopus. 'Ye sons of Aleuas,' he said, 'what have ye to say now at sight of this deserted station,—ye, the neighbours of the Lacedaemonians, who persisted in declaring that they never fled from battle, and that they were the first of all warriors? Ye beheld before how they shifted post, and now see with all the rest of us how they have run away under cover of night. As soon as the time came for them to be put to proof in battle against those who are really and truly the bravest of men, they have exposed themselves as manifestly of no account, even when compared to Greeks who are themselves of no account. For you, who praise them for what you know them to have done, and are quite without experience of the Persians, I make considerable excuse; but with respect to Artabazus, that he should have been frightened by the Lacedaemonians, and yielded from fear to the craven opinion that we ought to break up our encampment and go to be besieged in Thebes, has indeed astonished me. The King shall hear of it from me yet;—though this is a matter that will have to be discussed at another time and elsewhere. What we have now in hand is to frustrate this design of theirs and make pursuit until we overtake them, and exact penalty for all that they have done to the injury of the Persians.'

This threat against a haughty rival in the favour of the King, who, opposing the expedition from the first, had co-operated unwillingly, and, chafing at subordination, had taken every opportunity to thwart his chief, might not have been uttered had not Mardonius believed that no more work was before him than a triumphant slaughter of disorganised fugitives, or had he known how entirely the 40,000 seasoned soldiers under Artabazus—remains of the escort of 60,000— were by personal attachment at the disposal of their leader, and withdrawn from his own command.

In wild excitement the Persian division of the army was at once despatched across the Asopus to follow at a run on the track of the Greeks, who were supposed to be in hasty flight; Mardonius himself on a white Nisaean charger led on the mounted division of the Immortals—one thousand out of the ten thousand, who were all picked men; a corps distinguished by extravagantly rich accoutrements, supplied by a privileged commissariat and trains of camels, and accompanied in camp by the harems of the various officers, and by all the luxuries of [1] peace. The sally of the Persians roused the rest of the camp. The leaders of all nations, without

---

[1] Herod. ix. 58; vii. 83.

waiting for definite orders, which under the circumstances were possibly not sent, let loose their multitudes, who rushed on in entire neglect of ranks or array,—a shouting mob, the fastest only first,—with no thought but that the Greeks were to be had for the snatching.

The Athenians had wheeled at the summons of Pausanias, but were now threatened themselves, and indeed presently engaged, while still detached, by the Medising Greeks of the Persian right wing; and the battle was thus divided in the beginning into two independent conflicts.

The Lacedaemonians were overtaken first, drawn up— hoplites, light-armed, and helots—with the Arcadian Tegeans beside them. Strong in his post,—where, from the nature of the ground, attacks of cavalry, though present in more force, would have been of less avail, and awaiting the succour of the Athenians, or even the central forces of which the remoteness could not be known,—Pausanias again held his men in hand; and, galled as they were by the Persian arrows, commanded them—while still the sacrifices were unfavourable to action—to remain quiet, crouching on the knee, and protected as far as possible by their shields. The hostile arrows began to fall thick, and some horse approached near enough to engage; men were falling in the unmoved Greek ranks. It was now that Callicrates, the very stateliest and most beautiful man in the entire army, was fatally struck. When he died it was with the complaint on his lips, not at meeting death in the cause of Greece,—it was for that he left his home,—but that he should perish without having lifted a hand, without having given proof of the qualities apart from which pride in the possession of bodily beauty was admitted by the Greek to be unauthorised and incomplete. Still the attitude of the army as their confident assailants came on was perfectly tranquil; not a man started up, not a weapon stirred; as from one moment to another they expected the signal for opportune action from God and their commander. He meantime stood distressed beside the discouraging sacrifices, even when the Persian foot were coming within the distance where they planted in the ground the *gerrha* or wicker shields that were to protect their formidable and systematic archery, but where the closing up of their thickening ranks would impede their orderly retirement and even their action, and where the shock of conflict, if once successful, must be decisive.

It was just when opportunity and omens had, after renewed trial, been recognised by the Spartan general as still not coincident, that the Tegeans, less enduring of such stern control, broke the line, whether with or without command, and rushed to the attack; and now forthwith the expected omen appeared at last, and with a suddenness that was afterwards ascribed to a momentary prayer addressed by Pausanias in his trouble to the Cithaeronian [1] Here and the other Plataean gods. At his signal the whole Lacedaemonian host rose from its quietude, 'like a single wild beast roused from its lair, dangerous, [2] horrent.' In steady order, and shield to shield (a formation known as the *synaspism*), they closed upon the line of *gerrha*, which the Persians prepared to defend resolutely, and where, their bows being useless at such close quarters, they fought as from behind a breastwork, with a bravery sufficient to vindicate much of the confidence of Mardonius. With naked hands they grasped the Doric spears which were thrusting at their chests and faces with desperate effect, broke off abundance of them across the fence, and even when this gave way resisted as furiously : a sustained and stubborn conflict raged by the very fane of Demeter as they resorted to their knives and scimitars (*acinaces*), tugging at the wall of shields, and hanging upon them to obtain an opening for a stroke. This sustained valour, if taken alone,

---

[1] Thucyd. ii. 75; Plut. *Arist.* 18.   [2] Plut. *Arist.* 18.

would have made them no unequal foes, seeing that in
bodily strength they were on a par with the Greeks; but
in such a conflict they fought at serious disadvantage,
since, compared with the hoplites, they were naked of
defensive armour, while they were far inferior in dexterity
in wielding their weapons, and their attacks upon a line
as solid and continuous as a wall were made in spasmodic
onsets; singly even or in tens, or in bands of sometimes
more and sometimes less, they started forward upon the
Spartans only to meet their death. Yet as long as Mardonius survived, and the Thousand under his immediate [1] command were supporting the Median battle by pressing with
serious effect on the Lacedaemonians, there was no sign of
giving way. But even the Thousand were gradually reduced
by death and wounds; and when the leader disappeared,
dismay and flight at once took possession of the entire army.
A stone aimed by the hand of a Spartiat, Aeimnestus, struck
Mardonius on the head as he rode conspicuous on his white
charger, and broke his skull; and then, says Herodotus,
the compensation was discharged which, as the oracle had
found means of intimating, was to be paid to the Spartans
by Mardonius for the slaughter of their king Leonidas. The
historian omits a moral to the miserable fact which he records on the same page, that Aeimnestus, who was now so
well serving the cause of united Greece, was to meet his own
death afterwards in an intestine quarrel among the Greeks
[2] themselves. He pauses yet again before proceeding with
the incidents of the flight to note how observable it was,
that in the course of this battle, raging as it did about the
grove and fane of Demeter, not a single Persian died or
even penetrated within the *temenos*, though large numbers
fell in the unconsecrated ground without the precinct. 'In
my opinion,' he adds, 'if one is to have an opinion about

---

[1] Herod. vii. 40.   [2] Ib. ix. 64.

divine matters at all, the goddess herself refused to admit
them because they had set fire to the sacred *Anactorion* at
'Eleusis.' And so the Greek mind is set at rest from an
apprehension that Persians who might have taken refuge
in a sacred precinct encircled by battle might either have
escaped, or not have been spared even there.

The Athenian force had only arrived within hearing of the
clamour of this battle when they had themselves to stand on
their own defence. As their Hellenic antagonists approached
(Plutarch, taking his figures from the collective and conjec-
tural muster-roll of Herodotus, quotes them as 50,000),
Aristides advanced in front and appealed to them in the name
of their common gods to abstain from battle and offer no
hindrance to men who were on their way to the rescue of
Greeks. In effect it was only the Boeotians who fought
with zeal and resolution on the side of Persia against Greece;
they held the Athenians in check for a considerable time,
while the rest kept off entirely or were slack, and when
signs were visible of the discomfiture of the Persians, withdrew entirely. The Thebans however, conscious that they
were fighting for life or death, had been too deeply committed to give up so easily. Plutarch, as a Boeotian, naturally
pleads that only an oligarchical faction then in power was
traitor to Greece, and not the nation. Three hundred of
their first and [2]best—their aristocracy, the very sinews
of this faction—fell before the Athenians, and then the
Thebans turned and fled to gain the protection of their
city walls. The contagion of terror had spread from the
scene of confusion that was now visible all down the eastern
valley and across the Asopus. Not only were the remoter
Persians in flight, but all the mingled nations of the centre
which had come on in disorder were crowding back in double
confusion without having delivered a blow, to seek the refuge

---

[1] Herod. ix. 66.   [2] Ib. ix. 67.

of the entrenched and palisaded camp. The flying Thebans received considerable protection from their own and the Thessalian cavalry, which, though unable to rally them so as to make any independent stand of their own, interposed between them and the Athenians and brought them off with less comparative loss. But the victors of the subjects of Xerxes had freer play, and followed slaughtering the helpless and bewildered fugitives.

If any Persian bethought him in his terror of the help that might come from the 40,000 men of Artabazus, he looked for him in vain. Artabazus had anticipated the catastrophe with the cynical sagacity of a man who has both the will and the power to promote the conclusion that he prophesies. He had carefully preserved his own command and his own adherents from the impulsive onset of Mardonius. Marshalling them accurately, he led them forth as if for the battle, giving them a warning which would prepare them for some sudden turn (well acquainted as they were with his general discontent, and even apart from more explicit confidence as to his purpose), instructing them to be watchful of his personal movements, and so soon as he was seen to make a direct start, to follow in whatever direction it might be without hesitation. He was still only sluggishly on his way towards the battle-field, when unequivocal signs of defeat were apparent; he instantly wheeled about, the entire force following implicitly, neither to the Persian fort nor the Theban citadel, but to the well-known and well-travelled road to Phocis that marked a destination for the Hellespont.

The Greeks had also fought without aid from one large section of their forces, and these were now to be accounted for with varied fortune, some 37,000 out of 107,000. If not the din of battle, the flight of stragglers might suffice, perhaps even without messengers, to apprise the camp at the Heraeum of what was going on; but the endeavour to repair the error

of their distant retirement was, from whatever cause, not
made before the news of victory arrived. The Corinthians and
those next to them—counted up from the muster as 22,600,
over three-fifths of the whole—hastened, in no proper order,
along the hills and undercliff direct to the Demetrium; the
remaining two-fifths, from the Phliasians to the Megarians,
about 14,600, took the lower ground towards the scene of
conflict of the Athenians, and equally without precautionary
.order.   Here however they were caught sight of in their
defenceless disarray by the unbroken Theban horse under
Asopodorus son of Timander, who charged them and pursued them into the mountains, with the loss of 600 slain,
without reason or result in any way.

The defeated Persians and the panic-stricken mob were
already in large numbers within the palisaded fort, and, notwithstanding their confusion, were employed in manning
the towers and strengthening its openings (which must have
been left of considerable amplitude to admit of so speedy
a reception under such circumstances) before it could be
reached by the heavy-armed Lacedaemonians.   A stubborn
battle at the walls (*teichomachia*) now commenced, in which
the Spartans, little practised in fighting either against walls
or behind them, had decidedly the worst.   They were soon
joined by the more expert Athenians, who, apprised by a messenger of the state of things before the fort, willingly left
their Hellenic enemies, covered as they were in retreat, to
make their way to Thebes.   A stout contest from the wall
still continued for some time, but at last the Athenians, by
combined valour and pertinacity, established themselves on it,
and effected an opening through which the Greeks — the
Tegeans again leading—poured in a flood.   The barrier once
down, there was an end among the defenders alike of orderly
array and of any further exhibition of valour.   The mere
crowding of intermingled tribes and arms was enough to
extinguish discipline and to disable its operation if it existed,

while disaster upon disaster and the loss and disappearance of chiefs demoralised even the best. The fort became a slaughter-house, and a carnage ensued which even the entertainments presided over with satisfaction by modern princes and generals after centuries of improvement in the means of human destruction can scarcely hope to rival.

The spirit of vengeance for past sufferings was reinforced by a sense of the danger to be incurred by sparing any considerable proportion of such a multitude of enemies ; Pausanias forbade taking prisoners, and neither supplications nor promises of ransom stayed the hands of Athenians and Lacedaemonians, who emulated each other in the now merely laborious work of massacre. Penned up within the lines which they had toiled at as a refuge and protection, the wretched tribes of men, swept together from all parts of a vast continent to subserve without option the imperial greed of a despot and the military pride of his satraps, were killed in heaps like cattle, and piled in blood amongst the splendid tents, costly fittings, and the other apparatus of the pomp and luxury of their leaders.

Out of the enormous Persian army, which he sets down in round numbers at 300,000, Herodotus avers that besides the 40,000 who fled with Artabazus, only 3,000 were left alive.

On the side of the Greeks he only enumerates as killed :—

Spartiat Lacedaemonians	91 out of 5,000
Tegeans	16 „ 1,500
Athenians	52 „ 8,000.

The last are said to have all belonged to the single tribe Aiantis.

The losses of the heavy-armed Lacedaemonians—the 5,000 *perioeci* who were engaged, unless possibly comprised in the compendious term Spartiats, — and of the Plataean 600, are left unspecified here, and perhaps went to swell the total Greek loss, given by Plutarch at 1,360. It may be a question whether even this reckoning includes

the helots.   The Spartiats, and the Tegeans who fought
with them, are thus seen to have suffered much more heavily
in proportion than the Athenians.   In comparing the relative losses of opponents in ancient battles it must be borne
in mind that the victors had always a large number of
unenumerated wounded ; while of the vanquished, the
wounded for the most part, and often even the captives
when barbarians were in question, were counted among the
slain.   Any reservation of prisoners was quite exceptional,
and made only with a view to ransom, hostages, or sale as
slaves.

The entrenchment had been encumbered, necessarily and
unnecessarily, with non-combatant followers—purveyors of
supplies, attendant slaves, and women of all degrees, from the
favourites of the luxurious nobles downwards ; and these
probably constituted the majority of the spared.   Herodotus
describes one scene, which may serve to represent the aspect
of mingled horrors and splendours, the rescues, recogni-
tions, and coincident adventures that are implied by such
occasions.

While Pausanias was in the midst of urging and directing the slaughter, a woman, in the richest Persian ornaments
and attire, threw herself at his feet and clasped his knees,
claiming rescue, as a Greek, from Persian servitude.   She
declared that she was by birth a Coan, daughter of Hege-
torides son of Antagoras, and had been forcibly carried off
by the Persian Pharandates son of Teaspis ; an example of
a very extensive class of the miseries inflicted by the
barbarian domination on the Greeks of Asia Minor and
the islands, from which this victory alone had rescued the
Greeks of Europe.   In the Spartan commander she was
now addressing a host of her father's ; he committed her at
once to the care of some of the ephors, and dismissed her
afterwards at her desire to Aegina, in possession of all her
dignified appointments and ornaments.   The deliberate state

H

in which Herodotus represents her as arriving in a closed *armamaxa*, or covered chariot, with her gaudy attendants, seems inconsistent with the moment, and if the picture is to be preserved, must rather be transferred to the occasion of her departure. Precisely at this time, when all barbarian resistance was at an end, came in the lagging supports, first of the Mantinaeans, and then of the Eleians. Their regret, and still more their reproaches against their commanders, knew no bounds; to them they ascribed their non-participation in the battle, and on their return home visited it upon them in both cases by exile. The Mantinaeans would fain have obtained yet one chance of service by pursuing Artabazus on his road to Thessaly, but even this was refused them by Pausanias. The Corinthian and Sicyonian division,—Diodorus says the Phliasians [1] also,—too late for the battle, were sent forward, without further result than ascertaining that the retreat was remote and probably final.

Artabazus was indeed pushing on rapidly, to keep ahead, if possible, even of the never-resting tongue of Rumour. He told the Thessalians that he was called to Thrace by matters of importance necessitating speed, assured them that Mardonius and his army were close behind, and made a great point of the attentions it would be prudent to prepare for him. He then passed on through Macedonia by the indicated road for Thrace. Here he avoided the coast and took the inland roads, his numbers dwindling as he passed by hunger, by fatigue, and by the hostility of the native tribes who hung about his march. Herodotus is silent as to hostilities against the fugitives from Plataea on the part of the king of Macedonia, of which we have mention by [2] Demosthenes. Even so he was driven to make, not for the nearer Hellespont, but for the Thracian Bosphorus,

---

[1] Diod. xi. 32.   [2] *In Aristoc.* 687 ; *Epist. Phil.* 164.

which, from its greater remoteness from Greece by sea, and the strength of the Persian post at Byzantium, was more likely to yield a secure passage. He will reappear in the story in unimpaired credit with Xerxes, and, for the Greeks, in ill-omened communication with Pausanias.

CHAPTER VII.

AT Plataea the Greeks were occupied with the usual sequel*
of victory, the collection and solemn interment of their dead,
and the distribution of honours and spoil among both gods
and men. By proclamation of Pausanias all private appropriation of spoil was forbidden, and the large force of helots was
employed to gather the whole together from the camp and
field of battle. The worth of precious metals in coined money
(darics), personal ornaments, and enrichments of weapons and
camp furniture, in the vessels and table-services that were
carried about in such an expedition by the Persians, was
enormous; among the baggage-waggons gold and silver plate
was found in [1] sackfuls, so that of the abundance of merely
embroidered vestments which would at any other time have
been highly valued, no account whatever was taken. An
imputation upon the Aeginetans here occurs, which, though
possibly heightened by the historian's prejudice, still indicates a general feeling that the tone of Hellenic thought
had become vulgarised among these more purely commercial
islanders. He accuses them of dealing illicitly with the
helots for treasure that should have been brought to
the common fund, and even ascribes to this source, if we
adopt the most moderate interpretation of his language, the

---

[1] Herod. ix. 80.

origin of the largest Aeginetan fortunes. The district of Plataea gave up long after to fortunate finders deposits of plate and valuables that had been hidden away by those who never had a chance of recovering them, and the Aeginetans bought from the helots sometimes the secret of such stores, and sometimes the purloined objects themselves,—armlets, chains or torques, and golden-hilted scimetars that were found upon the bodies of the slain enemy all over the field. The helots, fresh from their secluded servitude at Lacedaemon, were as ignorant of the precious metals as the Swiss when they rifled the tents and stripped the bodies of the Burgundians at Granson, and were glad to get the price of brass for objects of gold which in any case they would have been unable to conceal or employ to any purpose.

A still more shameful fraud on the part of the Aeginetans against the victors in a battle in which they themselves had scarcely taken any part, was the suggestion made to Pausanias by Lampon son of Pytheus, one of their leading men, a member of a family distinguished for hereditary prowess in the public games, and a participator in the glory of [1]Salamis. He represented that the predicted penalty to be recovered from Mardonius still lacked completion; it would be exacted in full and the glory of Pausanias immensely enhanced if the head of Mardonius were cut off and exposed, as Mardonius and Xerxes had done with the remains of Leonidas. Pausanias repudiated the suggestion with contemptuous dignity; it was barbarian, not Hellenic, in spirit, and repugnant to Lacedaemonians, whatever it might be to Aeginetans. Lampon was bidden to bring no more advice, and might be thankful that even this time he got away with only a rebuke.

By next day the body of Mardonius was missing—withdrawn for burial, it was assumed; and more than one man afterwards claimed and received large rewards from his son

---

[1] Pind. *Isthm.* iv.

Artontes for the service : there was a report that it had been really performed by Dionysophanes, an Ephesian. A monument—probably a barrow—on the right of the road from Eleutherae to Plataea, immediately after the junction of the road to [1] Hysiae, was pointed out long after as that of Mardonius.

And now again, as after Salamis, questions arose as to the assignment of chief honours among the nations engaged. Some of the Athenian leaders, Leocrates and Myronides especially, were indisposed to concede any exclusive distinction to the Spartans for all their exploits and leadership, and Aristides could only prevail on them to remit the apportionments to the assembled Greeks. In the end, Athenians and Lacedaemonians each erected a separate trophy, and each nation honoured its own most deserving champions without drawing comparisons. [2] Pausanias speaks of the trophy as a single one, and situated about fifteen stadia (a mile and a half) beyond the city, towards Thebes. Here, as after Salamis, further heartburnings were said to have been evaded by the chief rivals renouncing their claims, at the suggestion of Megarians or Corinthians, in favour of an inferior power. The gods and heroes of Plataea had been specially invoked, and in consequence eighty talents (about £2,000) were set aside for the Plataeans, a sum which defrayed the cost of a temple to Athene Areia,—the Martial,—and of the paintings which adorned it, and which remained in preservation long enough to be seen by Plutarch and described by Pausanias. Herodotus however, giving voice to the common opinion of unbiassed Greeks, after the generous confession that among their enemies the first honours were due to the Persian foot (the horse of the Sakae), and among individuals to Mardonius, declares that of the Greeks, brave men as the Tegeans and Athenians had approved themselves, the palm of valour belonged to the Lacedaemonians,—belonged by this token, that though

---

[1] Paus. ix. 2.   [2] Ib. ix. 2. 4.

all alike had conquered their opponents, the Lacedaemonians had assaulted and conquered by far the most valiant. He had before stated his opinion that the one seat of strength in the army of Mardonius lay in the ranks of the native Persians of whom he was so proud. In place of Aristodemus, whose claims he thought were wrongly set aside, Poseidonius, Philocyon, and the rigid Spartiat Amompharetus were preferred; and of these again Poseidonius was chiefly honoured,—honoured, while Aristodemus was set aside, inasmuch as in his case daring had not been urged by contempt of the life he put in peril. It is highly characteristic of the Greek mind that Herodotus returns to Callicrates, and his premature death, as explaining how it was that a man so beautiful is absent from the list that signalises the most brave.

Among the Athenians, renown distinguished Sophanes son of Eutychides, of the deme of Decelea; the man of whom it came to be told—a valuable example of how fact was still liable to wander away through metaphor into myth—that he wore in battle an iron anchor or grappling-iron attached to a bronze chain, with which he moored himself to his station till his enemies were in flight, when he took it up again and carried it on in the pursuit. 'So the story goes; but there is another which conflicts with it, namely that the anchor he carried was not formed of iron and hanging to his corselet, but a painted symbol on his ever restless shield.' Opportunity is taken to record of this champion of Greek liberty, how at the siege of Aegina by the Athenians, when Greeks and Greeks, now allies, were in conflict, he challenged and killed the 'Argive Eurybates, a Nemean victor in the [1] pentathlon,'—'another brilliant exploit.'

The mention of the Decelea, as the deme of Sophanes, is fortunate, as it introduces an allusion to a later incident, the invasion of Attica by [2] Archidamus, and so informs us that

---

[1] Herod. ix. 75; Paus. i. 29. § 4.   [2] Ol. 88. 2 = B.C. 431.

Herodotus was finishing his history after that date; that he was in fact—anachronism as it seems for his comparative genius—a contemporary with Thucydides at the age of 40, and with Euripides when author of the Medea;—so near together in Greece was all that was archaic and most modern.

From the collected spoil a tithe was then reserved for the god at Delphi; and from this a golden tripod was dedicated, and placed on a three-headed serpent near the altar. Pausanias found that Phocian sacrilege had taken its way with the tripod, but the bronze support was still in its place. Constantine transferred this to the hippodrome of his new city, and there by rare clemency of fortune it stands to this day inscribed with a list of patriotic cities. It bore the inscription:—

Ἑλλάδος εὐρυχόρου σωτῆρες τόνδ' ἀνέθηκαν,
δουλοσύνης στυγερᾶς ῥυσάμενοι πόλιας.[1]

Further reservation was made for a bronze statue of Poseidon, seven cubits high, at the Isthmus, and for another of Zeus, twelve cubits high, at Olympia. Pausanias the traveller notes of the latter, apparently merely to guide the curious, that it was turned towards the east, and he copied from its base the catalogue of the dedicating cities already referred to.

Of the assignment of special trophies we are told that the Tegeans, who first entered the entrenched camp, had among other things from the quarters of Mardonius an elaborate manger formed entirely of bronze, which they dedicated in their ancient temple of Athene Alea, in the conflagration of [2] which it probably [3] perished.

In the temple of Athene Polias at Athens was long after shown the corselet of Masistius—an appropriate Athenian prize,—and a scimitar asserted to be that of Mardonius, the identity of which, however, is reasonably questioned by

---

[1] Diod. S. xi. 33.   [2] Ol. 96.   [3] Paus. viii. 45. § 3.

VII.]   *THE SPOILS OF PLATAEA.*   105

Pausanias, who refuses to believe in the resignation of such a trophy by the [1] Lacedaemonians.

A metrical inscription by [2] Simonides for a bow and arrows dedicated at Athens, recalls the specific services rendered by that weapon at Plataea :—

> Τόξα τάδε πτολέμοιο πεπαυμένα δακρυόεντος
> νηῷ 'Αθηναίης κεῖται ὑπορρόφια,
> πολλάκι δὴ στονόεντα κατὰ κλόνον ἐν δαΐ φωτῶν
> Περσῶν ἱππομάχων αἵματι λουσάμενα.

The general distribution concerned a miscellaneous assemblage of booty, such as ' concubines of the Persians, gold and silver, and other valuables and animals.' Whether the precise principle of apportionment with reference to [3] merit was determined by the numbers of [4] contingents must remain uncertain, but in any case the share of the Lacedaemonians could not have been less than enormous. Again, we are left in the dark as to the disposal of this share, whether as public or private treasure, in a polity of which a professed fundamental maxim . was to discourage and ignore accumulated wealth and the luxuries to which it could minister. Apart however from the laxities that creep into all organisations founded on the basis of asceticism, a populous state, of the influence and power of Sparta, could never dispense with the command of some considerable treasure or of stored wealth in some form. And even ascetic disciplinarians, especially when at the head of a system, can always find opportunities of expensive self-indulgence, which by some means are brought within the letter of the stern code. We read at this time of Spartans of great wealth ; and others will speedily, and not unfrequently, come before us whose common weakness is greed for that gold of which their laws forbade almost the mention ; and even when we look back to the reign of Darius, we find that if Cleomenes repudiated the invitations of Aristagoras to aid an

---

[1] Paus. i. 27. § 1.   [2] Sim. 200.
[3] Herod. ix. 81.   [4] Diod. S. xi. 33.

Ionian revolt, it was for other reasons, and not because he
was shocked at having it held out as a temptation that the
capture of Susa was quite within possibility,—Susa, the
treasure-house of the Great King, by acquiring which he
might confidently rival Ionia in [1] riches. The promise of
Aristagoras might now seem to the Spartans to have come
to pass ; general, ephors and Spartiats, perioeci and helots,
might all look round as if a new world had opened upon
them ; and men of the stubborn antique stamp of a Leonidas
or an Amompharetus were blind if they had not some mistrust of the working of this sight upon all classes of visitors
from the Eurotas, from the helots who had loyally contributed
to the capture, and yet were only to share in it dangerously
and by stealth, to the Regent himself on whom they were
lavished so abundantly. For him also, as if next after the
gods, the several classes of spoil—' women, horses, talents,
camels, and all the other wealth of whatever kind '— were
not tithed exactly, but put under contributions expressed by
tens, and with him rested of necessity the disposal of whatever
was most princely. Mardonius, though himself only a deputy,
or lieutenant, had remained in possession of all the splendidly appointed establishment of the fugitive King, and while
Pausanias gazed on the vessels and furniture of gold and
silver, the luxuriously covered couches and embroidered cur-
tains, a thought occurred to him of a contrast that should
give zest to his elation in victory. He summoned the Greek
generals to a feast in the royal tent itself, which they
found set out and prepared in every detail by the Persian's
own train of confectioners and cooks, as if Mardonius were
still alive ; and beside it he pointed with laughter to a spare
Laconian dinner that had been prepared in the usual order by
his own servants for himself, exclaiming with derisive scorn,
' Ye men of Hellas, I have brought you together for precisely

---

[1] Herod. v. 49.

this,—to exhibit to you the folly of the Median general, who having enjoyment of all this splendour, came here to plunder an existence so wretched as ours.' The turn of the moral is the same that is put into the mouth of Caractacus by a Roman writer, and of the hardy Swiss by [1] Philip de Comines; but in this case it strikes upon the ear as involving an appreciation of the more luxurious fare, when obtainable, that has scarcely the true Laconian ring.

The traveller Pausanias mentions finding the tombs of the Greeks very near the entrance to the city of Plataea as he came in from Attica, inscribed with the epitaphs of Simonides; the Athenians and Lacedaemonians having each their burial-place, and the rest of the Greeks a third. The Lacedaemonians made a triple division of their dead; commanders of companies—among whom were Poseidonius, Amompharetus, Philocyon, and Callicrates—occupied one depository, the rest of the Spartiats another, the helots a [2] third. But besides these veritable tombs, Herodotus avers that certain fictitious ones, fraudulent cenotaphs, had been afterwards raised by other cities anxious to assert their participation in the victory. One mound especially he charges with having been raised for Aeginetans—in disgrace again—some ten years afterwards by a friendly Plataean whom he names. Nothing is said of the burial of the enemies; and indeed a notice that the Plataeans found one skull without sutures—a case not unknown to modern physiology—when they gathered the bones together into one place, appears to imply that many at least were left above [3] ground through autumn and winter.

It still remained to deal with Thebes. But even before doing so it was incumbent to offer appropriate sacrifices for the great deliverance, and on this point guidance was solicited from the god at Pytho. The oracle enjoined the immediate erection of an altar to Zeus Eleutherius (the Liberator), but

---

[1] *Mem.* v. 1.   [2] Herod. ix. 85.   [3] Ib. ix. 83.

forbade them to offer a sacrifice upon it until all fire had
been quenched throughout the Plataean district, as having
been polluted by the sacrilegious barbarians, and re-lighted
pure from the common hearth at Delphi. The Greek officials
immediately made a general visitation, and caused all fire
to be extinguished, and a certain Euchidas left the city,
engaging to bring back fire from the god with the utmost
possible speed. Arrived and forthwith purified at Delphi,
and duly besprinkled and crowned with the sacred laurel, he
took fire from the altar there, started again to race homeward
to Plataea, and came in before sunset, having accomplished
the double journey, so the story goes, within the day. He ·
greeted the expectant citizens, delivered over the fire, and at
once sank down exhausted, and died on the spot. The Plataeans took him up and buried him in the sacred precinct of
Artemis Eucleia, inscribing on the tomb the following tetrameter—

Εὐχίδας Πυθῶδε θρέξας ἦλθε τᾷδ' αὐθημερόν.

'Euchidas running hence to Pytho here returned the self-same day.'

The full distance of one thousand stadia—115 miles—obliges
us to assign a very large interpretation to the 'single day' of
the tale and the inscription.

The enthusiasm of the confederates readily extended to
something more than the present occasional sacrifice. It was
resolved, on the proposal of Aristides, that the celebration
should be annual, and that every fourth year—a pentaeteris—
there should be a celebration of Eleutherian games, in the
presence of such sacred missions from general Hellas as the
various cities were wont to despatch to represent them at the
great common festivals, and perhaps of envoys (πρόβουλοι) for
political deliberation. To the Plataeans was to be committed
the function of offering sacrifices on the part and for the
safety of Hellas, as well as performing the annual rites at the
graves of the dead ; and in return, and as security for these
institutions, they were to be declared inviolable and conse-

crated to the god. The Plataeans thus obtained at least a
nominal guarantee from Greece at large for the extension of
their territory to the limits of Hysiae and the Asopus, which
had been wrested for them from Thebes by the Athenians in
[1] B.C. 519. The parallel between the arrangements which the
Greeks attempted to establish here and the sacred immunity of
Elis and the participation of all Hellas in its games is manifest; yet the suggesting influences are so natural that we may
less reasonably conclude that the correspondence is due to mere
rivalry or mimicry, than carry back the analogy, and infer that
the elevation of the Olympic games and territory to their
distinction was originally due to like combinations of events—
to the enthusiasm of a confederacy at some great conquest
which was connected with the seat of the festival in origin,
conduct, or conclusion.

These generous resolutions, made in the first heat of sympathy, proved of but insignificant or evanescent advantage for
Plataea. The site was unfavourable, to say nothing of the
Greek calendar being already well covered by festivals and
games which could not be superseded; and, as time went
on, the growth in popularity of the new institution was liable
to be checked by the very intimate attachment of Plataea
to Athens. Plataea had placed itself under the protection
of Athens as early as B.C. 519, at the recommendation
of Lacedaemonians—as Herodotus thought, out of no good
will to either; and the loyal city had approved the spirit
and value of its alliance at Marathon as well as in this later
war. It might even seem surprising that privileges should
now be conceded so readily which could scarcely but redound
to the advantage of the protecting state, whose aspirations
were so well known: but Athens was not then in a condition to excite alarm at a spirit of encroachment; patriotic
enthusiasm was blinding all but politicians of the most
special type to the still living germs of internal dissensions

[1] Herod. vi. 108.

and rivalries; and, above all, the common animosity of the patriotic Greek army against the especial enemies of Plataea, the Medising Thebans, still contumacious within the walls which had served the Mede as the fortified base of his most dangerous and hardly frustrated enterprise, would cause a proposition so appropriately honouring the patriotic rival to be carried by acclamation.

A further resolution, also it is [1] said on the motion of Aristides, had reference to a future Hellenic muster for the prosecution of the war; the numbers to be raised are given as 10,0c0 shields (that is hoplites), with a like number at least, we must infer, of light-armed men; 1,000 horses, to supply the want so grievously experienced in the late battle, and 100 ships. It is probable that these forces are to be considered exclusive of the power of the Spartans, to whom as directors of the whole it would be left to decide on the application of their own resources, as well as to dispose of the contingents of the allies.

On the eleventh day after the victory at Plataea the Thebans were summoned to surrender the members of the Medising faction, and especially Timegenidas and Attaginus, —the leaders of the leaders,— with the notice that the army would not remove from before the city till the demand was complied with. Refusal was followed up by the usual measures taken to reduce a fortified city in Greece; attacks were made upon the walls, but the main reliance was placed on the exclusion of supplies by investment, and on the openly expressed intention to damage the territory to such an extent that surrender would involve a less sacrifice. On the twentieth day a herald announced to Pausanias that the Thebans were prepared to give up the men demanded. The traveller [2] Pausanias in Roman times is as positive as the Boeotian Plutarch that the crime of Medism lay exclusively with an

---

[1] Plut. *Arist.* 21.   [2] Paus. x. 6. § 1.

oligarchy. Had Xerxes invaded Greece, he says, when the
Peisistratids ruled, the Athenians themselves would have been
open to the same charge. There is probably much truth
in this—certainly some; and at any rate, an anti-Medising
faction was sure to be born, if not to revive, on the failure
of the earlier policy. The oligarchs had made the best terms
they could, weakened as were their ranks by the slaughter of
so many of their class by the Athenians in the battle; and
Timegenidas made a patriotic virtue of the necessity of saving
Boeotia from further ravage, and the city from capture. A
futile attempt to induce the captors of Persian treasures to
be put off with a money ransom having failed, the utmost
that could be done was to appeal for such subventions from
the funds of the public—'that public which had in truth
gone along with their policy'—as would when applied in
bribery shrewdly help what they proposed to urge in
their defence. Everything was done to give the surrender
the air of being the voluntary act of Timegenidas and the
rest, and they were not without confidence that between
argument and corruption they might come safe through.
Attaginus, less sanguine or more fortunate, made his escape
in time. His children were given up in his place, but sent
back by Pausanias with the remark, in the spirit of his reply
to Lampon, that 'Medism was not a child's fault.' Divining
the calculations of the rest, he was no sooner in possession of
them than he cut off all opportunity of intrigues by immediately dismissing the confederate forces home; and then,
carrying the prisoners off with him to the Isthmus, he put
them all to death by his own authority.

Fifty-two years after this common triumph of Greece
the city of the Plataeans was besieged and subverted by
Greeks—by Lacedaemonians, at the commencement of that
intestine quarrel which was to be the ruin of so much that
was best in Hellas (427 B.C.). Restored again (386 B.C.),
they were again expelled (374 B.C.), to await a final restoration

(315 B.C.) two generations later; and yet, through all the tenacity of tradition and of race, this brave people carried over no insignificant traces of the institutions which had been intended to inaugurate a period of Hellenic unity, from the field where the blood of many tribes had been shed for one common Hellenic interest and hope. Plutarch of Chaeronea, who was probably an eye-witness, thus describes the ceremony with which the Plataeans of his day fulfilled the engagements of their ancestors at the tombs of the slain :—

'On the 16th of the month Maimacterion,—Alalcomeneis of the Boeotians,—the procession is marshalled at break of day. A trumpeter precedes sounding notes of war; cars follow laden with branches of myrtle and crowns, and with them a black bull; and young men of free condition carry amphorae of wine and milk for the libations, and vessels of oil and perfumed ointments ; no slave is permitted to give any assistance in the service which is being paid to men who died for freedom. Last of all comes the archon of the Plataeans, who, forbidden at other times to wear any colour but white and even to touch iron, is now arrayed in purple chiton and girt with a sword, as, holding a hydria taken from the public record office, he traverses the city on his way to the tombs. He then takes water from the fountain and washes the monuments, and anoints them ; and after sacrificing the bull on the pyre and praying to Zeus and Hermes Chthonios, he invites the brave men who died for Greece to the banquet and the blood ; and mixing wine in a crater, pours it on the ground, exclaiming, " I drink to the men who died for the liberty of the [1] Greeks." '

[2] Thucydides adds, 'honouring the tombs — ἐσθήμασιν — with robes ; ' the equivalents probably of the black scarves and fillets which we see attached to tombs on vases. The altar and statue of Zeus Eleutherius, both of white marble,

---

[1] Plut. *Aristides*, 21.   [2] Thucyd. iii. 58.

were erected just without the city of Plataea, near the bronze
monument over the slain of various tribes.   In Roman times
as late as [1] Pausanias the Eleutherian games were still held
here on the anniversary of the battle, the fourth day of the
Attic month Boedromion. The chief prize—a crown or chaplet,
for it was an [2] ἀγὼν στεφανίτης—was given for the race in
armour, for which the altar was the starting-point.

[1] Paus. ix. 2. § 4.   [2] Strabo, 412.

CHAPTER VIII.

THE battle of Plataea was truly one of the decisive battles
of the world ; the victory was not only decisive in the sense
that it left the worsted army disorganised and ruined beyond
all possibility of rally, but that it precluded for all time any
renewed attempt by Persia to subjugate continental Greece.
Upon this field was jeopardied and saved, if not the last and
single chance of the survival of progressive civilisation, much
at least of the prompt development of all its best characteristics;
the ripened display, within the next fifty years of Hellenic
independence, of that healthy and hopeful manhood of the
race that had been maturing through centuries, to be staked
at last on the turn of one day of conflict.   It would be rash
to infer that the germ of Hellenic genius would necessarily
have been lost to the world, though Oriental domination had
oppressed or even exterminated Hellenism at Athens and
Sparta ; but to the happier result it is at least due that the
world inherits a history, a literature, and art through which
Hellenic genius remains so prime an influence for instruction
and delight, for refinement and dignity in art and manners,
for guidance in administration of the intellectual powers,
for elevation of purpose, to noblest patriotism, and largest
theory of humanity.   A story opens before us which assuredly
is not free from many a discouraging incident ; our best
hopes are indeed disappointed at every turn ; but the

warnings, if we fairly read them, take an important place in the moral. The vices and errors of the Greek communities keep our eyes open to the imperfections which may intrude among virtues, that most approve themselves to be virtues when found strong enough to encourage humanity, for all its shortcomings and difficulties, not to despair.

All the importance of the victory could not however be seen at the moment. To many a Greek the power and wealth of the Great King could never have been realised so formidably as in sight of the ruin of his magnificent armament. Here, in the resources which he had forfeited, was apparent evidence of what he might still have in reserve; the magnitude of the danger that had been escaped, but only just escaped, was brought home to the senses amid the blood-stained spoil of the vast camp, with a liveliness that could not but have some effect on future apprehensions, while it strengthened resolution for the future. Self-confidence rose in more than equal proportion; the victory that had shattered the aggressive power and spirit of Persia animated the Greeks to prepare themselves against a revival of aggression, and strengthened a decision which had before been halting, to take securities against it with all the power of settled concord and alliance.

For although the host that, whether as ally or enemy, had devoured the plains of Thessaly, Boeotia, and Attica, might be assumed as accounted for, yet the hold of the Persians on their established conquests in Thrace; their command of the Hellespont, whether for reinforcements or interruption of the Euxine trade; and the strength and designs of their fleet, with all Ionia and Phoenicia to recruit from, were considerations of sufficient weight to give spirit to those in the Plataean council who advocated continued exertions and hearty adherence to the new-found value of confederation. The failure of Darius at Marathon had not deterred Xerxes from a second expedition, but had rather prompted more formidable preparation; and the defeat at Salamis had only induced the enemy to change the quarter of attack with a pertinacity that might still not be exhausted. On some of these points of apprehension the victors of Plataea were soon to be happily relieved, for on the very same day, the afternoon of the day which had been ushered in by the frantic onset of Mardonius, the Persian fleet was finally destroyed, and a not unimportant blow delivered even upon their army in Asia.

The commanders of the Greek fleet had of necessity more than reciprocated the anxieties that Pausanias and Aristides might have had time to feel on their account. While Mardonius was still in Thessaly they had not moved beyond the advanced station of Delos, from whence they could more readily obtain information about the enemy's fleet and act upon it with greater promptitude. Of their movements when the re-occupation of Attica drove the Athenians again to Salamis, we know nothing more than that the mission of the Athenian admiral Xanthippus to Sparta implies that the Athenian division, as might be expected, was not far from the shores of Attica. The evacuation of the latter country, however, soon set it free.

The Persian fleet might now have been expected to move back to the Hellespont, or still more probably to afford support or supplies to Mardonius; but in point of fact, besides the necessity of overawing the rising agitations in Ionia and the islands, the Phoenician mariners had not only been foiled by the weather on the unknown western coasts, but had forfeited all confidence by their behaviour at Salamis; their commanders were consequently discouraged from attempting even short voyages, and a renewal of the conflict seemed more hazardous still. Of this the Greeks could not be immediately aware, and to them preparation against any movement on the part of the Persian fleet was rightly a matter of most anxious interest. Western Greece could only be secured from the transport of aid to

Mardonius, or diversions in other directions, by complete command of the sea, and the time was at hand when this was to be actively asserted. The year was already far advanced, and the Greek force had received its last accession; the fleet of 110 ships all told, which we read of in the spring as assembled at Aegina, was now increased to [1]250 triremes. Of these the largest portion were Athenian; of the rest, besides Lacedaemonians, there were contingents from Corinth, Sicyon, and Troezene. The Corinthians brought in addition the highly esteemed contribution of the soothsayer Deiphonus from Apollonia, their colony on the Ionian gulf.

It was already autumn, and expectation was at its height for news of the conflict in Europe, which it was certain could not long be deferred, when Leotychides and the generals gave audience at Delos to three envoys who had left Samos unknown to Theomestor son of Androdamas, whom the Persians had established there as tyrant in reward for his services at Salamis. The spokesman was Hegesistratus son of Aristagoras, who set forth the case in every variety of aspect and with an Ionian fluency which might perhaps have damaged his cause had he in truth been the sole informant (ἔλεγε πολλὰ καὶ παντοῖα). Appealing to their sympathies as venerators of common gods, he supplicated them as Greeks to come to the rescue of Greeks and assist in expelling the barbarian; the Ionians at the first sight of them would rise in revolt, and the barbarians would as instantly retire, or, if they did not, might be pounced on as a prey. And never would there be another such chance: for the ships of the enemy were ill-found, wretched sea-boats, perfectly ineffective to cope with those of the Greeks. Never could an exploit be more easy or more certain of success. He added, as guarantee of the sincerity of the advice, that the envoys were ready to accompany the expedition as hostages.

The Spartan listened to the long-drawn pleadings and

---

[1] Diod. xi. 34.

beseechings without any indication that he accepted the information as correct, or that he sympathised with the orator, and then interposed abruptly, 'And what, Samian stranger! is your name?' Catching up the reply before the flow of words could re-commence, 'I accept, Hegesistratus,' said he, ' the appellation' (i. e. conductor or leader of armies); 'do you only, and these who are with you, take order to pledge your faith before you sail away that the Samians will be our zealous allies.' The decision thus curtly announced with true Spartan, affectation of suddenness and contempt for words, was as promptly put in action. The Samians, says Herodotus, took the oath and engagement of alliance with the Hellenes— that is with the Dorians, whom the historian seems here again to distinguish as specifically Hellenic, in contrast to the Pelasgic Athenians and Ionians. The other two envoys, Lampon son of Thrasycles and Athenagoras son of Archestratides, were dismissed the same day; and on the very next, the seer Deiphonus, son, or reputed [1]son, of the prophetic Euenius, having announced that the victims were favourable, the fleet put to sea; Leotychides, notwithstanding his rejection of the proposal of hostages, keeping by him Hegesistratus, the man with the name of good omen, a hostage in reality if not in [2]name. They moored at Calamei on the coast of Samos, and there made preparations for battle. The exact locality is uncertain; it is indicated by Herodotus to those who know the spot as being ' by the Heraeum, or temple of Here, that is in that place,'—terms apparently intended to distinguish the temple from the more celebrated Heraeum in or close to the city of Samos. A more remote station, perhaps the petty Ipnus, where Stephanus Byzantinus notes a temple of Here Ipnuntis, seems to be implied by the unperceived and unmolested retirement of the Persian fleet through the narrow channel between Samos and the continent.

---

[1] Herod. ix. 95.   [2] Ib. ix. 92.

The Persian commanders indeed were no sooner aware of
the advance of the Greeks than, as the envoys had predicted,
they gave up all thought of contending at sea, dismissed the
Phoenician vessels with their crews, and carried the others
from Samos to the opposite coast, where they could draw
them ashore and have the protection of fortifications and a
numerous army. They passed, says Herodotus, by the fane
of the Potniae of Mycale on to Gaeson and Scolopoeis, where
there is a fane of Eleusinian Demeter, founded by Philistus
son of Pasicles, when he accompanied Neileus son of Codrus
in the settlement of Miletus. The spot was on the coast
south of the mountainous promontory of Mycale, just before
it trends south-east to the embouchure of the Maeander and
the Latmian gulf. Gaeson, which is with Herodotus apparently the name of a town, was the name also of a river that
discharged itself into the lake Gaesonis and so into the sea.
[1]Ephorus spoke of the Gaeson and its lake as near Priene,
and another [2] author places it between Priene and [3] Miletus.
The ancient line of coast, owing to the accumulated deposits
of the Maeander, now lies, like the site of Priene, far inland ;
but the Gaeson is still represented by a stream which flows
from the mountains under the heights that are occupied by
the ruins of Priene. Pliny, immediately before coming to
Priene from the south, inserts the name Naulochus, which
indicates an ancient favourable station for ships. The plain
was here in communication with Ephesus and Sardis by the
road across the mountains, and again more circuitously by
the valley of the Maeander, past Magnesia. Here, previously
stationed, or rapidly concentrated, was the main body of the
force originally left behind by Xerxes to watch Ionia : it is
set down by Herodotus as 60,000 (Diodorus gives 100,000)
men, under Tigranes, a commander 'supereminent among the

---

[1] ap. Athenaeum, vii. p. 311.   [2] Ibid.
[3] Mela also, i. 17—Ionia 'cingit urbem Prienen et Gaesi fluminis ostium.'
Cf. Pliny, *H. N.* v. 31.

Persians, like Xerxes and Mardonius, for stature and beauty.'
The Persian admirals drew their vessels on shore and hastened
to enclose them by a vast fort, of sufficient circuit to shelter
the army in case of a reverse. Trees were cut down indiscriminately, and a wall or bulwark was formed of mixed stones
and timber, and strengthened by projecting stakes or palisades
—according to Diodorus by a trench also. The probability
of an Ionian insurrection had been a source of anxiety ever
since the reverses in Greece, and preparations for a campaign
in the collection of stores and provisions had in consequence
been in a state of [1] forwardness. What no vigilance or foresight could now supply was that spirit which is required to
give vivacity even to unbroken resolution, and to remedy
the despondency which comes over a multitude when under
misfortune, and foredooms to destruction an army which, however bravely, has suffered defeat after defeat, and a cause
which has never enjoyed one success. And then too a large
proportion of the muster—enormous doubtless, reduce the
quoted numbers as we may—were Ionians, who were justly
objects of increasing mistrust. From the Samians especially
all confidence had been withdrawn since the discovery that
some 500 captives, taken by the army of Xerxes from Attica,
had been purchased by them only to be sent home free and
restored to his enemies.

The aspect of the enterprise was now entirely changed for
the Greeks, who, with all their rapidity, at last found that
they had moved just too late to find the ineffective navy
the easy prey which they had expected. The tardy alacrity
of the reticent Spartan was probably due to some secret
notice of the preparations for the Persian retreat, in case
the signs of an approaching attack, which they were hopeless
to resist, should oblige them to forego their hold on the
now uneasy Samos;—information evidently passed over as

---

[1] Diod. xi. 34.

rapidly in one direction as the other. A suggestion which was made upon this disappointment, to return to inactivity at Delos, was set aside; and the project that still retained its hold as much on the imagination of the Greeks as on their reason, of making for the Hellespont and the bridge, had scarcely more to recommend it now than before, in comparison with the importance of striking at the hostile fleet. The Samians and Ionians would of course be more urgent than ever, and with more effect from the manifest justification of their former confident assurances. It was resolved therefore, but only after discussions had caused more [1]delay, to follow up the chase; the ships were provided with ladders and every possible preparation, to enable the forces, in case they should be disappointed of a sea-fight, to effect a rapid disembarkation and try the fortune of a battle on land. Not a vessel was afloat to oppose them when they arrived; all were seen drawn ashore under protection of the wall, while a numerous army of foot was in array on land. Leotychides, in imitation of the policy of Themistocles at Artemisium, passed along as near inshore as possible, and by the voice of his loudest herald invited the Ionians to bear in mind in the coming battle, in the first place Liberty and then the password Hebe—selected apparently as the name of the spouse of his ancestor Hercules, herself a daughter of the goddess of the Samian Heraeum: those who heard were urged to inform those who did not. The proclamation was made not without expectation of the effect it invited, but also with the indirect intention of rousing mistrust in the Persians towards the Ionians, to whom the herald affected to believe that his language would be alone intelligible. The Spartan seems to have applied his borrowed stratagem but clumsily, for in this case there was much fairer hope of considerable desertions than in that of

---

[1] Herod. ix. 98.

Artemisium; and an immediate result of the warning was that the Persians instantly disarmed the Samians, and assigned the Milesians a post too distant to allow them, in case of defection, to interfere in the expected battle.

The Greek debarkation, as it was effected without opposition, must have been made at some distance from the entrenched camp and army ; but by mid-day or later—Diodorus says the day ensuing—the troops were marshalled and moving forward to the attack. The Athenians, who were to sustain the main burden of the battle, were commanded by the archon eponymus of the year—Xanthippus, son of Ariphron and father of Pericles : and together with associated troops of other cities, Corinth, Sicyon, Troezene, they made up a full half of the entire force. These now advanced direct upon the enemy over the level ground by the sea-shore, while the Lacedaemonians and the other half of the army made a [1] circuit, and having to traverse on their way the rough ravines of torrents and spurs of the mountain, came into action later, as if intentionally, and only with the view to an effective flank attack. The spirit of emulation, of which the Greek was so susceptible in its noblest forms, was now at its height among the Athenians, who had recently had just cause to feel that by their warlike achievements they had already placed their country on a line with Sparta, hitherto the recognised leading power in Greece ; while in breadth and boldness of political views and in patriotic self-sacrifice alike they were far ahead. The present was an opportunity for winning yet another advance, and that on land—the very prerogative of the Spartans ; and the word passed from mouth to mouth to make such thorough and speedy work with their already despised opponents as should give them at least the largest share in the victory. It was afterwards believed that another influence, not independent of the supernatural powers, was at work to heighten

[1] Herod. ix. 102.

the general confidence and enthusiasm of the host. A sudden and instantaneous rumour, it was said—a φήμη—pervaded the ranks, to the effect that all cause for anxiety at home was happily at an end; that battle had at last been joined with Mardonius in Boeotia, and that the Greeks were complete victors. What may have been a bold assertion of the loud-voiced herald to the [1]Ionians became a belief all the more exciting from the uncertainty of its origin; it was indeed afterwards said that, as the troops marched along the shore, a herald's staff—confirmation unquestionable—was seen floating inland on a vast wave; apparently a mythical version of the incident of the coasting herald. The boldness of the present attack, by only half the men that could have been brought over by the Greek squadron, upon such a host and its entrenchments, might well seem to demand some unusual explanation. Herodotus—notwithstanding his recent mention of a falsified φήμη in the anecdote of the Medising Phocians—has no difficulty on the point; and why then the soldiers? and is not the 'interposition of the Divinity in human affairs' to be seen in the coincidence that at Mycale again, as at Plataea, the battle was fought close to a *temenos* of the Eleusinian Demeter? That the recognition of this locality may have been to Athenians as encouraging an omen as the name Hegesistratus was to the Spartan, we need not doubt. It was believed that during the battle of Salamis the mystic cry had been heard from clouds of dust along the Thriasian plain, avouching that the divinities of Eleusis were proceeding to protect their worshippers; and intimate indeed was the connection with Athens of a fane of their own goddess founded by a comrade of a son of Codrus, their own patriotic king.

The incidents of the battle in the afternoon correspond very closely with those of the same morning at Plataea: the Persians were first attacked behind their fence of *gerrha*, and

---

[1] Diod. xi. 34. § 4.

so long as it stood, maintained a not unequal war; when it fell they still fought bravely for a considerable time, but fled at last for refuge into the fortified camp: the camp however was nearer at hand to the Asiatic battle-field, and the Athenian pursuers swifter than the Lacedaemonians; so that Athenians, Corinthians, Sicyonians, and Troezenians entered pell-mell along with the fugitives. Resistance was still continued within, though by the Persians alone. Of the other troops, some took to flight; the Samians, who had been left in the camp, though disarmed, found means to assist the Greeks so soon as they were encouraged by prospect of success, while the other Ionians, incited by their example, and forgetting at once the faith of oaths and the fate of hostages, went over in a body, and turned their weapons on the barbarians. The contest was still undecided when the Lacedaemonians arrived fresh upon the spot, but the numbers of the Persians were already fast diminishing, and they fought only in knots, in uncombined onsets, at points where they could still oppose the entrance of the Greeks. Tigranes himself, the general of the land forces, died fighting, and with him Mardontes, who in the European expedition had led the islanders from the Persian gulf—the Erythraean sea. The admirals, Artayntes and Ithamitres, with Masistes, a son of Darius, who had been present at the action, were among the few men of distinction who escaped. They succeeded in gaining on the heights of Mycale a better refuge than the mountain afforded to many of their flying troops. The mistrusted Milesians, who had been posted among the defiles and declivities at the rear of the army, to act ostensibly as guards of the passes, but in reality in order to prevent their deserting to the Greeks during the battle, now found themselves precisely upon the line of communication and retreat of the routed army. As treacherous guides they led the hurrying fugitives into false tracks, and either deserted them in their bewilderment, or brought them upon the very enemy they shunned; at last turned openly upon them, in the spot which their knowledge of the localities pointed out as most advantageous, and, remembering the severities of Darius, were the most vindictive of their slaughterers. To this place, if it is to have place anywhere, we must transfer the [1]incident that the Greeks were for a moment checked by an alarm that Xerxes was arriving from Sardis with reinforcements by the road through the defiles of Mycale, but only to be presently reassured by finding that the apprehended enemies were Ionians in revolt.

The battle, thus at last won, had been strenuously contested ; Greeks and barbarians, says Herodotus, were animated to exertion by the feeling that the islands and the Hellespont were—a true Greek figure—set out as prizes for the victors. When the slaughter of both the fighting and the flying at last came to an end, the Greeks stripped the ships and camp of the booty, comprising the military chest with several stores of coined money, collected it on the shore, and then made a general conflagration of the palisaded camp and of the ships, which for some unstated reason they did not re-launch.

The Greek losses were considerable, but, like their original muster, are unenumerated; the Sicyonians are specified as having lost, along with many others, their general Perilaus. The chief honours of the battle were adjudged to be the right of the Athenians; after them are named in order the Corinthians, Troezenians, and Sicyonians, who fought in company with them ; while the Lacedaemonians and their associates are unmentioned.

Among the Athenians themselves, Hermolycus son of Euthunus, a pancratiast, was pre-eminent; though destined to perish later in an inter-Hellenic quarrel between Athens and Carystus in Euboea ; he was buried, apparently in recognition of his fame, on Geraestus, the extreme promontory of the island.

[1] Diod. xi. 36. § 3.

'And so,' says Herodotus, 'Ionia revolted from the Persians for the second time.'

In this expression we have to understand the defection of the islands also, and the emancipation of Samos, Chios, and Lesbos from the yoke of Persia, by a process of which we have no notice or particulars.

Xerxes had lingered at Sardis since his return from Europe, as if in expectation of couriers who should announce the full success promised by Mardonius. Since the announcement by the train of beacons of the reoccupation of Athens, he could have received little consolation beyond renewals of too hopeful promises. The European intelligence was at last to be anticipated by a disaster nearer home, as Sardis was reached by the scanty and disheartened survivors of Mycale. Salamis had cost him one brother, and he made the most of the escape of another, Masistes, from perils that were not at an end when he had eluded the Milesians. Masistes in his flight had taxed his fellow-fugitive Artayntes with having, by his miserable generalship, caused the entire disaster and the disgrace of the royal house, to which he now added the abusive charge of cowardice worse than a woman's: at this, the most poignant insult to a Persian, the self-restraint of Artayntes gave way; drawing his scimitar, he rushed upon the brother of the Great King, and would have killed him on the spot, if he had not been seized round the body just in time, even before the guards of Masistes could interpose, lifted from his horse, and flung upon the ground. It was a Halicarnassian, Xeinagoras son of Praxilaus, who rendered this service, and Xerxes rewarded him for it with the government of the whole of Cilicia. It had been more fortunate for both Masistes and Xerxes had the rescue miscarried. Even the catastrophe of Plataea, which must have been announced within a day or two, was less fraught with misery and disgrace than events, not on a distant continent, but within the royal palace, not wrought by foreign hostile hands, but due directly to the cruel passions and lust of Xerxes himself. With a narrative of these, which need not be repeated, Herodotus dismisses him from his history; clearly feeling, though he does not phrase it in a formal moral, that public violences and impieties were thus visited with retribution within the home, and within the tortured, or, even more severely, the seared and callous conscience of the man. With such an epilogue may be closed the story of too many a selfish scourge of the race!—an Augustus Caesar, a Norman William, a Prussian Frederic, a Napoleon, to take names almost at random.

On the 16th of February in the ensuing spring occurred an eclipse of the sun, which the superstition of the time may naturally have connected with the final disappointment of Xerxes and his retirement from Sardis; it was equally natural that by the time the tradition reached Herodotus the omen should have been carried back, as he records it, to the days of the King's inauspicious departure from Sardis for Greece.

CHAPTER IX.

It was difficult to realise that this check to the power of Persia on Asian ground might prove more decisive than the still severer blow inflicted in Europe. Memories were still fresh of the vengeance which Persia had before inflicted on Ionia for resistance or revolt; it was not so many years since the tragedian Phrynichus was fined at Athens for bringing into too painful prominence the horrors of the fall of Miletus. That disaster, and indeed the ruin and desolation of all Ionia, had followed upon provocation which present events seemed to repeat too exactly not to introduce like consequences. Athens had then interposed to encourage and abet a rising to which in the end she failed to give any effective support; while the transitory triumph of the burning of Sardis and the fanes of Cybele had infused into the quarrel the venom of religious vindictiveness. It is not surprising therefore that the policy of general migration before vengeance should arrive, which had been partially acted on by the Teians and Phocaeans at the original subjugation of Ionia, and the wisdom of which, as urged by Bias of Priene, was then recognised too late, should again be brought forward for serious consideration. The victorious Greeks returned to Samos, and there the Ionians of the islands and the continent had to face the question how they were to protect themselves with better fortune than before against the too probable consequences of the revolt to which they were again committed. Their elation at the victory of Mycale and their own participation in it might well have been tempered with apprehensions from which both Athenians and Spartans beyond the Aegean were naturally exempt. But the Athenians themselves were at this moment without a country or a city, without walls or temples, relying for re-establishment on their ships, their transportable wealth, and, above all, their population; and were known to have professed an intention under some contingencies of seeking new and distant seats. The project of abandoning the Ionian cities on the mainland, and apparently on the three great islands also, and of transferring their property and population to a region removed from such desperate liabilities, was therefore mooted with serious and even sanguine advocacy. It was the Homeric story of the happy resettlement of the harassed Phaeacians, or that of the later Phocaeans, over again. Leotychides, the Spartan leader, gave the proposal hearty support, and even affected to assume that it was decided conformably to his authority, and that the next point to be discussed was the particular destination. The Ionians could have no hope of disposing of Persian enmity without aid, and it was out of the question that their defence should be undertaken by the European Greeks under the conditions of maintaining a force on the spot for all time. If they were to be protected they must be within easier reach; and this might be compassed by putting them in possession of the trading ports (emporia) of the Greeks who had Medised, and who should now be expelled to make room for them. Boeotia, Locris, and Thessaly, where the Aleuad families were still to be punished, are most directly indicated; but Achaia, and more especially Argos, which had acted so equivocally, might also be considered as included, and in some respects affording a more tempting prospect.

This diplomacy on the part of Lacedaemon was perfectly natural and characteristic for a state still at the com-

K

mencement of its experience in remote and sustained enterprises. The traditional maxim, to limit external action in
respect both of time and distance, was in fact a constitutional
necessity when the predominant class at home was constantly
in an attitude of over-strained watchfulness and jealous defence. Leotychides in truth only discouraged present reliance
upon support the failure of which, as far as his own country
was concerned, he was quite right in assuming. The strength
of Sparta could not long be spared from repression of the
helots, and was moreover dependent on a discipline which could
only be enforced and sustained by keeping its employment
ordinarily within bounds, however it might be capable of
striking out suddenly at well chosen times with single,
forcible, and decisive blows. The difficulty experienced by
the Chians in drawing out the Spartans even as far as Delos,
and by the Samians in inducing them to attack the Persian
fleet before it had time to escape, are but moderate symptoms
of that fixed habit that could satisfy them with limiting their
efforts against Mardonius to defence of the peninsula, cut off
at the Isthmus by fortifications which, after years of notice,
were only completed at the latest [1] moment.

An opposition to these proposals, however, soon gained
head; and was the first revelation of that declared rivalry
to the supremacy of Sparta in thought and action, which was
destined to maintain itself with enduring effects on Greece
for the next half century, and on all history thereafter.
Short as was the period—not twenty years—since the first
Ionian revolt was quenched in blood (B.C. 494), Xerxes was
not Darius; nay, the men of the age of Darius were
rapidly dying out; and it was apparent to Ionians that
the genius of the Persian empire had undergone a degene-
racy, while the confidence and resolution of the Athenians
were what they had never before been. It was the Persian
command of the sea that had been fatal to Miletus; but

[1] Thucyd. i. 68.

the fair prospect that this had now been finally wrested from them altered all the conditions of the crisis for the islands and cities on the sea-board. The Athenians were not backward to foster, or even foment, these rising protests, and at last, when the issue was distinctly joined, they came forward with one of their own; they disallowed the necessity of leaving Ionia to desolation, and in any case repudiated the title of the Peloponnesians to take order respecting colonies of which Athens was the metropolis: it was from the prytaneum of Athens that the Nelid and Codrid leaders started to found these cities, and Athens was prepared to defend her proper relatives, as she claimed to have the sole right to do.

The arrival of the news of the battle of Plataea, while it added immensely to the glory and prestige of Sparta, insured the restoration of the Athenians to their city and country, and promised a revival of power corresponding with the energies her citizens had so uniformly displayed. The accession of strength to be gained for operations against Persia by attaching the islands and Ionia as allies, might suffice to decide Xanthippus in the assertion of an independent course, whether politic jealousy of Spartan designs against Argos came into consideration or no.

To the opposition thus developed the Spartans yielded with a good grace; and the Samians, Chians, Lesbians, and other islanders who took part in the expedition, were admitted into confederacy under an oath of steadfast [1] adherence.

And now at last the original passion of the Athenian fleet to make for the Hellespont could be satisfied. The bridge had indeed been broken by storms a year ago, before Xerxes recrossed the strait; but it might be capable of repair, and in any case it was desirable, if not indispensable, to establish control over the channel.

---

[1] Herod. ix. 106–120; Thucyd. i. 89.

The allied fleet moved northwards, past the now liberated
Chios and Aeolian Lesbos. Detained off the sheltering promontory of Lectos, the westernmost prolongation of the
range of Ida, by the late north winds that prevail through
the Hellespont, they proceeded at last to Abydos. Here they
found that the bridge which had extended from this point to
Sestos was fairly gone; while the Persians remained in possession of the Chersonesus opposite, and in a position to threaten
free navigation and annoy the opposite coast, or even to assist
the transit either of Persian reinforcements or retreating
troops. The Athenians were familiar from of old with the
Chersonesus, where some of their citizens—among them the
family of Miltiades—had property and rights, and for them
the liberation of the Hellespont was only an opening for new
enterprise. But Leotychides, hitherto the recognised head
of the expedition, now declined to make further concession
to the zeal and urgency of his allies, and would do no more.
He withdrew homewards, and with him went the ships of
the other Peloponnesian states—thus marking the future
breaking line of the great confederation. He probably could
not act otherwise under the strict limitations imposed upon
a Spartan king; but already, and especially after recent
differences, the course he took was equivalent to a temporary
abdication of Spartan headship, and a qualified resignation of
it to Athenians, who, elate in self-reliance, knew all the value
of the opportunity, and were secretly, if not openly, eager
to avail themselves of [1]it.

The words of Herodotus are very significant as to the
conditions under which a Greek of the time, whether as
member of a confederacy of states or under a separate
command, submitted his actions to authority. ‘It was determined by the Peloponnesians attached to Leotychides to
sail away to Hellas,—but by the Athenians and by Xanthippus their commander to remain where they were and make

[1] Herod. ix. 114; Thucyd. i. 89.

an attempt upon the Chersonesus.' Interpreted to the letter, Peloponnesians and Athenians assert as much independence of their respective commanders as these do of each other. As a matter of fact no more is implied—though this is much—than that the superior can only enforce orders which are in accordance with public feeling; the feeling being sometimes liable to be swayed, not to say forced, by the resoluteness of a commander, as the commander's resoluteness is sometimes by his sense of the inefficiency of obedience when not rendered with good-will.

The hostile occupants of the Chersonesus were taken by surprise, and hurried at the first alarm to take refuge in Sestos, the only place within reach of such strength as to be defensible, and which soon became over-crowded: to the native Aeolians and refugees from places around were added the Persians and their allies, and there, with no provision for enduring or repelling a siege, they were shut up by the Athenian investing force by sea and land. The Persian Oiobazus, who was in charge of all the tackle and materials for the bridge, had come in from Cardia on the northern coast, but the chief authority, both of the city and the district, was Artayctes, who had obtained his appointment from Xerxes, and afterwards abused it, under circumstances that made him the object of most vindictive rancour: a man, says Herodotus, both able and impiously unscrupulous (δεινὸς καὶ ἀτάσθαλος)—epithets which he justifies as follows. At Elaeus on the southern point of the peninsula, within a temenos or consecrated precinct, was the tomb of the hero Protesilaus, the sacredness of which was avouched by a large accumulation of offerings,—gold, silver, brass, costly robes or dressings (ἐσθής, as at Plataean tombs), and so forth. The tomb—apparently in form a naos, or at least a naïdion—stood menacingly enough, a memorial and emblem of the first collision between Asia and Europe in that war of Troy which Herodotus recognises as the prototype of all their subsequent hostilities. Protesilaus was a leader of Thessalians from Phylaké, and Homer relates how he was the first to leap from shipboard to land, and the first also to die, and that on the spot, by a Dardan weapon; so he perished, a youthful bridegroom, leaving a bride 'in frantic grief,—a house half finished.' Artayctes, the story ran, begged and obtained the temenos from Xerxes by the representation,—'Here is the house of a Greek who met his deserts when invading your territory; give his house to me that so there may be a lesson to others to keep off your ground.' He despoiled the fane of its valuables and transported them to Sestos, and gave up the temenos, apparently of some extent, to culture, and still worse to grazing, and worst of all, insulted wantonly the most sacred associations of the place. The story of Protesilaus was a traditional exemplar of conjugal affection most tenderly expressed, and its details point to an analogy with the equally Thessalian tradition of the self-sacrifice of Alcestis, which vindicates it as truly national, and not a mere late poetic development. By supplications to the gods, Laodameia obtained the return of her husband to earth for a three hours' colloquy, and then died with him as he died [1] again. This colloquy seems to have been a subject of mystic representation like the groups of Aphrodite and Adonis described by Theocritus — the Pietà of antiquity. In later accounts we read that she formed a lifelike image of her husband, kissed it, embraced it, talked to it as if alive and in connection with some sacred rites, and at last was burnt along with it. The tender sentiment clung to the locality, and gave to late Greek poetry the grief of Hero of Sestos over the corpse of her Leander. This is not the place to develop further the process by which a type of conjugal self-devotion—as given again in the story of Orpheus and Eurydice, and on the vase-paintings in a series of

---

[1] Ovid, *Trist.* i. 5. 20; Hygin. 103-4; Propert. i. 19. 7; Eurip. *frag. Prot.*; *Iliad,* ii. 695; Ovid, *Heroides,* xiii. 150.

interesting illustrations—became for the Greek a type for all
that is most solemn with reference to either the commencement of life or the circumstances and apprehended sequel of
its conclusion. It is enough to note that the barbarian could
only read such symbolism coarsely, and find a suggestion
for desecrating the [1] adytum by choosing it for the scene of
wantonness and gross debauchery.

Unprovided as the city was, the Persian garrison forced
it to hold out to the last extremity; so time dragged on
for the besiegers, the late autumn was upon them, and
even the Athenians, with so many motives to return
home, began to despair of success from seeing no sign of
progress, and urged the commanders—again not the single
Xanthippus—to give up and retire. In this case the will of
the commanders prevailed; they would persevere, although
the winter was close upon [2] them, until either the city was
taken or an order of recall arrived from the Athenian community (τὸ Ἀθηναίων κοινόν). That we hear nothing of
negotiations when the besieged had really no hope but in
tiring out their besiegers, was possibly due to the knowledge which Artayctes had of the feelings of which he
was the object, though it may just as easily be due to his
resolution.

At last subsistence failed entirely, the very thongs of
the couches had been cooked and eaten, and the Persian
garrison, who would be the last to suffer, were reduced
to the only chance left—to break out and escape. Early
one morning the besiegers observed signalling from the
towers, and speedily received intimation from the native
inhabitants that the Persians had vacated the town during
the night, descending from the wall and passing the
lines at an unwatched interval. The gates were immediately opened, and the city occupied by a detachment,

[1] Herod. ix. 116.   [2] Thucyd. i. 89.

while the main force started at once in pursuit of the
fugitives. They were in two parties. Oiobazus, who was
in advance, succeeded in getting clear off to Thrace, but
only to fall, before he could reach a Persian post, into
the hands of the Apsinthian Thracians, 'who sacrificed him
to their native god Pleistoros'—a deity of whom no mention
has been traced elsewhere—'in their peculiar fashion, and
slaughtered those who were with him in another fashion.'
Artayctes and his party, who had less start, were overtaken
a little beyond Aegos-potami, and for a short time maintained a defence: some were killed, and the rest, among
whom were Artayctes and his son, were captured and led
back bound to Sestos. We are further told how the captive's
conscience was touched by the miraculous antics of some
pickled fish, a fact not worth alluding to but for the historian's comment, which implies that the body, or at least
an effigy, of Protesilaus had been in some way [1] preserved.
His offers of ransom were declined—100 talents to the god,
200 to the Athenians. The Elaeuntians pressed for his well-
merited execution, as vengeance due to their hero Protesilaus, whose sanctuary he had defiled and desecrated, 'and the
disposition of Xanthippus inclined in the same direction.'
Elsewhere the historian, mentioning the offence by anticipation, attaches the name of Xanthippus to the [2] deed; and
the impression is conveyed that he was willing to stigma-
tise him, from repugnance either to cruelty unworthy of a
Greek, or to the general character of the persecutor of Miltiades. Artayctes was carried to the headland from which the
bridge of Xerxes had been constructed, or as some said to the
hill above the city Madytus, and there nailed alive to a plank
and raised aloft,—crucified in fact,—while his son was stoned
to death before his eyes. This refinement in cruelty would

---

[1] Herod. ix. 120. The relics, too valuable to be lost, were known to P. Mela.
'Sunt Protesilai ossa, consecrata delubro.' ii. 2.

[2] Herod. vii. 33.

alone have been sufficient to indicate in what direction
lay the motive of the hateful deed. It would scarcely be
a relief to think that it was to this same religious rancour,
and not to the cold policy of stimulating superstition, that
three of his sons by Sandace sister of Xerxes had already
fallen victims, having been sacrificed on the prow of the
galley of Themistocles at Salamis to Dionysus Omestes, in
concession to the clamours of a crowd, led on by Euphran-
tides the diviner. Plutarch gives this [1] story on the authority
of Phanias, a pupil of Aristotle.

The tomb of Protesilaus was, as might be expected, re-erected
and re-consecrated; and the mythical prototype of Hellenic
aggression on Asia was destined to be visited and invoked by
a more fortunate successor. When Alexander of Macedon
retrod the steps of Xerxes on his way to determine in what
sense the Great King's dictum as to the ultimate relations of
Europe and [2]Asia was to be fulfilled, he sacrificed to Protesilaus on his tomb at Elaeus, to obtain a happier landing;
then, after offerings to Poseidon and the Nereids while
passing the channel, which Xerxes was at least believed to
have scourged and chained, he reversed the omen for his army
by leaping on shore first of all, and in arms, and alighting
scatheless. It was probably not without the design of
counteracting a similar superstition, that at the end of his
first campaign he sent back from Caria to Macedonia every
newly married soldier—every Protesilaus—in his army, under
generals who were themselves bridegrooms, who were charged
to make the best of the good omen by bringing back with
them in spring the most numerous reinforcement possible of
both horse and [3]foot.

Sestos captured and Artayctes the sacrilegious punished,
the Athenians were at last free to make the longed-for
voyage homewards. Byzantium, upon the route by which

[1] Plut. *Themist.* 13.   [2] Herod. vii. 11.   [3] Arrian. *Hist.* 1.

Artabazus had escaped, still remained to be dealt with; but this was of necessity a work left over. Conspicuous among the spoils carried home were the cables of the Persian bridge, the ingenious workmanship of Phoenicians and Egyptians— as dedications to the gods. The Ionian allies also returned to their newly-liberated [1] cities. And so, with the winter, ended this eventful year.

[1] Thucyd. i. 89

CHAPTER X.

WE have now reached a point in the story where, but for a
few anticipatory hints, we are deserted by Herodotus, and
through the years that intervene between the fall of Sestos
and the Peloponnesian war have to make out a way for ourselves through difficulties and contradictions which enhance,
if it were possible, our appreciation of the guide we have
parted with. Some assistance, and in certain respects the
most valuable of all, is given by the few pages in which
Thucydides summarizes the history of this very interval of
fifty years—the Pentecontaëteris or Pentecontaëtia as it was
called in antiquity. But though the sequence of events is
observed in due order, there is unfortunately a want of
fixed dates and precise notes of intermediate intervals.
Other most important and interesting details are obtainable
from Plutarch's lives of Themistocles, Aristides, Cimon,
and Pericles, and even some notes of dates, though not
uniformly trustworthy; his narratives of incidents, again,
are sadly tainted with errors and contradictions too easily
detected not to oblige us to hesitate frequently over even
an unchallenged statement if it lacks corroboration. The
chronologised history of Diodorus Siculus is likewise of very
great value, but, as usual, has many drawbacks. It is even

more than usually unsatisfactory for the years that we are
concerned with.   Other confusions apart, we find some years
left entirely blank; while in another a complete series is
inserted of events which must have extended over several
or even many years, and we are left to determine as we may
whether in the assigned year they commenced, or culminated,
or came to an end.   Such are the limitations of our main
sources; but cross-lights occasionally visit us, reflected sometimes from the most brilliant, sometimes the most trifling,
remains of Hellenic literature, poetry and prose, of its best
period or its most debased.   Help also that is by no means to
be neglected in our dearth and distress is incidentally obtainable from monuments, from inscriptions, and, still more importantly for the history of that noblest progress in which
resides so much of the interest of our period, from works of
art.

Immediately upon the retirement of the barbarians from
Attica, and with complete confidence after the destruction of the army at Plataea, the Athenians for a second
time returned to a devastated country and ruined city,
bringing back the women and children from their refuge
in Salamis or Troezene, together with whatever moveable
property had been preserved.   Athens itself was found a
heap of ruins: except some of the better houses that had
served up to the last as quarters for Persian nobles, very few
were left entire, and of the circuit of the walls only short
interrupted portions remained.   The emergency was however
energetically met by the labour of the whole population, slave
and free; while Persian spoil, and fines exacted severely from
Medising islanders, came to the aid of the property which
had been rescued, in procuring means and materials.

Themistocles was the presiding genius of these operations, and in prosecuting them with zeal and forethought
he did but resume a career of which his conduct of the
Persian war had been only an episode; the dangers and

difficulties which he there overcame were indeed only a portion
of what he had been preparing to encounter, if not to provoke,
iu furtherance of a settled design for the aggrandisement of
his country. According to Herodotus, Themistocles in the
year of the invasion of Xerxes had but recently attained to
eminence, and the scholiast of Thucydides [1] notes that his
archonship was in the previous year,—an assertion apparently
corroborated by the absence of any other name in the lists for
that year. But the authority of the scholiast is not great,
nor is this interpretation of his words very satisfactory,
and there are considerations in the narrative of Herodotus
and elsewhere that oblige us to give a large interpretation to the limits of the phrase. The death of Themistocles
as recorded at the age of sixty-five must fall, as will appear,
about 460–459 B.C., and he would in consequence be thirty-
two in 493 B.C., when a Themistocles was archon eponymus of
the [2] year, thirty-five in the year of Marathon, and forty-two
in 483 B.C., three years before Salamis, when it was as the
conclusion of a rivalry with him of considerable duration that
Aristides was ostracised. The removal of such an opponent
is quite sufficient to explain the expression of Herodotus as
applying to his acquirement of predominant influence, and
there therefore appears to be no sufficient reason for questioning the earlier date of his archonship.

It was as early, then, as his holding of this office that, according to Thucydides, Themistocles had mooted the policy,
and even made a commencement of the plan, for fortifying
the promontory of the Piraeus, which he was now to resume
on an enormous scale. The stunning blow inflicted upon
Greece in the previous year by the fall of Miletus had been
due to the command of the sea by the Persian fleet, and
Chios, Lesbos, Tenedos, and the Chersonesus had succumbed
in rapid succession. Such disasters might well second the

[1] Thucyd. i. 93.   [2] Dion. Hal. 6.

arguments of Themistocles, who easily read in them the moral, that the freedom of Western Hellas must ultimately depend on maritime superiority; and his happy appreciation of the position and resources of his country and the genius of his fellow-citizens enabled him to discern that public confidence in wise counsel was alone required to secure that superiority to Athens.   There is every reason to ascribe to him at this early period the large conception which he was now to declare fully and urge on to execution; but in the meantime, as a still rising man, he had only been able to make gradual and cautious [1] advances.   The circumstances of the invasion of Datis and Artaphernes, while they confirmed the justness of his views, interfered prematurely with their realization ; and the splendid victory of Marathon was certain to give temporary strength to the party most disposed to thwart him.   It was only after a severe struggle that he succeeded, in opposition to the influence and supporters of Miltiades, in diverting the exclusive attention and resources of the citizens from the land force of hoplites, to ships, and ports, and arsenals.   It was felt on both sides that this change could not but involve some transference of power and ascendency from the settled proprietors and cultivators of land to classes of more restless habits and slighter local attachment, and it was contested accordingly.   His success, such as it was, was mainly due to his adroitly stimulating the jealousy and animosity of the popular assembly against Aegina, while he laid the basis of a system which had prospective reference to a struggle with Persia in case of need, and in any case to the assumption of a prime influence over Hellas.   It was thus that he obtained from the people their patriotic renunciation of the surplus profit from the Laurium silver mines, which had previously been distributed, and its devotion to the construction and maintenance of a fleet; and with such success, that the city, after having

---

[1] Plut. *Themist.*

been beholden to Corinth for twenty triremes to complete
an armament of seventy against Aegina in the year before
Marathon, could within ten years of that event place two
hundred of her own in line at Salamis.   Herodotus himself
ascribes the creation of this fleet, which 'was the salvation
of Greece,' to Themistocles ; a fact quite inconsistent with
his influence being of recent date, even though the statement,
that he gained a vote for the entire number of ships at once,
cannot be received against other evidence.

It was only in. respect of the fleet and its equipment that
these preparations were sufficiently advanced to be fully available against the invasion of Xerxes ; but now the original
plan, with all that it promised and all that it threatened, could
be resumed, and Themistocles exerted all his authority and
influence to hasten its fulfilment.

In former days the city had availed itself of the harbour
of Phalerum, which although exposed was at least spacious,
and had the advantage of being within the shortest distance
of the [1] city ; but on the representation of Themistocles it was
resolved to abandon this in favour of the three natural harbours formed by the rocky promontory of Piraeus.   One of
these, of smaller dimensions, appears to have been situated
eastward, at the foot of the steeply-scarped hill of Munychia ;
the larger and more important lay to the westward, thoroughly
sheltered, and accessible only by a narrow and easily protected
inlet.   The position of Munychia had been recognised in
earlier times as liable to be most dangerous for Athens if
held by an enemy—as indeed it was to prove more than
once long afterwards ; but the plans of Themistocles now
extended to the inclusion of this in a general circuit of
impregnable walls, defending the entire peninsula, and of
sufficient. extent to afford refuge for the population of the
city itself.   He urged upon the Athenians that it was from
a Persian naval force that they would have most to apprehend

---

[1] Pausanias, I. i. 2.

in future; that their safety depended on their own supremacy
at sea; and that should the time ever come for their country
to be again invaded, their true policy would be to decline
as before to rely on the defences of the upper city, and
fall back on those of the Piraeus as a citadel, where they
would have a refuge which would spare them the sufferings
of their late migrations, and be easily maintained by a few
of the least serviceable of the population, and give them the
opportunity to throw their whole able-bodied strength on
ship-board.

The locality itself provided stone in abundance, and
Thucydides refers to the walls as still existing for the
solidity which Themistocles proposed to give them: they
were sufficiently broad for two of the wagons that brought
materials to pass each other; they were not formed with
a core of rubble, nor was mortar employed, but they were
regularly constructed of great squared stones, the upper
surfaces of which were fastened with clamps of iron run
with lead. It was said that the height they were carried
to was not more than half of that originally intended, but
even at that height they were fully defensible.

Thus it was that Themistocles first gave shape to the principle on which the maritime empire of Athens was to rest,
and of which the parallel long walls were but a further
application, until at last the metropolis itself might be considered as within the impregnable circuit of the ports and
town of the Piraeus.

In the meantime however the city was too sacred to be
neglected: it had indeed to be attended to in the first
instance, though the subject of the fortified ports is duly introduced at a time when it was already a settled design and
a motive force in political action. It was in accordance with
these ulterior views that the walls of the city itself were
recommenced on a scale greatly in excess of mere repair
and restoration, and rather commensurable with the pre-

tensions of a state which had before been self-confident in energy and genius, and was now resolved to maintain pre-eminence as the due of its patriotic devotion and services in the course of the recent, and still existing, struggle. The area to be enclosed within the new walls was extended in every direction, so as to include the suburbs and to admit of future expansion.

The scope of these preparations was not unmarked or misinterpreted by jealous eyes; the apprehensions of Aegina were at once re-awakened, and with good reason. The predominance of the Athenian marine was already absolute, partly from the number of its triremes, and still more from the efficiency with which they were manned by a population whom the exigencies of the time had transformed into trained and dexterous oarsmen, whose daring and self-reliance had been heightened by success. If Athens were to be secured from attack by land also, the last check upon her ambition would be lost. Corinth complained later of the fatal indulgence allowed to these preparations, and might easily share with Megara the jealousies of Aegina; but it was from Lacedaemon—as head of the Dorian section, if not indeed of the entire confederacy—that a protest first arrived by the mouths of special envoys. The present relations of the two states and their mutual necessities caused the objections, though serious, to be couched in terms of advice rather than expostulation. Spartans, who on principle repudiated the protection of walls for their own city, might with a show of consistency from their own point of view urge the same magnanimous policy on others; but some other plea was necessary for them as representatives of alarmed Peloponnesian allies, who had fortifications of their own which they were not likely to renounce. They urged therefore that to fortify Athens would be but to provide the Persian, in the very probable event of a renewed invasion in still greater force, with one more such dangerous basis as he had already used to advantage in

L

Thebes; the Peloponnesus would be a place of refuge sufficient
for all, and the best basis for defence or action; it would be
better indeed that the Athenians, instead of adding to the
extra-Peloponnesian fortresses, should co-operate with them in
razing the walls of all the others.

Representations so moderately expressed might be as
moderately entertained, and meanwhile the progress of the
walls was not interrupted in the slightest degree. But the real
strength of the feelings in reserve was presently manifested
by the growing impatience of the Spartan envoys, who even
took upon themselves to interfere with the workmen by commands and threats. Themistocles was equal to the occasion:
for an opposition manifestly so serious he intimated his
serious respect, and stopped the works at once; and by his
advice the envoys were dismissed home without delay, satisfied
with this compliance, and with the engagement that the
Athenians would on their part send envoys to Sparta to deliberate further on the suggestion that had been put forward.
He himself in fact followed them forthwith, but for some time
after his arrival made no sign of bringing the business under
the consideration of the Spartan authorities. When questioned
by some of the leading men as to the cause of the delay, he
replied that he waited for his colleagues: he was surprised
that they had not arrived long ago, as promptly as himself; some hindrance must have intervened to detain them;
he had no doubt they would make their appearance in all
haste; and so with one excuse or another he made time draw
on. Theopompus states that the ephors were bribed by
Themistocles to connive at his dilatoriness; and such a suspicion is often found to attach as naturally to Spartan cor-
ruptibility as to Athenian craft; but the confidence placed
in the plausible negotiator needs no other explanation,
and possibly admitted of none, than the very frankness
of his plausibility, the unscrupulous positiveness of his assurances, and the reception that was appropriate to the

comrade and colleague of Eurybiades at Artemisium and
Salamis; he had before been welcomed at Sparta with honours
that were almost extravagant, and Hellas was even yet not so
secure against Persia that his friendliness could be dispensed
with or prudently jeopardised by unhandsome imputations.
But to delay thus gained there must necessarily be a term.
Rumours that the walls of Athens were rising all the while
received the positive confirmation of a message despatched
from the watchful Aegina by Polemarchus.   In point of fact,
Themistocles had arranged with the Council (*Boulé*) that the
work should be recommenced as soon as he had started, and
the departure of his colleagues delayed until the wall had
reached such a height that in an extreme case it would be
defensible.   All hands accordingly fell promptly to the
work, men, women, and children, slave and free, resident and stranger; and all available materials, whether of
private or public buildings, were seized and made use of
indiscriminately.   Thucydides adverts to the appearance and
miscellaneous materials of the lower part of the walls in his
own time, as evidence of the hasty energy with which the
work had been executed.   The stones were not properly
squared or fitted in courses, but laid together as they best
might be; and amongst them were visible even sepulchral *steles* and sculptured stones, which showed that not
even works of art or monuments of the dead had been
spared.

To the direct assertion of the fact by Polemarchus, as
just mentioned, Themistocles opposed a flat denial of its
possibility; he represented that so extraordinary a tale
should not be taken on trust from a source which was
prejudiced if not hostile; let men be sent from Sparta
to Athens of such character and dignity as really to command credit, and it would appear how grossly Athens was
calumniated.

The challenge made so boldly was accepted; and Spartan

envoys of the distinction demanded arrived at Athens to
open their astonished eyes on an effectually walled city; but
the reception that awaited them was governed by a message
from Themistocles to the Council, which had passed them on
the road. Abronichus son of Lysicles and Aristides son of
Lysimachus, his colleagues, had before this joined Themistocles with news that the requisite height of the wall had
been accomplished; there was no further use or motive
for dissimulation, but the indignation of the Spartans
might be dangerous; his instructions accordingly were
to detain the envoys, with as little appearance of coercion
as possible, but effectually, until he and his colleagues were
released.

The Spartans expressed themselves with great violence at
Athens, and it was not easy to conceal from them the
fact that they were under detention; but in the meantime, the hostages fairly in hand, Themistocles believed
that the shortest and frankest explanation at Sparta was
the best. His character for candour could in no case be
of use there again, unless indeed with the most credulous
and after lapse of time; he might always dispense with
it in dealing with those who had neither candour nor
scruples of their own: for the rest, he was not ill satisfied as a politician with the price for which he parted
with it.

He therefore presented himself to the Spartans, with the
plain announcement, 'that the walls of Athens were now so
far completed as to afford perfect shelter to its inhabitants;
and that in case the Lacedaemonians or the allies had any
communication to make to the Athenians, they would please
to address them as capable of knowing their own interest
no less than that of the general community. Of such capacity there was proof enough and notorious; their decision
that it was expedient for them to abandon their city and
take to the ships was a bold resolution adopted independently

of foreign counsel; while on the other hand it was well
known, and had been distinctly admitted at Sparta, that in
deliberating on common business their judgment had been
inferior to none. They were now of opinion, that it was
better for their city to be walled, both for the sake of
their citizens independently, and for the advantage of the
alliance at large; inasmuch as it was quite impossible for
states to deliberate fairly and equally on common objects
unless upon an equal basis. On this ground, either the
existing state of things must be acquiesced in as just, or
otherwise walls must be dispensed with by all members of
the confederacy indifferently, whether within or without the
Isthmus.' The Lacedaemonians suppressed their anger and
vexation perforce,—' they had interfered with no purpose of
obstruction, but had acted as public agents in communication of an opinion, moved indeed by a particular sense of
sympathy with the known zeal of the Athenians against
the Medes.' And so the two embassies returned to their respective homes without further difficulty or [1] challenge. But
the displeasure rankled at Sparta, and was to rankle, and
the time came one day for Themistocles personally to feel
its effect.

To this occasion, if we are to accept them at all, we must
refer some proceedings which, as obviously misplaced by Diodorus, are inconsistent with themselves, and as transformed
by [2] Plutarch, only reappear to be further involved in conflict
with most assured history.

We have seen Themistocles acting throughout with all
the freedom of absolute authority, though apparently un-
invested with any leading political office; and this at a
crisis when the people must have been in the liveliest agitation at their unprotected condition relatively to the
jealousies of the Peloponnesians. On no occasion could

----

[1] Cf. Schol. Aristoph. *Equ.* 811.   [2] Plut. *Aristides*·

he have appealed with more reason to the people in public
assembly (*ecclesia*) to be allowed an interval of uncontrolled
action in a business of the utmost importance to the
state, but which in the interests of the state might not be
divulged.   It is also perfectly consistent with the jealousy .
of the demus, that he should be called upon to confide his
plan to Aristides and Xanthippus, the latter of whom would
have reached Athens in the course of the winter,—men who
commanded public confidence not only from their general
character, but in such a contingency from their being at
least his rivals, if not his declared opponents.   The report
however which was thus obtained, that the scheme was both
advantageous and feasible, again only excited the popular
mistrust of a man who, already well known as an intriguer
of unrivalled ingenuity, had now enlisted his very competitors on his side and in favour of his most marked advancement.   They therefore insisted further—so the story
continues—that he should admit the Council into the secret
of his policy ; and that after this, if the report were to the
same effect, the liberty of action which he demanded should
be finally conceded to him.   The great advantage and
practicability of the plans were now affirmed ; and so at
last with difficulty, and with curiosity stimulated to the
highest pitch, Council and ecclesia gave up the control of
the state to a single man, who was to exercise it for a time
without check or supervision : and thus the stratagem obtained a success which, whether it might or might not have
been gained by a more direct method, was at any rate held
to justify the demand of the administrator, and the confidence, so cautiously bestowed, of the Athenian demus.

The city once walled, we hear of no further opposition or
protest at present from either the Lacedaemonians or their
immediate allies ; but the jealousy they had already displayed
could not but be enhanced and their animosity envenomed
by the consciousness of the contemptuous way in which

such clumsy schemes of interference had been seen through and set aside. To the Athenians, who were perfectly aware of these sentiments, they could only act as incitements to second the urgency of Themistocles to complete the defensive works at the Piraeus.

CHAPTER XI.

THE Athenian fleet, as we have seen, was detained at least
till the near approach of winter by the siege of Sestos, after
the Peloponnesians had retired, and only then at last made
the wished-for return to Athens, where the restoration of the
city and the resettlement of society and domestic life awaited
all available assistance. On this account, and inasmuch as
Aristides, who is next named in command of the fleet, was
occupied with the prolonged negotiations about the walls of
Athens, we cannot safely reckon upon it as having resumed
action so early as the ensuing spring of 478 B.C.

The most pressing services required of it were, first to
follow in the track of the Persian-Phoenician fleet, which
had escaped before the disaster at Mycale, and if not to
reach it, to provide occupation for it elsewhere; and then
to take Byzantium, which still insured to the Persians
a ready transit by the route of Artabazus from Asia to
Europe, either on some new expedition or to support the
garrisons in Thrace, and the power of interfering with the
trade to and from the Euxine. But the strong northern
winds which through the summer always set down the
Propontis and Hellespont, mark out the early part of the
year for the important expedition to Byzantium, and, under

all the circumstances, it seems to have been deferred to the spring of the next year, 477 B.C. This inference is in harmony with Diodorus, who assigns it to the archonship · of Adeimantus.

It would be inconsistent, however, to suppose that the intermediate year was entirely unemployed in the war, though it may have been mainly occupied with preparations for a more vigorous renewal, as soon as some past ravages had been repaired. To this year accordingly we must assign an expedition of great importance in its purpose, but of which, in consequence of its failure to realise any important results, we have but the most cursory notice.

A land force, we are told, was despatched by the Lacedaemonians, under the king Leotychides, to act in Thessaly against the Aleuad princes, who, replaced in authority by the Persian, had rendered zealous aid against Hellas to the very last. There was the best hope of native assistance, as a strong party of Thessalians had originally displayed hearty Hellenic [1] sympathy, and promoted, as long as there was reasonable chance of success, the defence of the passes of Olympus. On the occasion referred to a combined Athenian and Spartan force had been carried by the Euripus past Thermopylae to disembark at Halos, on the western Achaian shore of the Pagasaean gulf. The same route was probably adopted in the present instance, when Larissa was the object of attack. It is at least in harmony with this view that, according to a proposed correction of a text of [2] Pausanias, it was in the fourth year after the death of Leonidas (a period sufficiently covered by the duration of this expedition) that his remains were brought back from Thermopylae to Sparta by Pausanias, who thus acted appropriately as his nephew and regent for his son, and who is found the next year in command of the fleet.

---

[1] Herod. vii. 172.　　　　[2] Paus. iii. 14. 1.

Whenever this occurred, we cannot doubt that it was done in obedience to an oracle, though none is on record. The unaltered text of the Periegesis, however, gives an interval of forty years, which carries on the incident to the time of the grandson and namesake of Pausanias. Arnold Schaefer is unusually weak here, when he finds a motive for the transfer at this time in the possibility of danger from the Athenians to the sacred relics as at first [1] deposited.

It is, again, as connected with this expedition to Thessaly, that we obtain an available explanation of the notice that the combined fleets of Athens and Sparta were present, some time after the retirement of the Persians, in the bay of Pagasae, as they well might be now, for co-operating with or transporting the land force. How Themistocles had a private project for treacherously destroying the fleet of the allies of Athens ; how Aristides, to whom the demus required the plan to be divulged, reported that it was advantageous but dishonourable ; and how, thereupon, it was refused further entertainment,—this is a tale in which Plutarch gives new colour and details to what we have divined of the part played by Aristides in first learning privately the views of Themistocles in staying the works on the walls, and then in not denouncing, but very effectively furthering, the stratagem against Lacedaemon.

To the present occasion, however, we may probably refer the opposition of Themistocles to a Spartan proposal for forfeiting the ancient Amphictyonic rights of all cities that had failed to take part against the Medes. He apprehended the preponderance that would accrue to Spartan influence, but argued broadly against excommunicating all Greece, except some thirty-one cities, of which the majority were so small that the assembly would virtually be in the control of two or three of the largest ; and to this reasoning the Pylagorae gave in.

---

[1] Arn. Schaefer *De rerum p. bell. Pers.* p. 8.

A few lines of [1] Herodotus, which are confirmed as well as copied by [2] Pausanias, apprise us further, that Leotychides had a course of military success which it was believed that he only failed to push to completeness because he allowed himself to be corrupted by those whom it was his office to chastise. He had however been mistrusted by the oligarchical ephors as likely to be too eager, king as he was, to drive the Aleuad princes of Larissa to extremities. It was not so long ago as to be forgotten that king Cleomenes, who had been their instrument for putting an end to the tyranny of the Peisistratids at Athens, had attempted for his own purposes to install Isagoras in their place. Leotychides was watched in his very camp, and at least declared to be detected in the possession of a large bribe—a gloveful of money under his very seat. On his return to Lacedaemon—at latest, therefore, at the end of the campaign, the winter of 478 B.C.—the charge was pressed, and, rather than abide the result of a trial, he retired to Tegea in Arcadia, his house was razed to the ground, and he never was recalled.

He died at Tegea, and Diodorus, in agreement with better authorities, says after a reign of twenty-two years, which was succeeded by that of Archidamus of forty-two years; but he assigns his death to the archonship of Phaedon (=476-5 B.C.), and, so far consistently, the death of [3] Archidamus to 434 B.C. His own subsequent record, however, of the acts of Archidamus is at variance with this date, and in accordance with both [4] Plutarch and Thucydides, who enable us to fix the term of the life of Archidamus decisively in 427-6 B.C., and the commencement of his reign in 469 B.C. Diodorus therefore antedates the commencement of either reign by seven years.

The chronology of the succession is thus satisfactorily corrected; but it is not an unimportant question how Diodorus was led into the error that he carried forward so persistently.

[1] Herod. vi. 72.
[2] Diod. xii. 45.
[3] Paus. iii. 7. 9.
[4] Plut. *Cimon*, 16.

By one explanation he merely transferred an event to the
archonship of Phaedon from that of Apsephion by mistake in
the name, which in its place he certainly mis-copies [1] Phaion.
Another and more satisfactory view is, that his erroneous
date for the death is the interchanged date of exile. The
exile followed immediately upon the Thessalian expedition, of
which no date is given either for one year or another, but
which is quite in its place if undertaken to punish Medism in
477 B.C., though not easily accommodated to the circumstances
of 469 B.C. The expression of Herodotus, that he did not
live on to old age in Sparta, conveys with sufficient distinctness that his life was considerably prolonged after his retirement,—that he was to attain to old age, but elsewhere.

According to this supposition, therefore, the exile, or
rather flight, of Leotychides was not reckoned as formal de-
position, and it was only from his death that Archidamus,
whatever authority was allowed him in the interim, was
recorded as king. A parallel to a certain extent occurs in
the case of Pleistoanax, son of the regent Pausanias; he
also was charged with military remissness for the sake of
a bribe, was in exile eighteen years, during which time
his son, a minor, is alluded to as [2] king; was then recalled,
and has at last his term of exile included in the full tale of
his fifty years of [3] reign. The tale of his son's regnal years
only commences from this term, his previous dignities notwithstanding.

It is quite possible that Archidamus likewise was a minor
at the time of his grandfather's disgrace, though from
some considerations unlikely. It was before his exile that
Leotychides, in consequence of the death of his son Zeuxidamus, married a second wife; it is implied that a son by
this second marriage would have superseded Archidamus,
the heir of his deceased son Zeuxidamus, perhaps in accord-

---

[1] Ol. 74. 4.   [2] Thuc. iii. 26.   [3] Diod. xiii. 75.

ance with precedent, as the eldest born during his father's kingship. The only issue of this later marriage, however, was a daughter, Lampito, whom he gave in marriage to the presumptive heir Archidamus—son of her half-brother, his own grandson, and, in default of his further male issue, his heir; and this would seem more probably, though after all by no means certainly, to have taken place before his exile than after it.

The circumstances of royalty at Sparta about this time may be taken as representing many of the contingencies and consequences of its hard conditions generally. Leotychides only followed into exile his predecessor Demaratus, who had been supplanted by an intrigue to which he himself had been a party, and which involved corruption of a Delphic priestess; and the authority of the representative of the Proclid line of Heracleids, his grandson Archidamus, could scarcely be confirmed so long as his own return was a possibility. As regards the other, the Agid line, Cleomenes, the elder brother and predecessor of Leonidas, had been a party to the extrusion of Demaratus, and a feeling which arose from some discoveries upon the subject so far alarmed him that he retired to Thessaly, was then suspiciously busy in Arcadia, was at last and perhaps in consequence recalled, but soon died a maniac. The present king Pleistarchus, son of Leonidas, was still a minor; to what stringent control his cousin and guardian, the regent Pausanias, was amenable we shall presently see, and how soon the accession of Pleistoanax, the son of the regent, was superseded by an exile that was to last for some twenty years.

The position and authority of the kings would thus appear at this time to be about the least stable thing at Sparta. The relation indeed of the ephors to the kings was such, that kings and regents could scarcely but chafe under interference and control, and be uneasy as to constant peril from one trumped-up charge or another ; and the ephors on their side had cause, if only by their knowledge of this very uneasiness, always to exert their great power of self-protection early enough and vigorously enough.

It is not easy to read all the stories that are told to account for the setting aside, and no less for the reinstatement, of Spartan kings, without concluding that many of them can but represent pretexts for political or private objects, of which the true particulars are hidden far beyond detection. In a state so bound to the observance of rigid laws and constitution, changes of policy either requisite or desired, precautions against ambition or excessive influence, or even the substitution of another for the hereditary military commander, seem to have been effected as systematically by a charge of bribery or by a procured oracle, as they were at Athens more frankly, without any definite charge at all, by the process of ostracism.

The Athenian demus could not be more jealous of the independence of its command than was the Spartan oligarchy. It was in genuine aversion to tyrannies, and to the contagion of their example, that the ephors, by the not always zealous hands of their own kings, had rooted out the tyrants from Athens and other cities of Hellas ; and now the example of Athens in rebuking Miltiades for seeming to claim the entire credit of [1] Marathon, was followed at Sparta by a severe check administered to the first display of arrogance by the victor of Plataea. To the basis of the tripod at Delphi, which was a common Greek dedication for this victory, he had attached an inscription which Thucydides preserves, and which named himself alone, both as victor and dedicator.

The ephors had it instantly erased, and substituted

[1] Plutarch, *V. Arist.*

another reciting only the names of the dedicating confederate cities; his position was, however, otherwise at
present undisturbed. The signs of the erasure have been
recognised beside the inscription upon the bronze basis as
it still exists at Constantinople.

CHAPTER XII.

PAUSANIAS AND ARISTIDES AT BYZANTIUM.—ATHENIAN ACCEPT-
ANCE OF THE ACTIVE LEADERSHIP OF HELLAS.

B.C. 477 ; Ol. 75. 3 and 4.

BY the early spring of the next year, 477 B.C., a large
naval armament was afloat. Pausanias, son of Cleombrotus,
says Thucydides, was despatched from Lacedaemon as general
of the Hellenes, with twenty Peloponnesian ships; and with
them sailed the Athenians in thirty ships, and a considerable
number of other allies. Diodorus seems to include the other
allies in the proper squadron of Pausanias, which he gives
at fifty ships in all. They probably mustered on the coast
of Asia Minor, and their first attempts were made on Cyprus,
where the Persian garrisons were expelled from most of the
cities. The complete liberation of the entire island, however,
could not be effected, at least within the time available; the
attempt was renounced, and the fleet, anticipating the contrary summer winds, made for the north, and reached Byzantium, to find it probably all the more unprepared for defence,
from reports received of the direction of hostilities elsewhere.
The city was not taken without some [1]fighting; but we hear
of no considerable difficulty or prolongation of the siege. A
certain number of the defenders escaped; but on the capture,
Pausanias found himself not only a second time in possession

---

[1] Diod. xi. 44.

of the wealthy spoil of the chief refuge of the Persians in Europe, but also of a number of important prisoners—officers, and even relatives of the Great King. This second success, won by him at the head of the confederated naval force of Hellas, as he had won Plataea in command of the united land forces, seems to have filled the mind of the Spartan regent with dreams of emancipation from the control of his national constitution—the galling interference of ephors —of which the peril of Leotychides was a recent and perhaps an intentionally warning example, and which had but lately exposed himself to so public a humiliation.

We miss throughout the story of his treason any intimation of a really profound and promising scheme; no extensive connection of adherents among the allies is hinted at, no apparent opportunity of turning the discontents of a powerful class, the madness of many or of few, to the elevation of himself to the position of a tyrant—for nothing less was the project of Pausanias—of universal Hellas. Absolute self-contained arrogance, recalling the frequent relationship of pride to madness, brings to mind also that mania was the end of the wild life of his uncle Cleomenes I. Pausanias not merely disgusted the Ionians by injurious treatment in their intercourse with the Spartans, but even the Athenians and Peloponnesian allies by his superciliousness, and at last took to courses that put him in the wrong as much with his own countrymen as with the other Greeks, and threw him into desperate intrigues with the Persians which, for aught we can discern, were alike hopeless and senseless from the very beginning.

The discontent of the Ionian allies had been growing for some time. Unfavourably as the Ionians of Asia Minor contrast with those of Attica, even to an Athenian like Aeschylus, they were doubtless held still cheaper in respect of strength and discipline by the Spartans; but they were now under all the excitement of being consciously committed to a

perilous quarrel, were inspired by the sense of newly-recovered
liberty, and by emulation with the marvellous energy of
the Athenians, whom they were proud to claim as their
relations, whether accepted as such with entire cordiality
or [1] not. To the Ionians — the more so because of their
recent enfranchisement—it was galling beyond endurance
to be still treated like slaves; to be interfered with in
watering and foraging parties, till the Lacedaemonians gave
leave after taking precedence; to be subjected to arbitrary
punishments such as stripes, or picketing to iron anchors,
and even to blows from subordinates. To Dorians from
Peloponnesus a much smaller share of such treatment would
be intolerable. Expostulation was vain, and men in command, up to Aristides himself, who here as at Plataea might
claim the privilege of an associate in generalship, were refused
audience, and put off with studied airs of preoccupation or
more insulting disregard. An independent incident, of tragic
and shameful interest, brought on a crisis. Cleonice, a
daughter of a noble Byzantine family, was so unfortunate as
to attract the notice of Pausanias, and he forced her parents
by threats to surrender her to his desires. He had fallen
asleep when she was introduced into his apartment; aroused
by the sudden noise of a falling lamp, he seized the sword
that was beside him, and, under the momentary impression of
an enemy being near, struck out in the unexpected darkness,
to find that he had slain the unhappy girl, who was approaching his bed in shame and terror. It was believed
afterwards that her *eidolon* constantly haunted him at night,
repeating a warning and summoning hexameter; that, in
distress and excitement, he resorted to every form of atoning
purification, and to mystical rites at Heraclea and Phigaleia,
for evoking her soul and deprecating its anger; but only to
obtain a response which sent him back once more to Sparta
with promise of speedy conclusion to his miseries—a con-

[1] Herod. i. 143.

clusion that did speedily arrive, but only in a miserable death.
The tale, says [1] Plutarch, has been told by many; it was to be
told after him again by the traveller Pausanias, who had it,
he seems to suppose, as an unrecorded anecdote, from the lips
of a [2] Byzantine.

It was on [3] this that many of the Peloponnesian allies gave
up and returned home, to report how Sparta was being dis-
graced and the harmony of the Hellenic confederation endangered.

Mistrust still more serious soon arose, to add alarm to the
indignation of the recently emancipated Ionians. The satrapy
of Dascylitis, adjacent to the eastern coast of the Hellespont,
was held by the Achaemenid Megabates, who under Darius
had been appointed to co-operate with Aristagoras for the
subjugation of the [4] Cyclades, but, quarrelling with his associate, gave treacherous information to the Naxians, and so
frustrated the enterprise. From whatever suspicious circumstances, the report got about that Pausanias was nego-
tiating for an alliance with his daughter, in combination
with a treasonable scheme against Hellas. This version of
his designs is referred to by Herodotus as merely a report; but Thucydides could quote documents that came to
light at a later date—not later however than when Herodotus was writing—which proved that Pausanias aimed
higher, and indeed was on his guard against the treacherous
nature which had once before been fatal to another Hellenic
traitor. He took an opportunity of committing the charge
of Byzantium to a certain Gongylus, an Eretrian, together
with the custody of the prisoners, including some connections
and relatives of the Great King, and arranged that he should
liberate them without communication with the allies, and
proceed in person to the court of Xerxes, bearing a letter
in terms thus literally translated:—'Pausanias, general of

---

[1] Plut. *Cimon*, 6.
[2] Plut. *ibid.*
[3] Paus. iii. 17. 8.
[4] Herod. v. 32.

Sparta, out of a desire to gratify thee, sends to thee these
men, whom he took captive in war; and I am moreover
minded, if it is also agreeable to yourself, to marry your
daughter, and to bring into subjection to you both Sparta
and the rest of Hellas. If then you are at all favourable
to this, send down to the sea a man *who may be relied on*,
through whom I may communicate hereafter.'

The treachery of Gongylus to Hellas was gratefully recognised by Xerxes; such a service was least of all to be
expected from an Eretrian, whose country had been so merci-
lessly treated by Datis and Artaphernes. He was rewarded by
the lordship—in effect hereditary—of four towns in Aeolis,
near those which had been consigned to the equally unpatriotic Demaratus, and where Xenophon knew of the de-.
scendants of both as still established.

The proposal to negotiate was at once warmly embraced
by Xerxes; it confirmed all that Artabazus had ever impressed
upon him as to the true policy for subjecting Greece, the
policy which he had advocated all along, and which Mardonius had overruled with such fatal consequences. In all
haste he sent down Artabazus himself to supersede Megabates, with authority to forward a letter sealed with the royal
signet to Pausanias, and instructions to co-operate with him in
whatever he might propose to the best effect and in all good
faith. The reply so transmitted was in these terms:—'Thus
says King Xerxes to Pausanias. The act of kindness towards
the men whom you have preserved for me from Byzantium
beyond the sea, is laid up for you in record in our house
for all time; and I am gratified by your further communications. Let neither night nor day interfere to cause you to
relax in setting about what you promise me; and be not
hindered for any expenditure of gold or silver, nor for
abundant forces in whatever direction they may be required;
and deal in full confidence with Artabazus, a man of worth,
whom I have sent to you, in what is both my business and

your own, as will be best and most honourable for both of us.'
The custom here alluded to, of the formal registry of the
king's friends, is frequently [1] mentioned.

The receipt of this letter from the Great King seems to
have fairly turned the head of the Spartan regent; and if not
the more, certainly none the less, from the earnest of a large
treasure conveyed to him by Artabazus for employment in
[2] corruption. He at once assumed the state and the arbitrary airs of a Persian satrap. He had already abused the
dignity which the Greeks could not but willingly concede to
the head of Sparta in any case, and still more to the victor
of Plataea ; but he now assumed the ensigns of Persian
rank in dress and attendance, and adopted in serious in-
fatuation the display which in the Boeotian camp he had
sarcastically contrasted with Spartan simplicity. He left
Byzantium to make a round through Thrace, where there
were still considerable Persian garrisons, even as near as in
the Chersonesus, with which the royal signet would probably
enable him to open communications. On his return he appeared with a body-guard of Medes and Egyptians, had his
table served with all the pomp and apparatus of Persia, and
could not restrain himself from giving hints, or rather notice,
in trivial matters, of the designs that he was harbouring on
a larger [3] scale. But he returned to find the confederates and
their commanders by no means in the merely irritated and
unsettled state in which he left them. Suspicions were
abroad, and general alarm at common danger had ripened
into a common understanding as to the means by which
it might be averted. Alike in demeanour and administration, the Athenian commander Aristides was in absolute
contrast to Pausanias — as the steadfast to the fitful, the
deliberate to the capricious, the just to the arbitrary, the

[1] Herod. iii. 140, viii. 85; Diod. S. xvii. 14; Joseph. *Antiq.* xi. 6; Esther,
ii. 23, vi. 1.
[2] Diod. xi. 44.   [3] Thuc. i. 130.

truly dignified to all that was supercilious, offensive, and arrogant. The Ionians had had warning before the battle of Mycale, and also at the siege of Sestos, that Sparta was less to be relied on than Athens for rendering such aid as they required to maintain their newly-recovered independence; and the temper of the Athenian commander Aristides, and of Cimon also if, as is possible from the tenor of some accounts, he was already associated with him, gave assurance that such aid would be rendered with a good faith and Hellenic loyalty, which plainly could no longer be counted on from Pausanias.

The crisis must have seemed dangerous to Aristides himself; and there was every reason for his readily entertaining the advances of the insular and Asian allies, who were now prepared definitely to transfer their recognition of leadership from Sparta to Athens. It was only from patriotic concession to the predilections of the confederacy—predilections rooted in immemorial tradition—that Athens had conceded the leadership to Sparta at sea also, where her own preponderant naval power gave her a fair claim to pre-eminence. This preponderance had been gradually becoming still more decided, and no one knew better than Aristides the future which Themistocles was at this very time preparing for it, by his improvements at the Piraeus. The Peloponnesian allies, the peculiar adherents of Sparta, not sorry perhaps (as at Sestos) to have again an excuse for giving up, had already retired in disgust; those that remained were the Ionians, whom Athens had already protected against Spartan interference, by assertion of her metropolitan claims, and whose continued zeal could be relied on. The same tradition of colonial dependence was now willingly urged by the Ionians themselves; and in truth, whatever change of character may have supervened from foreign admixture and under Asian skies, there was still enough of original tribal character remaining to account for a very lively sympathy of relationship, especially as compared with Spartan Dorians. The heroic traditions of these cities, and their conspicuous monuments, kept ever in mind that their reputed founders were of the old royal race of Athens, or had carried from its prytaneum their sacred [1] fire; and the motives involved in these associations were ever most powerful with the Greeks at periods of excited enthusiasm.

The signs of relaxation in Spartan energy, and worse still, of a tendency to corruption or treachery in her most powerful leader, were thus declaring themselves at a time when Athenian energy, so far from exhaustion, was in the first flush of sanguine resolution. It is beside the question at such a point to consider whether Aristides was most influenced in his policy by ambition for the power of Athens, or concern for the defence of Hellas. His course could only be the same in either case; much indeed remained to be done to secure the result of past victories for the benefit of Hellas at large, and only by Athens coming frankly and boldly to the front could this security be taken. It was on the occasion of a distinct insult being offered to Aristides by Pausanias, that an opportunity seemed afforded to the Ionian malcontents for gaining him over to a policy which he had resolved not to precipitate, nor even to appear to invite. On his seeking a hearing from Pausanias for expostulations, and with intent to inform him of the offensiveness of his conduct, he had been superciliously put off; the mimic satrap would not listen to him, would scarcely look at him; he was not at leisure. Counting on his indignation, the captains and generals of the allies, chiefly of the Chians, Samians, and Aeolian Lesbians, made a direct proposal that he should assume the leadership (*hegemonia*), and thus attach to himself the allies, who

---

[1] Herod. i. 146.

had long been anxious to give up the Spartans and would
at once range themselves with the Athenians. They quitted
the interview however without having elicited either pledge
or proposal from Aristides to undertake what was suggested
to him ; and yet every word he had said was confirmatory
of the pressing necessity that something should be done,
of the justice of their complaints, of the zeal and good-
will of the Athenians, and even of the principles of the
best settlement in the event of such a change. He was
only cool in his expressions, when he might have been
expected to declare his reliance on the resolution of the
malcontents to encounter the consequences of a quarrel.
There were some among them who could interpret the
demand which this attitude conveyed, and Ouliades of Samos
and Antagoras of Chios — it is noteworthy that Aeolian
Lesbos is not even yet included—resolved to commit themselves boldly to an irreparable breach, in confidence that the
rest would follow them, and that Aristides might be relied on
to interpose between them and the Spartans if violence were
[1] attempted, and so give permanence to an alliance already
approved in principle. As the general's trireme was moving
in advance on the waters of Byzantium, the conspirators—
so they are called—on a sudden brought their own vessels
wantonly into collision with it, catching it violently amid-
ships. Pausanias came forward in a rage, and seeing who
were the offenders, vented a threat that the time would
not be long before he would show them that it was not
his ship that they had damaged, but their own native
countries. They bluntly retorted ' that it was high time
for him to be gone ; and he might be thankful that the
recollection of his connection with the Greeks in the Plataean victory restrained them from inflicting the punishment
he merited.' There and then they moved off to range

<hr>

[1] Thucyd. i. 96; Plut. Arist. 23.

their squadrons in station with the Athenians, and were joined at once by all the allies but the Peloponnesians. Such was the first decisive rupture which marked the line which, for such important consequences, whether in emulation or collision, was to separate the Ionian and Dorian confederations.

It was precisely at this juncture that further complications were relieved, by the recall of Pausanias to Lacedaemon, there to reply to charges of wrongs against individuals, which in various instances were established. On more serious public charges he obtained acquittal; but still too much was notorious of how he had comported himself in his appointment of general, as if it were a tyranny, and too much was suspected of his inclination to Medism, to allow of his being again entrusted with command.

It was apparently at the approach of winter 477 B.C. that he returned home, and his fleet with him; it would then be, at the earliest, in the spring of 476 B.C. that Dorcis was sent out in his stead, associated with others, and with only an inconsiderable force. Dorcis found on his arrival, as under these circumstances was probably anticipated, that the resolution of the seceding allies to acquiesce no longer in Spartan leadership was fixed; and after a short stay he returned home, 'nor did the Lacedaemonians afterwards send out other commanders.' The example of Pausanias, following so closely on that of Leotychides, alarmed them as to the corrupting effect of prolonged absence from the discipline of home; and they were in truth well content to be rid of the Median war, in which they had only taken part at all when it approached their doors, and to leave the distant prosecution of it in the hands of the Athenians, who were not only fully as competent to conduct it, but were disposed—especially when so engaged—to remain on good terms with themselves. According to Plutarch they were the better satisfied with this course from the conciliatory assurances, and if so, we must infer from the growing political influence, of Cimon. Diodorus dates this revolution in the archonship of Adeimantus = 477–6 B.C.

Such was the commencement of the hegemony, or leadership of Hellas, by the Athenians.

CHAPTER XIII.

DORIAN AND IONIAN GENIUS AND GENEALOGY.

THE sternness and stability of the peculiar institutions of Sparta had in the course of years produced a national character so distinctive, that her statesmen and citizens might seem to stand in almost as strong a contrast, in respect of maxims and manners, and even language, to other Dorians, as the Dorians at large did to the Ionians. The Dorian colonists of the shores of the Euxine, of Rhodes and Cos and the borders of the archipelago, of Sicily and Italy, were drawn of necessity into habits of general intercourse and free communication with foreigners and aliens, quite unknown to the Spartans, secluded as they were from even the stimulant proximity of an Ionian frontier. Commerce was fostered at Dorian Corinth, with all its consequences of foreign haunt and intercourse, and luxury in the coarser forms affected by commercial wealth; and innovation and invention were promoted there as eagerly as they were repressed at [1] Lacedaemon. At Corinth, as in her western colonies, the plastic and the graphic arts flourished with a vivacity that communicated no trifling reaction to Ionian genius; and Dorian Megara, besides being the home of such a master of elegiac poetry as Theognis, was the

---

[1] Pindar, *Ol.* xiii. 15; Thucyd. i. 13, 69; Herod. ii. 168.

very birth-place of imaginative Comedy, of which Dorian
Syracuse was the nursing-mother. There is every presumption that this contrast, at least in respect of its strongest
lines, was superinduced mainly by the special legislation of
Sparta, which, overstrained by the police requirements of
its institution of helotry and in the interest of military
prowess, carried more than military discipline into every
detail of domestic life.

Lacedaemon anterior to the Dorian conquest is presented
in the Homeric legend as a centre of refinement, or indeed of
luxury; and the picture is by no means extravagantly out
of harmony with such intimations as reach us of its earlier
Doric times, in no sparse notices of archaic Spartan monuments and art — of Spartan sculpture, and poetry, and
music.

Bathycles, Terpander, Thaletas, Alcman, Tyrtaeus, if they
were not Spartans, are so associated in fame with Sparta,
as to prove that appreciation for art lived on with considerable pertinacity even after the germs of the native faculty for
creation had been ruthlessly trodden down and stamped out.
In later days these proper Hellenic characteristics only
appear in a lively devotion to certain religious and athletic
festivals and their accompaniments; beyond this it seems
left to predominating political power alone to constitute a
bond between Sparta and the general Hellenic community,
and to preserve it from forfeiting in its isolation all sympathy
with the busy related tribes beyond its jealously-guarded
barrier. This predominance, however, was during a long
period sustained and decisive, uncontested and unquestioned;
it was asserted intermittently, but still on occasion with such
promptitude and force, as to give the impression of jealous
watchfulness as well as power. The larger Dorian Hellas
in consequence, for all its varied qualifications and divergences, never renounced a traditional regard for Sparta as
chief of the Dorian race, and peculiarly as chief and leader

on all occasions of rivalry and complication with the other great Hellenic section—the Ionian.

The deepest line of division that we know among the people who in historical times were designated collectively as Hellenes, runs between these Doric and Ionic sections; another line divides the Aeolians from both, but much less decisively, for among the varied and widely-spread tribes of Aeolian descent and dialect and characteristics, while those on the west of the Aegean approximated very nearly to the most distinctive Dorians, there were others in the islands and colonies eastward that exhibited many signs of Ionian sympathy. This approach, however, of Aeolians to Ionians is ambiguous and accidental, and historical indications go far to show that their distinction was all but primitive; that Dorism developed independently from an Aeolism with which Ionism was already in marked contrast, at some point of earlier departure, rather than that Ionism and Dorism together were collateral shoots from an original main Aeolic stem.

Strabo, who, late as he is, merits even on these points especial attention, remarks, with his usual good sense, that the earlier divisions of the tribes of Hellas must needs have followed, and may be tracked by the broader distinctions of dialect, the innumerable minor subdivisions being left aside. Under this guidance four families are obtained, which however, by the derivation that he points out, may again be reduced to a primitive pair, the Ionian dialect being virtually the same as the old Attic, and the Dorian not to be distinguished from the old Aeolic. The specialties of Attic speech of the fully-developed period were thus deviations from primitive Ionian, and those of Sparta from primitive Aeolian.

According to this view, the Ionian and Aeolian dialects were in contrast from the beginning, and were continued among certain sections of the race with less change in their

forms, though still by no means exempt from slighter variations, than when they came to be spoken in the predominant
states of Attica and Sparta. Modern criticism has eluci-
dated in detail the diversities of Attic and Ionic, as well
as of Lesbian Boeotian and Thessalian Aeolic, and the purer
[1] Doric.

The geographer supports his analysis by the remark that
the inhabitants of Attica at an early period were recognised
as Ionians, and that the colonies in Asia who used the Ionic
dialect were notoriously of Attic origin. Even up to his
own time, he proceeds, all the Hellenes without the Isthmus,
except the Athenians, Megarians, and the Dorians about
Mount Parnassus, were still called Aeolians, and the districts within the Isthmus were also previously in complete
Aeolian occupation, the Homeric Achaeans having been an
Aeolian tribe. Then two interferences took place; a population from Attica, who, according to his own account, were
already known as Ionians, established themselves in the
district along the Corinthian gulf, that was afterwards the
best-known Achaia, but only to be driven back again to
Attica by Achaians, when the latter were expelled from
their more easterly seats in Peloponnesus by the intrusive
Dorians. The Aeolic dialect, continues Strabo, was still
retained after this revolution by the Eleians, who had sided
with the invaders, and by the Arcadians, who, safe among
their mountains, defied them; though even among these,
despite their political independence, there was a sympathetic
tendency for the dialect of the dominant tribe to prevail.
In the case of subjection, as might be expected, the dialectic
modification was decisive; even as Herodotus witnesses, that
Ionians who were left isolated in Cynouria and fell into
subjection to Argos became ultimately Dorised. Allowing
for these influences, it is less surprising that in Strabo's time

[1] Grote, ii. p. 452.

every town in Peloponnesus Dorised, than that most of them should still retain some dialectic peculiarities of their own.

The Dorians then, according to the view of Strabo, had already acquired their characteristic dialect, as well as certain peculiarities of manners qualifying their primitive Aeolism, before this invasion, and he ascribes these changes to the special climatic and social influences that affect a tribe in secluded and crowded occupation of a bleak and rugged territory. Upon this view no distinctive Dorism is recognised prior to the residence of a teeming population in the rough and limited Doris. But Doris about Parnassus was only the late seat of a tribe that had previously had many migrations. Herodotus, who speaks with an absence of hesitation that carries much authority, from its apparent harmony with uncontested traditions, knows of it first as occupying Phthiotis, to the south of the Pagasaean gulf, at that time conterminal with the Thessalian [1] Pelasgi, and including the Hellas proper of Homer; and, in fact, in close proximity to the original, or at least the primaeval Achaia. Here it would be in possession of a sea-board, and hence might perhaps have extended the early Dorian influence, that is afterwards declared so powerfully, to Rhodes and to Crete. Hestiaeotis, which Herodotus bounds by Ossa and Olympus, is given as the next seat of the tribe; expelled hence by Cadmeians, who seem to be represented in mythus by the eponymn Cadmus, and migrating from Thebes to Illyria, they occupy Pindus under the title of Macedonians, thence pass southward to Dryopis, and so at last move across the Crissaean gulf to their final establishment in Peloponnesus. Such a story is by no means too wild for a period of general unsettlement, and implies a series of warlike enterprises and collisions, by a vigorous tribe under a succession of vigorous leaders, and tribal cohesion of a fibre that, in view of numerous parallels in later

---

[1] Herod. i. 57.

history, it would be presumptuous to disallow; but we can
no more circumscribe the regions successively taken possession
of, than we can limit times of occupation, or the possible
association and reaction of other tribes as such events went on.

This broad implication of Strabo, that the grand distinction
between Dorians and Ionians was but inherited from a prior,
and equally marked, distinction between Ionian and Aeolian
(the Doric Spartans being to primitive Aeolians what the
Athenians were to primitive Ionians), is matched by as broad,
and at first sight a more surprising, assertion of Herodotus,
that the Athenians as a Pelasgic race were contrasted in origin
with the Lacedaemonians as a Hellenic one.   Interpreted
strictly and literally, this statement would exclude the Athenians and Ionians generally from the list of Hellenes, and so
far would agree with his habit of speaking of Dorians as
specifically Hellenes; these Aeolo-Hellenic populations would
confront Pelasgico-Ionic in the ultimate bifurcation of the
race; but it is manifest that he would have admitted no
such extreme interpretation of his statement, and we must
compare other evidence before we pretend to extract from
what he here seems to say, what he can only in reasonable
consistency mean.

Pelasgic is as widely distributed an appellative in legend
as Aeolian in history, and though we are not justified in
pronouncing that they are convertible with only a difference
of epoch, the geographical range and the incidents ascribed
to both are curiously similar.   Thessaly northwards is Pelasgic, is Pelasgiotis, as all Peloponnesus on the [1] south, in
legends that it were vain to set aside as nugatory, and so
are the islands and the eastern coast of the Aegean.   Two
views in consequence are open to us; either that the Aeolians
superseded alien Pelasgi, or, more probably, that they were
a vigorous overgrowth from their midst—a section taking

---

[1] Eurip., *Iphig. Aul.* 1473.

such a start as the Dorians afterwards took from amongst themselves; and then, that the Ionians were another, and possibly a later, that made a separate leading shoot upon a different congenial soil and under contrasted climatic and social influences. The first of these tribes that rose to a self-consciousness of independence and superior power might well be apt to consider the differences of the races left behind as little worth regard. ' When Hellas was Pelasgic,' says Herodotus, ' the Athenians were distinguished as Cranai Pelasgi ;' he marks other epochs in their history by the titles of Cecropidae, Athenians, and, still later, Ionians; each change being attached to a change of king or leader—Cecrops, Erechtheus, Ion—in no case to an expulsion from the country of the tribe already in possession. With perfect consistency so far, he again affirms that the Ionians of Asia were a Pelasgic race, that so also were the Ionians of the Cyclades, and that the Ionian colonies were founded by a population which had been expelled by the Achaians from Peloponnesus, where they were called Aegialian [1] Pelasgi. Strabo, we have seen, asserts that it was from Attica that they had originally passed to Aegialea, and calls them even then Ionians, which agrees with the story of the settlement of Ionians at Cynouria, where they remained to be subject to the Dorian Argives.

But these statements appear to involve the consequence that if the Athenian race was Pelasgic, the Pelasgic must have been Hellenic; which would contradict the principle of the distinction drawn by Herodotus himself. He is indeed in the difficulty that the Pelasgi appeared to have spoken a barbarous tongue, whereas the Athenians spoke the Hellenic; but he still does not doubt that they ' broke off' from the main Pelasgic stem, and is therefore driven to conclude that they changed their language on becoming

---

[1] Herod. vii. 94, 95.

N

Hellenised. In any case the opinion of Herodotus goes for very little in a question as to fundamental difference of language, and cannot be taken to establish a positive diversity of race between tribes that proved themselves so happily susceptible of reciprocal influence.

It must be borne in mind throughout that the name Pelasgian, like Aeolian afterwards, in all probability comprised a diversity of sub-tribes which, even if upon a general level of civilisation and relationship, might easily differ among themselves as widely at least as Celts, Gaels, and Cymri, in tendencies, dispositions, capacities, and susceptibilities of influence, good or evil.

There is temptation to infer that Herodotus, being possessed by the Athenian claim to be autochthonous—to have never immigrated into their country and never to have been expelled—and at the same time by the persistent tradition of the range of the Pelasgic period, merely adopted as a necessary conclusion that the Athenians so unremoved must be Pelasgians, and shut his eyes to inconsistent consequences. But how evanescent an ethnological distinction he was prepared to accept as involved in Pelasgic origin appears in the fact of his noticing, without serious demur, that the Hellenes charged such an origin even upon the Aeolians of the [1] archipelago; whence it seems clear that, according to his conception, Pelasgism might well lie deep down at the basis of both Aeolian and Ionian antiquity.

Such a charge could mean no more than that settlers of purer race and more imbued with the nobler culture that was recognised as characteristic of a new epoch had coalesced with a comparatively, but only comparatively, alien population. The growth and assumption of national character by the nations of modern Europe after the break up of the Roman empire furnish many examples of dis-

---

[1] Herod. vii. 94, 95.

proportion between the numbers and the influence of commingling tribes, conquering or conquered. As time went on, and according to the capacity of the secondary race, it might well be that though contributing at first most largely to the numbers of the population, it perpetuated but little of its primitive unculture. Only in one sense could Ionians and Aeolians be conceived of as members of a non-Hellenic Pelasgic race, and that is, that a large, perhaps the largest proportion of the population of either was of a non-Hellenic stock which had become absorbed—transformed by the superior energy and genius of the smaller Hellenic portion, of Aeolic genius in one case, of Ionian in the other. Herodotus himself gives an account of the expulsion, by his own Pelasgic Athenians, of a depressed tribe of Pelasgi. One version of this quarrel connected it with molestation of free maidens drawing water from the well Enneakrounoi. This water, we learn from Thucydides, was used for sacred purposes, especially on occasions of marriage, and the story—which has many an ancient analogue—reads much like a mythic translation of a dispute as to a privilege of intermarriage, a constant source of disagreement between tribes and cities of antiquity.

What is most surprising in the result thus obtained from analysis of the reports, is the extremely limited area, even if we include Aegialia and Cynouria with Attica, which is allowed for the primitive Ionians, and a difficulty arises how this can consist with the conditions of the grand figure that is made in historic times by the Ionian race as correlative and in competition with Dorian and Aeolian conjoined. But Herodotus himself is a witness how comparatively insignificant were the commencements of Ionia. 'At a time,' he says, 'when the Hellenic race generally was weak, the Ionian was by far the weakest of all and of least account; for except Athens there was no other Ionian city of [1] importance.'

[1] Herod. i. 143.

It is characteristic of a vigorous stock that it will from time to time throw out a fresh shoot that is more productive than any that have gone before; and not only is a population thus suddenly prolific and suddenly prosperous, but it presently manifests new characteristics, assumes new energies, and, in respect of civilisation, is a true birth of an original species. It is likewise characteristic of the commencement of new epochs of history, that a particular tribe, sometimes it may be said a particular family, makes its way out of the indiscriminate crowd and cluster, and by conjoint development of numbers and characteristic energy moulds the entire course of after history. History must usually accept genius of this value as an ultimate fact; it may trace some secondary obligations to circumstances, to happiness of geographical position or political surroundings; but no combination of these has ever yet been competent to account for the genesis of the chief motive characteristics of the genius itself. Still, with nations as with men individually, while the power to mould circumstances is much,—is energy in any case and may be genius,—yet for greatest results the circumstances must be such as are capable of being moulded ; and moral and physical endowments within and happy combinations and opportunity without, nay, even what we are driven to call accident or luck, must conspire, and at critical periods occasionally do conspire, that the very greatest success that is conceivable may actually occur.

The situation of Attica had doubtless many advantages; and even the poverty of its soil, which rendered it a less tempting prey to invaders, would help to divert industry to maritime adventure, for which its spacious and well-protected harbours gave aid and encouragement. Accordingly, when the time arrived that moral conditions were in happy coincidence with material opportunities, Attica became a centre of most active colonisation, and the colonies she planted again proved secondary centres of most active colonisation. So was filled up and occupied a period all but unrecorded of marvellous development and activity and prosperity; the prosperity that makes its mark by the speedy growth of a few associated families into a tribe, of a tribe into a nation; growth with which the world is so familiar in the stories of modern colonies and their mother countries.

We have no direct and explicit trace of this vast Ionic development in the Homeric poems; Pelasgians are noted as still existing, as tribes or hordes, but of no coherence or marked distinction, and seeming to have already receded into almost as much obscurity as shrouds them for Herodotus or Thucydides—dwindling, dwarfed, and unprogressive sections left behind, as poor inheritors of possibly a once great name. What indeed is not implied of the original greatness of the name when in the most solemn and ceremonious adjuration of Zeus in the entire poem, he is invoked under the titles Dodonaean, ¹ Pelasgic? The Achaian nation of Homer is not yet even by name Hellenic, though the fact that his chief hero Achilles belongs to the district that includes Hellas proper already indicates with what seat was to be associated the hearth of the ultimately dominant tribe. Still though the period that the poet depicts was that to which he was carried back by the legends he dealt with, the characteristics of which were familiar in the early scattered poems which his own work was destined to supersede, it was at the same time impossible for him not to be influenced by the interests and circumstances of his own time. There is much appearance that this was when the Ionic development was already in active movement; and a hint has even been detected in the possibly not unintentional disparagement of Athens— sometimes direct and sometimes by neglect—that the pre-

---

¹ *Iliad*, xvi. 233.

dilections of the poet were engaged less for the intrusive energy than for the elder races.

A single mention of Ionians (Iaones) in the Iliad brings them curiously into equivocal connexion with the [1] Athenians, and with the characteristic epithet—ἐλκεχίτωνες—but not much can be made of the passage. The flowing draperies of the older Athenians were in contrast to Doric costume, and together with their peculiar seclusion of women seem to argue Asiatic affinities or reactions, which were perhaps contracted in the course of the great Ionian colonisations.

It was the great pride of the Athenians that they were autochthonous, a boast which was founded on the principle that neither their history nor their legends, which would have been accepted as equal in authority, could tell of their nation having ever been, like so many others, ejected in a body from their territory. Something may have been due to the defensibleness of the country on its northern mountainous frontier, something to its occupying a position aside from the route of armies, or—which is the explanation of Thucydides—to the uncovetable poverty of its soil. Attica is just such an angle of a continent as populations are apt to be driven into as a last refuge in violent times—like Cornwall or Biscay, Wales or Scotland. Such refugees, if able or allowed to maintain themselves in independence, sometimes only perpetuate a dull and ineffective race, even though they may not have been merely the most ready to be fugitive, but the most resolved to resist to the last rather than submit to conquerors. It may be otherwise if they accept the influence of immigrant populations, or even of leaders and dynasties from without; and great results ensue when the original population is so endowed as not only to respond to happiest stimulus, but, while accepting an influence, to stamp an influence in return. In the circumstances of Attica

---

[1] Hom. *Il.* xiii. 685-689.

we may recognise the same process, though resulting in a different form of character, that produced in England what Shakespeare has called a 'happy breed of men,' from the mingling of Roman, Dane, Belgian, Saxon, Norman, Fleming, Frenchman, with the by no means homogeneous original Celtic tribes. Only in later times did Attica become irreconcileably jealous of aliens. Legislators even as modern as Solon and Cleisthenes consolidated its power by incorporating strangers with full franchise; and it seems clear that each change of dynasty in mythical story expresses the reception of a new wave of foreign, and possibly cognate, population. To these contingencies, always reserving the chief value of the truly native, autochthonous genius, we may fairly ascribe no little of that restless activity and versatility of mind which distinguished the Athenians even among the generally so restless and mobile Hellenes.

CHAPTER XIV.

THE CONFEDERATION UNDER LEADERSHIP OF ATHENS.—THE
ASSESSMENT OF ARISTIDES.—THE DISGRACE OF PAUSANIAS.

B.C. 476; Ol. 75. 4. and 76.

As early as 490 B.C., fourteen years before the present
date, Aristides had taken a position of eminence at Athens.
He was one of the generals who were associated with Miltiades at Marathon, where by setting the example of deference
to his single authority, he contributed still more to the victory than even by his services in the battle; the next year
he was Archon Eponymus. He was related to one of the
richest families in Athens represented by Callias, though
accounted, for his position at least, a poor man; and his
immediate connexion was not so much with the oligarchical
as the aristocratical party, and with the party perhaps even
less than with the class. He had been an associate of
Cleisthenes the Alcmaeonid, a very personification of that
class, who yet had discerned the necessity and the occasion
for giving more decision to the institutions of Solon, and
had effected this by original measures which caused him
to be celebrated as even more truly than Solon the founder
of Athenian [1] democracy.

The Cleisthenean constitution owed its birth to a sagacious
recognition of the requirements of new circumstances in a

---

[1] Isoc. π. ἀντιδ. 232; Herod. vi. 131.

new time. By a liberal admission of new citizens, and by subdividing the tribes and redistributing them on a new principle, and thus breaking up many inveterate local and narrow influences, it did as much violence to sectional prejudices as had been done to the rights of property by the *seisachtheia* of Solon, to which measure the innovations of Cleisthenes acted as an appropriate complement. The example so confirmed was destined to be followed again, and have the further support of Aristides, though he had first to overcome the general inclination in Athens to think that a change which had cost so great an effort was necessarily final, and could be so maintained. It was in the interval between Marathon and Salamis that Themistocles entered public life. He was younger than Aristides, and yet we are not on that account obliged to set aside as impossible the tradition that their rivalry began in a Greek competition for the regards of a beautiful Ceian youth Stesilaus, to which Solon himself at an earlier [1] date might have been a party. Themistocles, son of Neocles, was destitute of the advantages both of fortune and family, at least of more than just sufficient to give him an opening to a public career. Confident in energy and resource, ready and incisive of speech, he measured the scope of his genius against the foreseen contingencies of a coming period, and dared to set his ambition on a glory that should match even the trophy of Miltiades, by which he was haunted sleeping and awake.

Politicians of this stamp, who labour under such initial disadvantages, are apt, whatever may be their ultimate or fundamental patriotism, not to be over-scrupulous as to the persons or things which they attack in their resolve to let the world know early what men it has to reckon with and will have to find employment for. It was in the face of the opposition of Miltiades himself that Themistocles carried his

---

[1] *Frag.* 13 and 15, Bergk.

first great measure, the appropriation of the annual state revenue from the Laurian silver mines to the increase of the fleet; and this appears to have been only one out of many of his novel and adventurous propositions.   He is not named—Xanthippus has that bad distinction—among those who turned the failure at Paros into a capital charge; but he was the main cause (in 483 B.C.) of the ostracism of Aristides, who had supported Miltiades in more partial attention to a land-force.   It was thus at any rate that he secured the direction of the next three years, invaluable for the timely furtherance of the naval preparations which were to be effective at Salamis. The opponent of his policy was honestly converted by its triumph; Themistocles himself moved for his recall, and thenceforward the two acted in concert to an extent truly wonderful, considering the contrast of their natures.   Aristides is said to have been conscious, even in earlier days, that, in his apprehension of the general prejudicial influence of Themistocles, he had opposed him sometimes with too un-fortunate effect; once he had even candidly admitted that it was high time, if such contests were to go on, for the Athenians to throw one or other of them into the pit; and ostracism intervened in fact as a solution of the difficulty. This, however, had now gone by; he appeared to recognise that the occasion had arrived for him to follow in the steps of his master Cleisthenes, though as a master himself, and that he could not do better service to the state than by giving aid to inevitable changes with a frank cordiality which would at least enable him to impress them with some character of his own, and to regulate violence into ordered energy.

Another contemporary of Aristides still younger than Themistocles was Cimon, son of Miltiades, who will soon come before us in command of the fleet at Byzantium. He possessed a large share of the best qualities of both his elders, without attaining to the heroic disinterestedness of Aristides, and certainly falling short of Themistocles at the

point where nature has set the eternal limit between endowments however distinguished and unquestionable genius.
He began life under mingled conditions of hardship and brilliancy.   He inherited the renown of Marathon, which could
not but be a power as time went on with the men who had
fought there.   They were however for a time ungratefully
jealous of it as too great a power, and resented some self-
assertion of Miltiades by seizing the opportunity of inflicting
on him a monstrous fine of fifty talents, which, remaining
unpaid at his death, carried on the obligation and the stigma
to his son.   The son had the buoyancy both of youth and
of temperament; he was disinclined to the more finished
intellectual or musical culture that already distinguished the
Athenians above other Greeks, as it did the Greeks from
barbarians.   In speech and manners he was more in harmony
with the Dorian type, and proved himself always naturally
more in sympathy with Sparta than even Aristides, who set
up as his legislative model the severity of Lycurgus.   Severe,
in early life at least, Cimon was not.   He was free of life and
of love, and contemporary poets told of his weakness for the
Salaminian Asteria, and again for a certain Mnestra; told
also, however, of his affection for a legitimate wife Isodice,
daughter of Euryptolemus, a son of Megacles, in elegies
written to console him in his desolation at her death.   By
these characteristics, combined with a generous and open
nature and energy in public lofty aims, he was recognised
as bearing resemblance to the Euripidean type of Hercules:

φαῦλον, ἄκομψον, τὰ μέγιστ᾽ ἀγαθόν.

A wealthy marriage of his half-sister Elpinice was the
means, it is said, of relieving him from the inherited fine,
and his military services at Salamis and onwards commenced
a popularity which was confirmed by an unaffected manner
which transmuted a blunt bearing into gentleness itself.   In
Cimon we recognise an antique type of what in modern times

we designate with admiration as truly 'sailor-like.' It was as quite a youth that he adopted the maritime policy of Themistocles, which he was to devote his life to carrying out. In the midst of the dismay produced by the resolution to abandon Athens for the ships, Cimon was seen in cheerful style—Ion described him as of noble stature, with a head of abundant close and curly hair—leading a troop of companions through the Cerameicus to the Acropolis, and holding in his hand a bridle, which he was on his way to dedicate to the goddess in token that the class of knights with whom his fortune was then perhaps only sufficient to rank him, were for the time renouncing land service. He exchanged bit and bridle for one of the shields—probably his father's spoils from Marathon—which were suspended about the temple, and then, after a prayer to the goddess, descended to embark, communicating to no few the spirit of his enthusiasm. In the actual conflict he acquitted himself with such brilliant manfulness as to mark him at once for a career not unworthy of his [1] origin. The first time that his name appears afterwards is as the colleague of Aristides, by anticipation possibly of his successorship, in command of the fleet at Byzantium: that Cornelius Nepos, by confusion with a later exploit, puts him in the place of Xanthippus at Mycale, may be due—and that is all that can be said—to his name having really occurred there in a secondary command.

Nothing is more comprehensible than the attraction which is said to have been felt by Aristides towards the comparatively youthful Cimon, and to none could he resign more hopefully the responsibilities of active warfare which he now seems to have relinquished for organic statesmanship.

The Ionians did not adopt Athenian leadership in place of Spartan unspurred by a lively sense of their requirement of aid, and of their most likely chance for obtaining it.

---

[1] Plut. *Cimon,* 5.

Neither the seaports of the Asian coast nor the islands could reasonably feel themselves safe from further attack and cruel reprisals, sooner or later; too much cause had they to remember Persian pertinacity and [1] vindictiveness. To secure themselves against such renewals of violence by weakening or overawing the common enemy was now recognised as a genuine common object in the interest of both the parties to the new arrangement, with as much fervour as it was afterwards believed to be a mere pretext for exaction on the part of the Athenians, and with more reason. Revenge for sufferings and the hope of recouping losses by conquest and plunder, were no doubt also not uninfluential motives; the strength of all combined is proved by the serious arrangements which were not only agreed to with alacrity, but realised and sustained. A permanent confederation was formed for the prosecution of hostilities and the protection of Hellas and her colonies against Persia. To Athens, as decidedly the preponderant power, both morally and materially, was of necessity, and also with free good-will, consigned the headship and chief control of the affairs and conduct of the alliance; a position that carried with it the responsibility of the collection and administration of a common fund, and the presidency of the assemblies of delegates. As time went on and circumstances altered, the terms of confederation were modified in various instances; but at first the general rule was the contribution, not only of money or ships, but of actual personal service. The important insular communities of Lesbos, Chios, and Samos occupied from the very first that position of exceptional independence as compared with the smaller islands and the separate cities of the coasts which they long retained. They were able and willing to yield their full share of assistance to the main object in manned and disciplined war-ships, and did

---

[1] Diod. xi. 48.

not make themselves liable for a money assessment, for which,
as time went on, both the supply of ships and service of men
was elsewhere willingly commuted. We have no precise
enumeration of the allies of Athens at this early time, but
the course of the history brings up the mention of many;
and on two occasions—at the outbreak of the Peloponnesian
and Syracusan wars—Thucydides gives lists which are comprehensive, though in disappointingly general terms. Crete
was never directly affected by these events, and Cyprus was
also soon to be left aside; but otherwise all the Greek
islands of the Aegean northwards—except Melos, Thera,
Aegina, and Cythera—were contributory, including Euboea;
as were the cities on the coasts of Thrace and the Chalcidic
peninsula from the Macedonian boundary to the Hellespont;
Byzantium and various cities on the coasts of the Propontis,
and less certainly of the Euxine; the important series of
cities on the western coast of Asia Minor—though apparently
with considerable exceptions—Aeolian, Ionian, Dorian, and
Carian, as far as Caunus at least on the borders of Lycia, if
not even round to the Chelidonian isles.

The sacred island of Delos was chosen as the depository
of the common treasure and the place of meeting of the
contributors. Apart from its central convenience and defensibleness as an island, and the sanctity of the temple,
which had been respected, and more than respected, by
Datis, who even burnt lavish incense there,—it was a
traditional centre for solemn reunions of Ionians from either
side the Aegean. Thucydides quotes the Homeric hymn
as proving that these festivals in very early times were of
the same character as those which in his day collected the
entire Ionian population of every age and sex at the Ephesian
celebrations. Both Polycrates of Samos and Peisistratus as
tyrant of Athens had displayed a pious regard for the
seat of the nativity of Apollo and Artemis, no doubt
of much the same value and significance as the jealousy

which has involved modern politicians in war ostensibly upon
a quarrel about the keys and custody of holy places. The
annual *theoria* of the Athenians to Delos is memorised in the
story of the death of Socrates.

At the distinct request of the allies the Athenians appointed Aristides to superintend the difficult process of
assessing the various forms and amounts of contribution.
This implies that his fairness and probity must already
have gained general approval; though it is possible that
it was his strict observance of justice in the performance of
the task that obtained for him that universal character under
which he is recognised by Herodotus, who declares him to
have been to his mind the very best of the Athenians and
the most just. We are fain, however, to admit that he
may have merited and obtained that title previously, for it
were pity to sacrifice the story that he had, necessarily at an
earlier date, written his own name on the oyster-shell for
a clown, who could give no better reason for his vote of
ostracism than that he was utterly tired of hearing about
Aristides the Just—the Just.

The total annual amount of the assessment was the large
sum of 460 talents (£112,125), and this perhaps not inclusive of, but only supplementary to, the costly supply of
equipped ships furnished by some of the cities in lieu of a
money payment, and exclusive again of any payment by
Athens, whose navy was most important of all. We know as
little of any basis on which the required total was calculated
as we do of the proportions in which it was distributed. We
are only assured by the satisfaction expressed in the settlement
—perhaps heightened in its echoes from experience of later
changes—that the total, like the distribution, was held to be
perfectly justified.

According to [1] Plutarch, the Greeks had made payments

---

[1] Plut. *Arist.* 24.

towards the war even under the leadership of the Lacedaemonians, but not on the principle of such a distinct
survey and estimate of their respective resources as was
now carried through by Aristides. The assessor came forth
from the trial a poorer man than he entered upon it—to the
great astonishment of Athens, and somewhat to the amusement of Themistocles, who professed to recognise that as but
poor praise for a politician which was not too extravagant
a merit for a money-bag.

The prospect of peace and security might well reconcile
these industrious cities to payments, even exceeding in
amount the tribute formerly exacted by Persia, which in
most important cases had been levied by tyrants or satraps, who could enrich themselves with all the recklessness
of arbitrary power. The tax so willingly paid by autonomous states who had joint votes in its expenditure was
first called the φόρος; it is not quite clear whether an inheritance of the former title of tribute, or a euphemistic modification of it on occasion of the change. Thucydides thinks
it necessary to explain the term as an equivalent of φόρα. In
later days the Athenians found even the term φόρα for a tax
odious, and substituted for it σύνταξις, as implying a burden
not imposed but agreed upon. The immediate officials who,
according to Thucydides, were intrusted with the receipt of
the fund, and according to their title, with the dispensing of it
also, were the Hellenotamiae, whose appointment rested with
the Athenians. This title, by its very parallelism with the
Hellenodicae of Olympia, and indeed of Sparta [1] also, carries
with it an implied responsibility for the common interests
of Hellas, and we must assume that their functions were
supposed to be exercised under certain agreed conditions
of audit and control by the periodical congress. The
whole arrangement was based on the model of the ancient

---

[1] Xen. *Rep. Lac.* xiii. 11.

amphictyonies, but vastly dilated both in scope and scale. Themistocles may have had no hand in its organisation, but he who had urged elsewhere so cogently, that the more insignificant cities, whatever the theoretical equality of their vote in such assemblies, would always be controlled by one or other of the few more powerful, must have been well satisfied with the prospect for the power of Athens in such a combination, where she stood in her preponderance unrivalled and alone. When assessment, collection, and distribution were exclusively and immediately in Athenian hands, no check of general supervision, at whatever seat of the treasury, could long be counted upon, by those who knew Greece, to prevent distribution being mainly biased towards Athenian policy and purposes. We hear nothing directly of any negotiations with Sparta with reference to this fund and the further prosecution of the purpose to which it was to be applied; and yet a confederacy that was to be the common bulwark of Hellas, and that proposed to itself the task of so dealing with Persian power as to render her hitherto periodical aggressions impossible for the future, had surely a claim upon the Peloponnesians generally. The peninsula that had hardly roused itself before to move its arms beyond the Isthmus until alarmed for the immunity of its own coasts, could scarcely but be urged now to further the efficiency of the fleet on which it might again have to rely for its immunity hereafter. The Spartans however did not at this time naturally look very far ahead; it was enough for them and satisfied their traditions to see that there was no danger immediately pressing; in any case they could not now appear as allies subordinate to Athens, where they had lately been superiors; their own power and that of their immediate dependents and allies—Corinthians, Arcadians, and the rest who had sallied with them to Plataea— would always be in reserve; the conduct of Leotychides and Pausanias abroad had moreover not only put them more than

ever out of conceit with detached enterprises, but to some
extent had disarranged their political and military system.
All such difficulties and objections only operated to enhance
the value of the opportunity to Athens, and we may with
much confidence assign to this time an embassy that arrived
at Sparta from the Athenians to move—perhaps in the common
Hellenic *synedrion,* which was still considered to meet there—
the further consideration of the relations of Hellas to Persia.
Its announcements and proposals were not received without
producing considerable agitation. They included at least a
vindication, which we may suppose was rather challenged
than in the first instance volunteered, of the scale on which
the harbour of the Piraeus was being extended as necessary
for the security and reception of the combined Hellenic fleet—
now so very numerous from the accession of the colonies—
and on which the security of Hellas would henceforward depend. The strong argument of an oracle that commanded
the Spartans to beware of admitting a halting leadership was
urged, it is said, against their renunciation of maritime
hegemony, the natural complement of that which they
retained by land. The ambition moreover that had been
so fostered at Athens by glory and success could scarcely
but spring up under like influences among the younger
spirits of Lacedaemon; the excitement that crazed Pausanias
was not without its effect on minds by many degrees more
sober. The passions however that were now so born had
to wait their time and their turn; at Sparta the power of
the elders was supreme, and the aspiration of the new
generation had to survive if it could, and as in effect it did,
the sexagenarian predecessors in possession. To a Heracleid
Hetaemeridas is assigned the ingenuity of propounding
reasons that sounded sufficient for leaving the Athenians
to take their own way undisturbed, as it was clear that
they intended to take it in any case. Such at least is the
point of view from which the certainly perplexed and

disarranged notices of [1] Diodorus seem to fall naturally into coherence. He concludes that the Athenians, being entirely relieved from apprehension of a breach with Sparta, were at undisturbed leisure to apply themselves to the advancement of their own city; and from his last date (the archonship of Dromoclides, 476–5 B.C.) there certainly ensues an interval of several Olympiads—the δμαιχμία of [2] Thucydides, a period short enough, and yet how long for Greece!—within which the two great powers of land and sea, of Dorian and Ionian stock, are at least not in hostile collision. One transitory difficulty only was to occur, or had already occurred, that bore such a semblance, and this again was due to what must be called another extravagance of Pausanias. He reappeared at Byzantium in a ship of Hermione, professedly to take part in the war, though without any public authorisation from Sparta, and in reality with intention to proceed with his criminal intrigues. Between his personal authority with those who could not suspect him of treason, and his connections with the party which at Byzantium, as in Athens itself, would through rivalry or in consideration of bribes concur in such designs, he managed to establish himself in the city in such a position, that when the allies under the conduct of Cimon took the alarm, their ejection of him is expressed by phrases implying either direct violence or starving out. Plutarch, who does not here copy Thucydides, employs the same expression. He went off southwards, but only to fix himself at Colonae in the Troad, within easy reach of Artabazus, if not of Demaratus and Gongylus also. Information of his practices however went past him to Sparta, with no favourable account of his ·doings; and the ephors forthwith despatched the formal summons of a *scytale*, bidding him return in company with the herald who bore it, and never quit him on pain of being accounted a national enemy. Unwilling to excite further suspicion, and in

---

[1] Diod. xi. 43 and 50.   [2] Thuc. i. 10.

confidence that with the treasure at his command he could
escape from existing charges by bribes, he returned a
second time. On arrival he was placed in confinement,
and retained there some time by the ephors, in the exercise
of their independent authority even over a king, not to
say a regent; and it was only by treating and management
that he obtained a formal trial at an opportunity for
bringing the accusations against him to a favourable issue.
Nothing was established against him, either by his enemies
or the state, with such positiveness as to warrant severity
towards one, who, himself of the royal blood, was also the
official governor and representative of the minority of his
cousin, King Plistarchus, son of Leonidas. His acquittal
however left him not the less under grave suspicions, on
account of his infringements of Spartan discipline and his
manifest leaning to the ways of the barbarians; he remained
therefore for years unemployed, and not unwatched, until
impatience was again to overmaster him and hurry him
to a wretched catastrophe.

It must have been about this time that intrigue with
Persian gold from the satrapy of Artabazus, and possibly with
some reference to the invitations of Pausanias, was brought
home to an agent in Peloponnesus. This was Arthmius,
son of Pythonax of Zeleia, a town rather of Phrygia than
the Troad: he was a proxenus of Athens, and at Athens indignation was vehement accordingly. [1] Demosthenes quotes
textually a decree, alluded to in like terms by both [2] Aeschines and [3] Deinarchus, which remained inscribed on a
bonze stele in the Acropolis, and by which, on the motion
of Thucydides, Arthmius was declared 'degraded and hostile,'
and warned under penalty of death, not only from Athens
itself, but from every territory under Athenian control; and
the exclusion extended to his family and his [4] descendants.

---

[1] Demosth. *Phil.* iii. p. 122.   [2] Aesch. *c. Ctes.* sub fin.
[3] Deinar. *c. Arist.* 25, 26.   [4] Plut. *Them.* 6.

CHAPTER XV.

THE command of the combined fleet had in the meantime been taken over at Byzantium by Cimon, who, arriving from Athens with a small squadron of only four ships, had nevertheless found an opportunity for a brilliant achievement by the way. In the absence of the chief Greek force at Byzantium, the Persians, who were not quite cleared out of Chersonesus, and some garrisons further west, were giving signs of renewed activity and intriguing for the co-operation of Thracian allies from the north. With his four triremes, which no doubt were provided with the improvements introduced by [1]Themistocles, he successfully attacked their flotilla of thirteen vessels, and then followed up his victory on land by beating and driving out both Persians and auxiliaries, with such effect as to set the fertile peninsula entirely free for Athenian re-occupation. We can scarcely refuse this exploit as related by Plutarch a place in the history, and it is not easy to find a better, or indeed another, for we must demur to accepting it as introductory to the reduction of the important rebellion of Thasos some years later, when the fleet employed was necessarily much more numerous and powerful.

[1] Plut. *Cim.* 12.

The full force of the Byzantine fleet being now required,
was directed by Cimon, energetically and without delay,
to unfasten the hold which the Persians, though ousted
from the straits, and, as we may infer, from [1] Lemnos and
Thasos likewise, still retained upon Thrace. Their opportunity for receiving reinforcements from Asia was now finally
cut off, and the time had come to deal with them in detail.

Far añd wide over Thrace, as well as along the Hellespont,·
the officers of the Great King had held posts ever since the
European expedition of Mardonius under [2] Darius. It was
then that the island of Thasos had been reduced by them, and
compelled to demolish its walls and surrender its navy, to
the formation of which it had devoted the profits of the
mines on the mainland—an anticipation of the policy that
was to have better fortune at Athens. One chief Persian
stronghold was at Eïon, at the mouth of the Strymon, over
against Thasos, commanding the access to the gold regions
of Mount Pangaeus, which, as worked by the Thasians, had
rivalled in productiveness those of their own [3] island. The
district, however yielded silver as well as gold, [4] and was
occupied partly by the Pierians, between the mountains
and the sea, partly by the Odomanti, and most especially
by the Satrian Thracians, all ·most warlike tribes, whose
seats extended northwards, among thickly-wooded or snow-
covered mountains, and who never had been to the knowledge of the historian otherwise than independent. On their
loftiest mountains they had an oracle of Dionysus, which
implies the culture of the vine on the lower slopes, and
corresponds with what might be inferred from the mythological aspects of the region ; it has even been conjectured,
not unplausibly, that the Dionysiac Satyrs were in origin
no other than these wild Satrae. The limits of Macedonian sway were already advanced very close up towards

[1] Xen. *Hellen.* v. 1. 31.   [2] Herod. vii. 106.
[3] Herod. vi. 46.   [4] Id. vii. 112.

the [1] Strymon, between which and Mount Dysorus lay other most productive mines. Herodotus had visited with marvel the mines at Thasos, which he ascribes to early Phoenician colonists; Greeks possibly in direct intercourse with Phoènicia, who had brought thence their knowledge of mining, even if they had not, which is probable enough, Phoenician associates. The resources which were appreciated so early, were still and long after unexhausted, at least on the mainland; the Persians levied rates upon them during their occupation, and Thracians, Athenians, Thasians, and Macedonians fight over them down to the extinction of Hellenic autonomies by the kings, who drew from them the very sinews of their military power. The liberation of Thasos from Persia, after the destruction of the fortifications by the Persians themselves, is passed over as a matter of course; but the reduction of Eïon was attended by some difficult and remarkable circumstances. The Persian in command was Boges, a man of desperate resolution, who held out to the last. He relied on his fortifications, and was in correspondence for supplies with friendly Thracians of the upper Strymon, in the district of Siris, which had been subjugated and cleared of its earlier Paeonian inhabitants by Megabazus, lieutenant of Darius, and in which Xerxes had deposited his sacred chariot.

It is an illustration of how far the successes of Leotychides in Thessaly, incomplete as they were considered at home, had transferred power to the Hellenic party, that Menon of Pharsalus aided the Athenians here with a subsidy of twelve talents, and a squadron of 300 Penestae mounted at his own [2] charge. There is only a question whether his great recompense was citizenship or somewhat short of this—*ateleia*. By the time the armament of the allies arrived, under the command of Cimon, such a force had been concentrated by Boges,

---

[1] Herod. v. 17.   [2] Demosth. *Aristoc.* p. 687.

either from allies and stations inland or from the garrisons which controlled the numerous cities of the adjacent Chalcidic peninsula, that he was encouraged to stand a conflict in open field ; he was worsted, however, and driven within the walls, where his numbers only gave the besieged additional embarrassment. Cimon's force was sufficient to invest the city, and the hoped-for relief never made its appearance; the Athenian general had cut off all chance of it, by detaching a force against the Thracians and driving them before it in all directions. Famine was now imminent, but the place still held out; and the offer of conditions of surrender, including safe-conduct to Asia, which was made readily by the besiegers for the sake of speedier possession of their prize,—the very citadel, and also the treasury of the wealthy province,—was rejected. The difficulty of holding out, however, was not dependent alone on pressure of famine, however urgent; there was a danger more urgent still. The walls of the city were of unburnt brick, that would yield readily to the action of water; and Cimon, by a stratagem that was long a favourite subject of celebration, and was one day to be imitated against the walls of [1] Mantinea, so dammed and diverted the Strymon, that under its action the speedy formation of a breach was unavoidable. The catastrophe that ensued has many parallels, especially in Eastern history ; Butes, or Boges, slew his children, wife, and concubines, on an enormous pyre, disappointed the besiegers by scattering from the wall before their sight into the Strymon all the treasure of gold and silver out of the citadel, then fired the city and the pyre at once, and entered himself and his friends with him into the flames. 'On this account he is still to the present time praised by the Persians,' says Herodotus, 'and rightly [2] too.' It would be rash, however, to conclude that this immolation was so complete that no spoil whatever, nor Persian prisoners

---

[1] Paus. viii. 8. 5.　　　　　[2] Herod. vii. 107 ; Plut. *Cim.* 7.

of birth available for ransom, were left over for the victors. The terms of Thucydides imply a selling into slavery as consequent on the [1]capture, and an anecdote relates how on such an occasion, at least, Cimon enriched himself by sagaciously taking his share rather in naked prisoners than their rich accoutrements.

This conquest at once freed the Greek cities of the seaboard of the westward gulfs from annoyance, and added them as contributors to the Aristidean assessment; as such we find distinctly enumerated Argilus, Stageirus, Acanthus, Scolus, Olynthus, and others come in by implication. Thucydides names the capture of Eïon as the first of the exploits by which Athens advanced to empire, and so distintinguishing it above others unnamed must, I think, be held to imply that the Athenians from the first held the place in their own possession. It thus became their basis for advancing some years later to a position higher up the river, and of most admirable natural advantages. Old traditions gave the Athenian, what he accepted as a title, to feel himself no stranger in this region. He was accustomed to the tale that the sons of Theseus, Demophon and Acamas, had, one or the other, or perhaps both, touched here after the taking of Troy, and close at hand was the scene of the loves of [2]Demophon—or of [3]Acamas—and Phyllis. Phyllis is the eponymous nymph or heroine of the district Phyllis, that lies between the northern slopes of Mount Pangaeus and the river Angites, that flows parallel to it to join the Strymon in the lake Prasias above Eïon. [4]Aeschines appeals to this mythus —how Acamas (his Scholiast says Demophon) had received the site of Amphipolis in way of dowry—as being notoriously ancient, as well as, at any rate to the satisfaction of his hearers and his argument, authentic; and it implies an inaccurate and modern apprehension of the characteristics of a period given to limited variations of mythus, if one should imagine

[1] Thuc. i. 98.   [2] Serv. in Virg. *Ecl.* v. 10; Ovid, *Epist. Her.* 2.
[3] Lucian. *de Sall.*; Schol. Aesch. *de Fal. Leg.*   [4] Aesch. *de Fal. Leg.*

that the story had its origin after this campaign of Cimon. We may far more probably assume that it is a genuine, though of course mythical, record of some primitive transactions between Athens and this region; a consequence of it no less real than that hankering after power in this quarter by the Athenians, a passion which returns again and again, like an ineradicable impression of early youth, which owed much of its force quite as probably to unconscious inheritance as to any later influence. The story of this love, as fully told, was not encouraging; Acamas was no more constant as a lover than his father Theseus. Ever expected to return according to his promise, he was looked for in vain, and Phyllis destroyed herself. Poetry, of whatever date, told of her transformation into an almond-tree, of which the premature blossoms await the dallying leaves; they burst forth when the belated lover arrived to throw his arms around the yet warm and not yet quite unconscious stem.

In the same year as the capture of Eïon (476 B.C., during the archonship of [1] Phaedon), is given in an isolated notice, and very unsatisfactory terms, the disaster of an Athenian force under Lysistratus, Lycurgus, and Cratinus, said to have been destroyed by the Thracians after their conquest of Eïon. If we accept this at all, it must be as a corrupt record of some serious mishap, after the reduction of the place by Cimon, to the land force which had at first operated successfully to check Thracian attempts to raise the siege.

More disasters were to follow thereafter through a series of years, until the Scholiast of Aeschines could tell how it was, because Demophon had broken tryst with Phyllis in nine several appointments—there seems a hint of suggestion here in the name of the important locality, Nine ways—that the nymph in bitterness had doomed the Athenians to expiation by as many defeats; the Scholiast accurately reckons them up,

---

[1] Schol. Aesch. *de Fal. Leg.*

and so accurately no doubt would the ascribed denunciation of the nymph keep level pace with Athenian misfortunes.

Besides the general commercial advantages of such a position, the precious metals of the adjacent mines were to prove too tempting not to determine the Athenians to assume, as time went on, the position and rights rather of conquerors of the Persians, than mere liberators of their oppressed subjects, Hellenic or other, the Thasians or Thracians who had previously shared these productive sources of revenue between [1]them. It was not long before, between claims for restitution and resentment at encroachment, they became very seriously embroiled with both.

Herodotus makes mention of another hold of Persians on Europe, respecting the fate of which there is considerable difficulty. This was Doriscus, at the mouth of the Hebrus eastward, opposite Samothrace, on the border of the vast plain where Xerxes reviewed his army. It had remained a Persian fortress since the Scythian expedition of Darius. For the governor appointed by Darius, Xerxes substituted Mascames, son of Megadostes, and by him the post was so stubbornly maintained, that after all the other Persian officers had been rooted out from Thrace and the Hellespont, he alone defied all the numerous attempts to eject [2] him. This is the only notice we find of the defence of Doriscus; it is perhaps presumable that it came to an end at the death of Mascames, for though the honours that Xerxes accorded him were continued by Artaxerxes to his sons, it does not follow that they succeeded to his command. The city of Ainos, again, a very short distance to the east of Doriscus, was certainly associated with [3]Athens. It was Mascames probably who animated the movement that Cimon had countervailed in the Chersonesus.

The future political position and influence of Cimon were

[1] Herod. ix. 75.   [2] Id. vii. 107.   [3] Thuc. iv. 28; vii. 57.

not only advanced by his success as a commander in these
northern wars, but also by the brilliant retrieval they induced
of his private fortune, so low at the time when he only
inherited the liability to a crushing fine. Opportunities of
enrichment legitimate enough, from share of spoil and so forth,
were doubtless open ; but these operations had moreover
brought under Athenian control the Chersonesus, where
under other circumstances Cimon might have succeeded his
father Miltiades as tyrant, and where the present would no
doubt reinstate him at least in an extensive proprietorship.
It is thus that, the embarrassment of the fine notwithstanding,
we read of him as indulging in lavishness which was accepted
as ungrudged display in a man, if not of hereditary wealth, yet
of hereditary title to be wealthy. It is even inviting to conjecture that he may have had some proprietary rights in the
neighbourhood of Eïon ; the notion is suggested by curious
hints, so significant as to demand collating, of relations and
relationships to each other and to this part of Thrace, of the
families of the tyrants Miltiades and Peisistratus and the
historian Thucydides.

Miltiades I colonised or obtained possession of the Chersonesus, when he quitted Athens out of disgust at the rule of
Peisistratus ; and there, after death, received the recognised
heroic honours of a 'founder'—an οἰκιστής. As belonging to
the Philaid gens he claimed descent from Ajax, as the Aeacid
Philaeus had obtained Athenian citizenship and settled at
Attic [1] Melite. The demus Philaeus was connected with the
same [2] hero, and to this Peisistratus belonged. The gens, not
the demus of Miltiades, and the demus, not the gens of Peisistratus, who was a Nelid, have thus a common relation to
Philaeus ; and this is the first of several hints, individually
inconclusive, of their connection with each other. Peisistratus
may indeed have claimed to rank as a Philaid also, through

---

[1] Herod. vi. 35 ; Etym. M.   [2] Plut. *Solon*, 10.

some maternal [1] connections, as Pericles was attacked as an Alcmaeonid, though only so by the mother's side. A half-brother of Miltiades I, by the mother's side, was Cimon, to whom the nickname Koalemus imputed dulness of intellect. Of his father Stesagoras we have no particulars; for anything that appears then, his descendants, among them Miltiades of Marathon, have no claim to the Aeacid descent of Miltiades the first. His wealth at least is avouched by his winning three Olympic chariot-races; he gratified Peisistratus by causing him to be proclaimed as victor for the second, and so gained recall from banishment; he disappointed the Peisistratidae of like honour on the third occasion, and was assassinated in [2] consequence. Stesagoras II succeeded his uncle Miltiades I at the [3] Chersonesus, and was himself succeeded by his brother Miltiades II (515 B.C.), in whom the Peisistratids took such interest as to despatch him thither in a [4] trireme. Of the concern of the Peisistratidae with any other part of Thrace we hear nothing; but Herodotus furnishes the curious and isolated fact, independently of any notice of conquest, that Peisistratus drew considerable revenues from the [5] Strymon.

Miltiades II, by a first and Athenian wife, had a son Metiochus, whose fortunes were remarkable: he was captured by the Persians when they drove out his father, 493 B.C., and Darius either restrained or gave loose to resentment, so far as to give him a Persian wife and family, and so denationalise him. An own sister of Metiochus was Elpinice. But their brother Cimon was the son of a second wife, Hegesipyle, daughter of a king of Thracians—[6] Olorus.

As regards Thucydides the historian, he too, by his own statement, was son of an Olorus; by that of [7] Marcellinus, of a Hegesipyle also; and according to the same authority and Plutarch, he was buried in the 'Cimonia,' the family

[1] Plato, *Hipparch*, p. 288. Ael. *V.H.* ix. 32.   [3] Herod. vi. 38.   i. 121.   [6] Id. vi. 39.   [2] Plut. *Cim.* 4; Herod. vi. 103; [4] Id. vi. 39.   [5] Id. [7] *In vit.*

cemetery of Cimon by the Melite Gate, close to the tomb of Elpinice. Thucydides, on his own showing, had, like Peisistratus before him, property on the Strymon; and [1] Hermippus explained, not unplausibly, his intimation of peculiar knowledge and his rather anxious tendency concerning the Peisistratidae, by his asserted relationship to the [2] family. [3] Plutarch, at variance with other authorities who put the catastrophe at Athens, says that it was at Scapte-hyle that ho was assassinated.

---

[1] *Ap. Marcell.* 18; Schol. Thuc. i. 20.　　[2] Thuc. vi. 35.　　[3] *Cimon,* 6.

CHAPTER XVI.

THE DEVELOPMENT OF ATHENIAN DEMOCRACY.

AFTER the restoration of the walls of Athens and the speedy resettlement of domestic life and civil order, the ancient local influences led to a resumption of ancient habits; but along with much that reappeared unaltered from of old, there came up much that was surprisingly novel, and not more in the material, than in the moral and intellectual, equipments of strenuous civilisation in the capacities and aspirations of various competing classes. It was soon recognised by some, who were by no means forward to invite innovation, that changes must be admitted in the distribution of political power, conformably to new manifestations of political energy. The exceptional powers of the crisis involved in their lapse something more than mere return to previous arrangements. In the difficulties of the conflict, necessity had reconciled the citizens to entrusting unusual discretion to a restricted body, and the vigorous tone which was in consequence communicated to the action of the state had for a time confirmed the authority, perhaps enhanced the pretensions, of a Council which is referred to constantly in general terms; we learn by a casual notice of Aristotle [1]alone, that this was not the Council of 500 to which Miltiades had

---

[1] Arist. *Polit.* v. 3, p. 683 a.

been responsible during the earlier invasion, but the more limited Council or Court of the Areopagus. The time had not yet arrived for this venerable authority to be directly assailed, but otherwise all traditional respect was becoming seriously weakened during the later prosecution of the war; a spirit of proud and even arrogant self-reliance spread among the mass of the population, when each man, fighting with zeal as if the event depended on himself, was almost persuaded that not even the general had contributed more to its result. The urgency of the times gave opportunity and prominence to men who never before had a chance of either, but, when so put to the proof, were as worthy as the best. The urgency of the strain might relax, but not so the ambition of the many, who were ill-content to fall back in civil life into places below those with whom they had ranked in the face of danger as equals or superiors and who now had only a privilege to plead and no sufficient reason. It was a familiar principle and experience with the Greek, that political franchise should and would be co-extensive with military service; and now for the first time a victory at sea had been so important and so glorious, that the familiar maxim carried its application to the entire nautical multitude.

The spirit, the enthusiasm, of democratical encroachment at Athens was far from originating in these events, however it might be revived and reinforced by them; the germ was of far earlier origin, had made good several stages of progress, and to its movement was not inconsiderably due the vigour of the Athenian patriotic exertions at this time as on some earlier occasions; so manifestly is concentrated energy associated with [1] freedom. Athenian poets were fond of dating democratical institutions as far back as mythical times, extravagantly enough, though more plausibly than when they imputed Spartan characteristics to the subjects of Menelaus. But

---

[1] Herod. v. 78.

enough of Solon's institutions—which, if within, are only just within the scope of true historic ken—survived the lapse to the tyranny of Peisistratus, to attest a very positive democratic tendency, and indeed intention, and, for all their deficiencies, to explain how he came to be regarded in time as the universal legislator and author of the Athenian free constitution. ·

According to the conception of Aristotle, what Solon founded was indeed worthy of the high title of a proper polity,—a *politeia*, which is, in modern phraseology, a 'free constitution,'—inasmuch as it aimed at, and to a large extent effected, a harmony of diverse powers.   He found and left the council of the Areopagus with its general supervision of morals and manners and guardianship of legality; this was the Upper Council,—ἡ ἄνω βουλή—as distinguished from a second, the Probouleutic or Preconsidering Council, which was elected annually, and as its members held office for life, its principle was strictly oligarchical.   Again, the Preconsidering Council, which was also of a time before Solon and of which a main function was to determine and prepare what business should be submitted to the popular [1] ecclesia, is defined by Aristotle, and even in virtue of being elective, and that annually, as an aristocratic institution.   In fact, in the most democratical of ancient societies it was well understood that offices which were obtainable through election must needs be gained by those who could intimidate or bribe or command deference even independently of special qualifications, must fall to an aristocracy whether of birth or of wealth.   It was only a change therefore in favour of aristocracy as contrasted with oligarchy, that the privilege of birth was now superseded by the limit of a high property qualification.   The democratic element, however, but for consideration of which 'the demus would be too nearly

---

[1] Plut. *Solon,* 19.

P

enslaved for any tranquillity to be 'expected,' was then admitted with no little decision. Of the four classes of citizens upon which Solon successively imposed an advance in his graduated income-tax, the lowest and most numerous, although still remaining incapable of magistracy, was for the first time allowed to participate in the full elective ²franchise.

It was to his innovation at this point, and its consequences that Solon chiefly, and with a degree of justice that would perhaps have surprised himself, owed his democratic fame. By the demus, thus largely interpreted, magistrates and functionaries, archons and council, were elected in the first instance, and to this demus they were required, at conclusion of their term, to render account' and apply for certificate, undergoing at the same time close scrutiny. As some check on the recognised aristocratical tendency of the accepted conditions of election, and (so far in the interests of democracy again) to take security as far as possible against the exercise of undue influence by clubs and associated cliques, its *dicasteria*, or committees for special purposes, were taken from the general number by the chance of ³lot. How vast was the power that such privileges delivered over into democratical hands under able guidance we shall see hereafter.

In the meantime, the liability of public interests to be hampered by the factious conflicts of class interests, was still overlooked and left unprovided against by these arrangements. A pre-historic settlement which was ascribed to Theseus, and due, if Theseus never existed or had no concern in it, to some great organising genius, had laid deep foundations for the strength if not predominance of Attica in Hellas, by associating the freemen of its scattered townships in dependence on the legislature and courts of ⁴Athens. This is the policy by which Thales of Miletus afterwards urged that

¹ Arist. 661 a.   ² Plut. *Solon*, 18.
³ Arist. *Polit.* 2.   ⁴ Thuc. ii. 15.

still one chance remained for reinvigorating [1] Ionia; but even suppression of the narrow rivalry of townships left uneradicated that of wider districts, a feeling which was perhaps only more likely to burst forth amongst the enlarged constituencies of Solon. The political subdivisions that followed the natural limits of highland, lowland, and seaboard districts, were too conformable to the groups of real or supposed conflicting interests, especially between the poorer and wealthier citizens, for local disagreements not to be reproduced in compact parties in the assembly and there to break out into political contentions. It was immediately through the opportunities which these provided, that tyranny— a transformed pernicious demagogy—found an entrance, and after the opportunity had been seized by the able Peisistratus, never long relaxed its grasp during thirty years; it is difficult not to believe, though there is no direct evidence of the fact, that aid was rendered by discontents on the part of the large class of residents in Athens and Attica for whom, as not being members by birth of any of the Ionic tribes, there was no protection by political franchise.

When relief was at length obtained and the Peisistratids were expelled, an heir to their opportunities and an aspirant to their succession rose up before long in Isagoras, son of Tisandros, but only to be as promptly confronted by the Alcmaeonid Cleisthenes.

It was the belief at Athens that Cleisthenes, during the time that he was at Delphi in exile, had contributed importantly to their former liberation from the son of Peisistratus by inducing the Pythia to attach to every response to Lacedaemon, public or private, an injunction, which was effective at last, to suppress the tyranny at Athens. Himself a grandson of Cleisthenes, tyrant of Sicyon, he learnt a lesson from his policy, but only so to apply it as to deprive tyranny of its last chance at Athens. He got the better of

[1] Herod. i. 170.

P 2

his rival Isagoras by 'taking the demus into [1]partnership,' and well he requited the assistance. He gave a safer and a broader basis to the democratical element of the constitution by liberal admission to citizenship of foreign [2]metics, that is by naturalising resident foreigners,—residents no doubt in numerous cases of long standing or through generations,— and if the record may be trusted, even foreigners who, though not slaves, were servants. By the latter we may understand foreigners, artisans and others, who were free but worked for hire, like many an Athenian of old stock, and who often, like many metics of superior station, might only be known as of foreign descent by absence from tribal registry.

Besides thus swamping the faction-infected constituency by an extension of privilege that for the first time was made independent of scrutiny of ancient pedigree, Cleisthenes furthered his purpose of giving steadiness to the state, by redistribution of electoral groups and districts. For the four Ionic tribes into which traditions of worship made it impossible to foist the new unrelated citizens, he substituted ten, to which, following a Sicyonian precedent, he gave new names, entitling them, after Attic heroes, as eponymi. Each tribe comprised a certain number of demes or parishes, but as a rule by no means adjoining each other, and as the tribe was the electoral unit that sent its several representatives to the Council, this altered arrangement naturally tended to a disruption of ancient partizanships and to elections on a better principle than the representation of narrow local cabals. What precise scheme of grouping was employed further we are not told, nor how acquiescence in such a disturbance of ancient associations and recent alliances was secured. Traditional family and religious ties were beyond legislative reach, and would and did inevitably remain in force; but it appears that some simplified religious sanctions and

---

[1] Herod. v. 66-69.   [2] μέτοικοι, Arist. *Polit.* iii. 1, p. 66a.

celebrations, attaching probably to the mythic associations of the heroic eponymns, were appropriated to the new tribes, both severally and in [1] common. This hint assures us that the policy of Sicyonian Cleisthenes in the same direction had, like that of his grandson, some motives which Herodotus, if he suspected, has at least not cared to tell.

The democratic concession that was now further demanded by what Aristotle calls the 'nautical multitude,' or, to translate more honestly, 'rabble,' in the pride of their achievements and eager for tangible advantage from the splendid ascendency that Athens had won by their valour and perseverance, was the eligibility to office of every class of citizens, even the hitherto excluded Thetic or very poorest. The limit of this political privilege originally ruled with liability to taxation and to service in war either as hoplite or light-armed, but the new importance of war service afloat (if only as oarsmen, still as highly-trained and disciplined oarsmen) had now given the lowest class a technical right to equal participation; Salamis could be cited, and was cited unsparingly and for ever—long after Comedy had made a stock-joke of the common-place—as a claim to political power superior to every other—to all others together.

Themistocles, it would seem, was the natural vindicator of the pretensions of the crews who were the main strength of his peculiar policy aboard the navy that was his own creation, and with whose glory in their greatest achievements hitherto his own was so immediately associated. That the truly revolutionary measure that gave effect to their pretensions is connected immediately with the name, not of Themistocles as we should expect, but of Aristides, implies most naturally that it was obtained at last as a concession after a more or less considerable struggle of interests and parties. The world is familiar with the

---

[1] *Arist. Polit.* vi. 2.

experience that a political party does not at once relinquish
the reins of power because all independent guidance is so
utterly lost as no longer to leave choice between repugnant
alternatives.   Then the veriest Eupatrid partizan, whether by
descent or predilection, can anticipate sagaciously at last,
though it may be only after prolonged resistance has proved
useless, that from the vantage-ground he holds the influence
of class may be made to tell but little less effectively in the
new state of things than in the old.   Aristides, there can be
little doubt, was superior to many if not most of the Eupatrid
party with whom he acted and who were brought over to
this concession; otherwise a Eupatrid is not unfrequently
developed into something very like a revolutionist by well-
grounded confidence that his personal genius—let his class
fare as it may—will secure his own leadership all the more
certainly from the exaggerated violence that he volunteers
to hold under restraint; and then there is the case of the
politician who can foresee and dares to face the fact that
the thing must be, accepts the risk with the resolution to
deal with consequences as best he may when they arrive—as
some one must deal with them—and in the meantime keenly
appreciates the mere exercise of power in carrying through
a great measure however inconsistently adopted by him, and
knows that popular gratitude does not look back beyond the
hand from which it actually takes its benefit at last.

In the case of Themistocles, it is probably not unfair to
ascribe some of the persistency in democratical purpose which,
notwithstanding his advance in fame and fortune, he continues to give proof of still later, to the circumstances of
his origin.   He was comparatively to his most powerful
competitors a new man; and neither by marriage nor
descent connected with any of the historical Eupatrid
families to which, notwithstanding their notorious conservative tendencies, all political parties were still accustomed
and best content to look in the first instance for leaders

and statesmen. He was of an old Attic race of Lycomidae, but no brilliance accrued to him thence that would compensate for some defect in Attic purity on the side of his mother, whether of Thracian or Carian blood, or for the limitation of his fortune, which originally did not exceed three talents. These disadvantages had come home to him very early in life, but only to exercise him early in breaking down by force of resolution and genius some social barriers that divided even the palaestra.

As regards the elements of the less eagerly innovating and the conservative parties, it must always be understood and borne in mind that at this period at Athens, as in other important states of Hellas, there ever lived on the germ of— more than oligarchical—even dangerous and tyrannous reaction, confined to a few it may be, discouraged, discredited, latent, vehemently disclaimed of course by many who amongst themselves were consciously sympathetic, and disallowed by the superficial as having any real existence; but it was of indestructible vitality nevertheless, and moreover instinctively and nervously dreaded by the new inheritors of power, even while they were laughing with the comedian who ridiculed it as an obsolete absurdity. The intrigues at Plataea were of recent memory; but even the earlier sting of the Peisistratid tyranny, so we are assured by [1] Thucydides, lingered in the wound that shuddered at a touch, and an oligarchical tyranny came round in time to justify the popular resolve that, with an assignable reason or without, the experience should never be forgot.

Any seeds of such desperate hope among Eupatrids could only be entertained furtively, as in absolute opposition to a more powerful section, which was represented now by Aristides, Cimon, and Ephialtes, who honestly aimed to make the oligarchical and aristocratical conditions of the government work harmoniously with the democratical,

---

[1] Thuc. vi. 53.

which they strove to restrain or regulate when they might
not rule.   Of Ephialtes son of Sophonides we know too
little; in his poverty and highmindedness he is a parallel
to his associate Aristides.   He is said to have protected
his independence even against his own party by refusing
the ten talents with which they would have increased
his [1] means.   Another colleague of Aristides, who is to
us but a name, is Alcmaeon, but a name that intimates
connection with the great Alcmaeonid family, of which
Xanthippus, who is not heard of in these transactions, was
at present the protagonist, and Pericles after a few years
was destined to be.   With this family Cimon, who had a
noble pedigree of his own, was connected by marriage.
These were times of scrupulous records of relationships by
the phratries, of formal and religious celebrations of births,
and of commemorations of deaths in worship of remoter
and immediate ancestries; and records so long back were
so preserved as to seem to authenticate the claims by
which they were attached to primeval ages and heroes.
A descent from Ajax or from Hercules was claimed and
conceded in such cases with perfect faith on both sides;
to the claimant it gave an ideal to emulate, an obligation
which Pindar's odes take for granted in every strophe, the
influence of which is seen in the numerous great names that
cluster round these associations.   Such recognised descent
was a real power in politics; it imparted special grace to
well-assumed popular manners, and the most democratical
accorded to it some indulgence in extravagance and even
licence, forgave it more and forgot for it more and more
readily than in other instances of merely equal desert.
And so in Athens, as elsewhere, democracy had a certain
affection—a very weakness—for the guidance and leadership
of an aristocrat by birth.

---

[1] Aelian, xi. 9 ; V. Max. iii. 8 ex. 4.

The faith, one might almost say the sense, of the continuity of mythological with historical and current times, was all but universally prevalent, and few politicians of power before Themistocles are found independent of it. Solon himself was reputed a Codrid; Peisistratus, said also to be his relative, was a Nelid; both thus connected with the families that first had reigned at Athens and then given leaders and kings to the Ionian colonies. The Alcmaeonids also carried up their genealogy to Neleus, with Nestor, not to say Poseidon, still in the background. This family furnishes Megacles, the slayer of Cylon; Alcmaeon, the guest of Croesus; Megacles, the son-in-law of Cleisthenes tyrant of Sicyon, in a line that had ruled there, not undeservedly, for one hundred years; Cleisthenes, the founder of Athenian democracy; his sister married to Peisistratus, but only to increase of discord; Agariste, wife of Xanthippus and mother of Pericles; Deinomache, wife of Cleinias and mother of Alcibiades; and Isodice, wife of Cimon.

The father of Cleinias was the earlier Alcibiades, who was the colleague of Cleisthenes, and on his part claimed descent from Eurysaces, son of Ajax. Another traditional son of Ajax and fellow-settler in Attica was Philaeus, whom the first Miltiades claimed as ancestor,—as, by the mother's side at least, did the second also, his successor in tyranny of the Chersonesus, the victor at Marathon, and father of Cimon by a daughter of a Thracian prince.

Cf the remoter ancestry of Aristides we hear nothing, but he was at least related to the wealthy Callias, and there can be no doubt as to the order to which the colleague of the reforming Alcmaeonid Cleisthenes must have belonged.

We now learn from Plutarch that [1] Cimon, who had acted

---

[1] Plut. *Cim.* 10.

in harmony with Aristides at the Hellespont, made common cause with him at home to resist the extreme democratic measures which Themistocles was urging forward, and so commenced a new rivalry that was destined to have important consequences. At present the command lay with Themistocles; the passion for the development of democracy was ablaze, and no other public man was found to lend aid of any importance to countervail it but Ephialtes. His views in this direction and at the present time, as a partizan of Aristides and Cimon, were probably as perfectly in harmony with those of the Alcmaeonids, as when at a later date he was in opposition to Cimon and promoted an assault upon the time-honoured privileges of the Areopagus in concert with Pericles.

To what extent the policy of Themistocles may have been checked by such an opposition, what other concessions may have been made to it besides the opening of the elections to magistracy, or indeed whether any, it is impossible to say. But the direction in which progress was being made was at any rate certain and is known to us, and led, sooner or later, to such further changes as the application of the democratic lot to the elections of Archons and even members of the Council (Boulé), and important reductions of the powers and privileges of both.

The progress of constitutional change at Athens, the anticipation of which is necessary for a clear apprehension of the import of its present condition, is thus sketched by Aristotle: 'When the power of the popular dicastery came to be fully recognised, the demus received all the court that is payable to a tyrant, and so the polity (the duly regulated Constitution) was turned into the democracy that we are witnesses of.' One demagogue after another helped a little; but the decisive blow was struck when Pericles and Ephialtes 'docked' the powers of the Areopagitic Council, and habitual participation in the dicastery was opened to the very poorest by carrying a [1] payment.

At present, however, the step in legislation which if not promoted by Themistocles, was certainly carried by Aristides in the direction of his policy, introduced a period of tranquillity, and Athens for a time had leisure from internal dissensions, as well as from conflicts with Persia.

Questions of policy in abundance, that would open serious struggles for supremacy of thought and action, were certain to arise full soon, with respect to the prosecution of aggressive war with Persia, the treatment of the lately Medising states, the management of the Delian confederacy, the attitude to be maintained relatively to Sparta and her special allies, and so forth ; but in the meantime Hellas took a long free breath after her unwonted effort, and, while her strength and population were being insensibly restored, found vent for the enthusiasm of her triumph in an outburst of energy applied to Arts which, after long maturing, now suddenly leapt to perfection, within the limits of a single lifetime.

[1] Arist. *Polit.* ii. 9, p. 661 a.

CHAPTER XVII.

POETRY, LYRIC AND DRAMATIC, IN THE AGE OF THEMISTOCLES.
PINDAR, PHRYNICHUS, AESCHYLUS.

476 B.C.; OL. 76. I.

At the summer solstice of 476 B.C., under the commencing archonship at Athens of Phaedon, came round the first celebration of the Olympic games since the great victories of Salamis, Plataea, and Mycale, since the time when Xerxes at Thermopylae enquired how the Greeks were occupied, and the reply had elicited a foreboding as to the dangerous qualities of opponents who could strain energies to the utmost, not for the sake of a prize in money, but to gain the honour of a simple olive [1] crown. Again recurred the festival which was the most expressive pledge of Hellenic unity; when Greece was free from intestine conflicts, and, moreover, in the first glow of self-gratulation and pride at delivery from a foreign enemy. If jealousies between her states could ever be lulled at all, surely it might be now; and, in fact, when Themistocles appeared at the stadium, the contests that were proceeding were disregarded—he was hailed with a general outburst of applause, and throughout the day was followed and proudly pointed out to admiring strangers. His nature was peculiarly susceptible of pleasure from such homage, and he professed to his friends that Hellas had herein fully compensated him for all his labours. He was, however, by no means a man to

---

[1] Herod. viii. 26.

disregard more material compensations; and the very rapid progress of his fortune showed conclusively that he knew well how to opportunely help himself. A fragment of an attack upon him remains which attests both his passion for display, in spite perhaps of the inadequate means he once could command for it, and by what dealings he was accused of providing these means to an extent that had certainly enabled him by this time to undertake the most chargeable public offices.

Timocreon, the *melopoios* of Rhodes, complains in bitter verses, which apparently date before the disgraces of Pausanias and Leotychides, of the falsehood, injustice, and treachery of Themistocles—of Themistocles who, when propitiated by only a moderate sum, did not care to restore him, his friend and host, to his native Ialysus, but for the sake of three talents that he sailed away with, recalled some from exile, banished others, and put others to death, without regard to justice. 'Praise Pausanias, or Xanthippus, or Leotychides who will; he, for his part, applauds Aristides as the singly most excellent man of all who came from sacred Athens. Themistocles is the detestation of [1] Latona.' He further ridicules the shabby entertainment that Themistocles had given at the Isthmus, when the guests prayed that it might not be an apt omen for the coming harvest.

Meagreness on this occasion, however, may have been but the parsimony of an ostentatious man, who does not care to be lavish when ostentation will not have the reward he chiefly covets. At Olympia, but probably four years later than our present date, he made such a show of magnificence as to be provocative at home of dangerous dissatisfaction.

On the other hand, I think we must assign to this present Olympiad his own encouragement of popular indignation against Hiero, tyrant of Syracuse. It is precisely this date

---

[1] Plut. *Them.* 21.

that is given for the subversion by Hiero of the Ionic city of
Catana ; he had transferred the inhabitants in a body to
Leontini, and was proceeding to settle in their stead a new
colony of Dorians in a city with a new name, Aetna, where he
should enjoy for all time the heroic honours which by ancient
custom were accorded to a founder—an *oikistes.* Syracuse
furnished half the new population, the other half he invited
from Peloponnesus. It is quite intelligible that such arbitrary
courses at such a time should have encouraged a denunciation
of his ostentatious magnificence, as the offensive intrusion of a
tyrant among Hellenic freemen, to the ruin of his tent and
exclusion of his horses from the [1]contest.

The victory of Theron, tyrant of Acragas, with the four-
horse chariot,—that triumph that still remained to be coveted
by Hiero when he was victor with the single horse in the
next [2]Olympiad,—is usually assigned to this occasion, though
an argument may be combined that would transfer it to the
next, and is perhaps worth stating, though I have disregarded
it elsewhere. The testimony of the scholiast halts between
the two dates, and cannot be adduced as deciding for either ;
that Diodorus dates the death of Theron in the very year
of the next Olympic festival might doubtless seem inconsistent with the elaborate poetic celebration of the victory by
Pindar, though not necessarily with the victory itself. But
the year, as reckoned by archons, commenced at the same
season as the games, and the terms of the ode are quite
susceptible of being interpreted to imply that Theron was
at the time declining in health, was not remote from the same
anticipated migration to those rewards of the just that Pindar
here so beautifully indicates, and that he did not deem it
inappropriate to promise afterwards still more, and yet scarcely
more pointedly, to Hiero, when he too was touching on the
fatal [3]term.

[1] Plut. *Them.*   [2] Pind. *Ol.* 1, sub fin.   [3] Pind. *Pyth.* iii.

One short but very beautiful ode of Pindar remains to
us that is certified as written for a victory gained this year
in the stadium of boys by Asopichus, of Orchomenus in
[1] Boeotia.

Lyric poetry had now touched its very acme in Pindar, who
at the age of forty-five was in the full might and glory of his
genius.   Theban by birth, and from early years the associate,
as poets had ever been up to this time in Greece, of aristo-
cracies and tyrants,—of Aleuads in Thessaly, of Alexander in
Macedon, of Hiero and Theron in Sicily, of Arcesilaus in
Cyrene,—there is not a line in his preserved works that can
be strictly challenged as unnational, unpatriotic, unworthy of
a spokesman who has at heart the best interests of general
Hellas.   Tradition retains at least a rumour that if he ever
offended party feeling at all, it was at his native Thebes, by
expression of sympathy with the Hellenic services of hostile
Athens.   He recognised it as the function of the lyric poet
to shed the glow of poetry over every occasion and incident of
contemporary life that was worthy of a noble interest, to
exalt and purify the feelings it excited, to dignify motive and
aspiration, and represent humanity as then only verging
towards its natural perfection, when it tended to realise in
itself as far as possible the best conception it could form of
the divine.

The extant remains of the poet are almost exclusively odes
on occasion of victories in the games; hymns, paeans, dithy-
rambs in honour of gods, and hymenaeals congratulatory of
men, and threnes or dirges that were consolatory, not without
promise of a better life, are lost to us but for fragments—
fragments that enhance our regret for what has been in part
engulfed by the common injuries of time, but partly destroyed
wilfully by fanaticism.

In prolific variety of metrical arrangement and mastery of

---

[1] Pind. *Olym.* xiv.

rhythm, Pindar was and still is without a rival; the secret
of his art in this direction must be considered as still, after all
the labour and learning bestowed upon it, very imperfectly
explained.   The key to it is probably lost with the secret
of the music which originally accompanied the poetry, and
was indeed a very important part of the composition of the
poet.   It was also the poet's part to train the choruses by
whom his odes were sung, and to instruct them in sedulous
rehearsals; and what we miss now of the 'immortal man,'
with only the written words before us, is comparable in a
degree to the enhancement, lost for ever, which Shakespear
superadded to his dramas by direct communication to the
original actors of the effects he aimed at, and his conceptions
of how they were to be produced.

That the music did not interfere with the perfect hearing
of the words is most certain, so delicate are the transitions, so
uncompromising are the suspensions of the theme for the sake
of divergence, to what are in truth indispensable and heightening, although to the unintelligent unintelligibly irrelevant
episodes.

Simonides, who was held worthy to be a rival of Pindar, and
even to have surpassed him in pathos,—the fragment of his
'Danae' approves the tradition,—was now at the end of a long
life; but even as late as 476 B.C., at the age of eighty, is recorded
as victor with a dithyrambic chorus.   The chief remains of
him that we possess—and however brief, at least complete in
themselves—are the elegiac inscriptions or epigraphs, many
applying to the incidents of the Persian war, in which his
combined ingenuity, propriety, and terseness were unrivalled.
Simonides, like Pindar, was familiar with the courts of the
Sicilian tyrants, as he had previously been with those of Hipparchus at Athens and of the Thessalian dynasts.   It was
only at a centre where wealth was abundant and willingly
lavished upon refined superfluities, that lyrical art, at the
degree of elaboration it had now attained to, could be fur-

nished with means and opportunities for its fullest display. A composition of Simonides might require a chorus of fifty performers, who were to be carefully and expensively trained, and the requirement would be vain unless such productions were frequent and habitual; it required also an audience of refined sensibilities and culture, such as in any state of society must be exceptional, and which during the earlier period, when popular aspirations were under strong repression, was found in highest perfection among those who, few or many, were elevated above the general mass as an aristocracy, and engrossed participation in active government.

The almost universal sentiment for artistic beauty which at this time prevailed among the Greeks of all races and classes was naturally most lively amongst the families of hereditary culture and wealth, the same from which, if not by virtue, not slightly by the aid of their sympathy with popular tendencies in the like direction, had ever come forth the men who gained command of their states as tyrants. Hiero was preceded in his love and patronage of art by such men as Peisistratus at Athens, Cleisthenes at Sicyon, Polycrates at Samos, Periander at Corinth, to mention no more men, who, by their furtherance of what Greeks had so much at heart, seemed almost to vindicate their position. The continuance of such rule would no doubt have been presently fatal to much for which the best art affords only poor compensation; and the better art itself was imperilled seriously. Under such circumstances, when, in a second generation, nobler impulses—which can only for a time and under a deception be associated with usurpation—are flagging or extinct, it cannot but decline to a purely personal and parasitical application. Hiero and Theron are to be credited with personal qualities and patriotic services that go very far to excuse, if not to vindicate the enthusiasm of Pindar; but it is well that he was not committed to celebrate their immediate successors.

When tyranny was abolished throughout Greece, from end

to end, the fortunes of art in its most elaborate and expensive developments were rescued primarily from wreck by the care and appreciation of the same class from which the tyrants had sprung—by such families as the Alcmaeonids, who were even allied to them, whose wealth had enabled them to contend in the chariot-races at Olympia, and even when they were in exile to promote gratuitously the enhancement of the architectural splendour of Delphi. A democracy that such men founded or fostered was not likely to miss them as its leaders and administrators; and they 'took the people into partnership,' to extend the words of Herodotus, in their artistic projects now, as before in their revolutionary. The guiding minds might still be aristocratical, might still be in many social respects an exclusive few; but not only was the sanction of the people asked and obtained, but their sympathies too were regarded, were appealed to, and the result left little discontent at what in effect was equivalent to a delegation of popular control; and this was especially the case when the fund disbursed was less immediately from the public treasury than from private fortunes.

The system of the 'liturgies,' or services for the public, by which this was brought about, seems to have been at least as old as Solon, and may have been one of his political inventions. It was the principle of this institution that citizens of exceptional-wealth were liable to be called on, out of the tribes in rotation, to make exceptional contributions to the public service; for the equipment of a war vessel only occasionally, but in usual and regular order to furnish forth public spectacles and festivals and amusements. Such a demand is manifestly an extension of Solon's graduated property-tax, and in principle challenges a like justification. At Athens at least the institution seems to have had the justification of success, and there is no slight case to be made for the principle as demanding even general application. It is too usually the opprobrium of civilised communities that, by whose fault or unwisdom soever, a large mass of the population, which subserves the social requirements not unimportantly, though in the lowest functions, receives no more advantage from the imposing result than if civilisation did not exist ; with regard to this large section at least, civilisation is a failure. Count up the numbers, and they are a vast nation that lags behind in squalor and hopelessness ; shall it be said, as a necessary condition of the grace and glory of the superior ranks, any more than are their own crapulence and gaudiness or the merely self-indulgent listlessness which misuses a superflux so sorely missed elsewhere? What the narrower political economy insists on as the natural laws of the distribution of wealth, are no more to be trusted to bring out spontaneously, without any adjustment of human intelligence, the fairest or the most desirable result, than are any other natural laws. In this, as in so many other cases, the opportunity and the faculty of regulative power that is confided to us demands to be taken into account, and 'the art itself is nature.' It is in perfect accordance with natural laws for the water-shed which is indispensable to the fertility of a district, to form, if left to itself, pestiferous marshes or desolating inundations. To say nothing of disgrace, society may be threatened by dangers as serious, through the aggregation of wealth by one accident or another in a single or a few extravagant masses, or even by such an unchecked irrational apportionment of the results of labour among the labourers as constantly ensues even when competition seems most free. The division even then, though under all the forms of peace and legality, is sometimes of the nature of a promiscuous scramble and sometimes of a lottery, and the shares prove at last to be only coarsely proportionate to the values of the co-operating labour, either mental or manual.

It is not however the sense of very palpable injustice that has usually induced a legislative interference; sufferers and spectators alike are rather apt to acquiesce in this as a hardship inherent in the inevitable course of the world; but the extreme

of social contrast engenders blind discontents and violences
which cannot be disregarded, and the prudent dealing with
which at once postulates the main principle of corrective taxation. Corrective self-taxation—the dispensing of alms—has
always been applied, however unequally, rudely, wastefully; and
in modern times we are most familiar with attempts to redeem
wild nature by the application of funds raised by taxation to
the relief, somewhat indiscriminately it must be said, of the
destitute victims of misfortune or of vice. Further applications of the principle come in when the gathered gains of
commerce are mulcted in a poor subsidy to a genius or his
descendants, or the well-to-do and wealthy are taxed not only
to support but to educate the poor, or for the adornment
of parks and establishment of public galleries to afford recrea-
tion chiefly to classes that are much too poor to be in any
sense contributory. So does the prudence at least, if not the
obligation quite so readily, become in some degree recognised,
of giving more unity to the system of society by a better
diffusion of enjoyment as well as comfort, than is the outcome
of the vaunted, of the so often misstated and misunderstood,
law of supply and demand.

On the other·hand, there is the danger of adjustment de-
generating in ungoverned hands into confiscation; and the
historical outcry—*panem et circenses*—is warning that justice
itself had need be very wise if the sinews of industry are not
to be relaxed and the remedy of civil discord not fordo itself.

The *leiturgia* was an ancient contrivance for equalising in
some degree the advantages of civil society, at least for dis-
tributing some of the best of them, and went far to reconcile
free poverty, if not penury, to co-existence with a class of
acquired or hereditary opulence. Opulence on its own part
had a pride which was compensated by the opportunity of
public display—a pride which was not ignoble when its gratification depended on addressing successfully the acute sense
and fastidious taste of such a public as the Athenians. These

functions were no doubt often burdensome enough, though
only through ambitious competition ruinous ; if there were
some to complain, there were more to rejoice, who were eager
for the distinction, and prepared with hearty good-will even to
damage their fortunes seriously.   The prize was certainly not
always bare renown, and sometimes the influence that ensued
upon a great success was counted on to more than reinstate
the outlay; but even so, the renown was the basis of the
influence.

In England the costly entertainments of a mayoralty but
weakly represent, or rather parody, the Athenian tribal liturgy ;
and modern instances of noble employment of immense wealth
are not so frequent as to have ceased to be matters of surprise.
We have otherwise, in substitution of the ancient system, only
the precarious enforcement by public opinion of aids to chari-
ties that spare an intermediate class, or of contributing to the
amusement of a class still narrower by 'hunting a county.'
The Italian opera lives by exceptionally liberal subscriptions
of the wealthy, but not out of public spirit or to the relief of
very extended public participation ; the higher drama lan-
guishes, or rather is extinct, in default of unmercenary support and subvention.

The most chargeable of all the ordinary Athenian liturgies
was the dramatic—the Choragia—of which the first mention
occurs in the year 476 B.C., just preceding the present
Olympia, and associated with the name of Themistocles as
Choragus.   The inscription which was read on a commemorative tablet that he dedicated, ran thus :—'Themistocles of
the Phrearian tribe was Choragus, Phrynichus was Master
(i. e. the teacher of the chorus or poet), Adeimantus was
Archon.'

The name of Phrynichus dates an epoch in the history of
the drama, particularly of tragedy, as standing between
Aeschylus, his immediate successor and younger contemporary, and Thespis, contemporary of Solon.

It is the peculiar glory of Athens to have originated and perfected tragedy, though not the drama generally, for comedy had already taken birth elsewhere,—taken very highly developed form in Sicily certainly, if not previously at Megara.

The essential characteristic of the drama may be said to be the representation of human action by impersonations, by assumed characters. In this barest sense it may be recognised as independent of spoken language; inasmuch as mere dumb show of even an individual, not to say of several conjointly, suffices to tell a very complicated story. Whether as mimicry of individuals or general pantomime, impersonation of this kind has been in vogue everywhere and always, and has sometimes been raised by men of peculiarly apt endowments to the dignity of an art. In its purest form it is independent even of mimicry of costume. Such an exhibition is then capable of being enhanced by music; predominance as between music and acting being variously adjusted, accordingly as music is accompaniment to acting or acting to music. In either case, whether as telling a story or merely expressing a train of sentiment, there is intervention of the dramatic principle.

A further modification arrives, and it would seem a demand for still more distinct acting, in such a performance as we read of in the Odyssey, where the bard sings the adventure of Mars and Venus, including the dialogue of Hermes and Apollo, Poseidon and Vulcan, and is accompanied by the dancing of a chorus of youths. In other instances a pair of performers, gesticulators apparently rather than dancers, are associated with a chorus and the singing and playing [1] bard. In such exhibitions the dancing, as a visible expression of general sentiment, seems to have had the same relation to more definite pantomime, as the accompaniment

---

[1] *Hymn. Apoll. Pyth.* 15; *Iliad,* xviii. 590.

of pipe or lyre to the audible words. The genius and the passion for expressive gesture manifestly conduct to the completest possible development in dramatic impersonation. Hellenic comedy and tragedy proper are accordingly both traced by Aristotle—with whose amount of knowledge we may be content—to developments from choral celebrations of Dionysus; tragedy from the enthusiastic dithyramb, and comedy from the phallic extravagances, such as in his time were still in vogue in many cities in their rudest naturalistic form. Each form of the drama seems to have advanced with considerable independence of the other, and even severally at several centres, though it is impossible not to infer from the great start which was taken so early by comedy in Sicily that her more dignified sister at Athens might well have some considerable obligations to own to.

When history first took note of comedy it was already familiar with the use of masks, of speeches, of words spoken not sung, and of plurality of actors, by whom introduced was not known; nor were many names of dramatists on [1] record. It was Epicharmus however and Phormis in Sicily who first advanced beyond simple dialogue or insignificant incidents, and dramatised fables (= stories) — and ‘ from Sicily therefore this first came.’ Epicharmus was from Megara, Phormis from Arcadia, and it was admitted that comedy had its primitive commencement among the ruder, the rustic and unceremonious Dorian populations, whose capacity for humour is recorded and exemplified for us in Theocritus. But comedy at this Sicilian epoch is drama with all apparatus and capabilities full blown; Phormis attended to the draping both of his actors and of the stage, and so it appears certain that the plays of Epicharmus, to which [2] Plautus owed obligations, had more resemblance, as plays of general character and with proper plots, to the new comedy

---

[1] Aristot. *Poet.*   [2] Hor. *Epist.* ii. 1. 58.

of Athens than to the old.   An attempt of Crates as late as 450 B.C. to establish comedy of general character at Athens seems even then to have been premature, and could not compete with the stimulant personalities of Aristophanes and Cratinus.

Epicharmus was still writing in 477 B.C., but apparently towards the end of a very long life; and at this time Phrynichus was exhibiting what is most authentically recorded as a very early form of tragedy, a form which is indeed characteristic still of a play of Aeschylus—the Persae— represented four years later.

Every manifestation of religion, however festive its general character may be, has necessarily a serious—a solemn side; and there are abundant proofs of this in the Dionysiac— elsewhere also, as for instance at [1] Argos, but especially in Attica, where all religious sentiments were peculiar in intensity.   The god who became associated, and not on inferior terms, with Apollo at Delphi, was an assessor no less with the awful goddesses of Eleusis, and shared with them in the respect which is ever inspired by concern with the gravest responsibilities of another world—of a future [2] life.   It was therefore quite as natural and spontaneous a process for the severest form of dramatic poetry to be engrafted on the dithyramb of the god, as for the most cheerful, the most extravagantly vivacious on the turbulent excitement of his coarser celebrations.

To Thespis in the time of Solon was ascribed the relief of the choral performers by introduction of recited speeches, but as yet with no mention of dialogue.   For anything that appears, the chorus was uniformly composed of representatives of Satyrs, the mythical train of Dionysus, a modification superinduced on the ancient dithyramb by Arion at Corinth, and already involving the principle of impersonation.   How

---

[1] Paus. ii. 37. 5.   [2] Herod. ii. 123.

rapidly the same principle extended to the *exarchon*, the leader of the chorus, to the variation of the characters that he might assume, to the substitution or addition of other characters besides Satyrs for the chorus, it may be to the incorporation of an independently developed system at once, these are matters unrecorded; when the door was once opened for innovation, the emulative spirit of gifted imaginations at a period of high intellectual excitement did not allow it to prematurely close.

To Aeschylus Aristotle ascribes the introduction, into tragedy at least,—if we may not with Epicharmus in mind say into the drama,—of a second actor, an innovation equivalent to the commencement of dialogue, and then still further the curtailment of the choral sections of the piece in favour of extended dialogue; and it may be asked, what then remains intermediately for Phrynichus? But there was abundant opportunity for variety of artistic elaboration and novelty, even within the limits of composition restricted to lyrical chorus and narrative speeches. It is to the value which these latter now attained that we must ascribe the affection with which they were retained in later Greek tragedy, whether delivered by messengers or in the prologues that Euripides peculiarly affects, but that were not rejected by [1] Aeschylus or [2] Sophocles. In these we have relics, traditions, of the time when such narrative speeches, an epic element in fact, were the sole interruptions or reliefs of the choruses, but their reduction to such an extent may have been but gradual. So we cannot say by whom it was effected, nor whether it was by one of the many gradual transitions, to which Aristotle alludes as unrecorded, or by a bold stroke, that the chorus of Satyrs was extruded from intercourse with the more severe action, and relegated—as from tradition of hereditary claim to all it could not be denied a

---

[1] *Eumenides.*   [2] *Trachiniae.*

residue—to a separate and final satyric entrance or play. Still less can we certify that the system of trilogic and tetralogic combinations of dramas may not have had its origin long before the first recorded example that comprised the Persae of Aeschylus.

It is characteristic of early art to rely on repetitions in the very simplest form as at once the great resource of variety and composition; to proceed from more absolute parallels to such contrasts of type and antetype as Gothic art delights in, the coupled subjects of the Old Testament and New, of sacred and profane, and so to climb by degrees towards truly aesthetic principles of composition.

From the scattered notices that are obtainable of Phrynichus we must conclude that his merits were still rather distinctly poetical than specifically dramatic. A caviller at Aeschylus in Aristophanes—at Aeschylus who combined both qualifications—ascribes the effect which he produced to his luck in having to take over the simple-minded auditors of Phrynichus, who were easily astonished. But the poetical merit of Phrynichus, in addition to his very considerable [1] originality, must have been very great, and the melodiousness of his versification is particularly celebrated. The careers of Phrynichus and of Aeschylus overlap, and each may have borrowed from the other,—the elder from the younger quite as probably as the younger from the elder of natural necessity. Phrynichus was said to have first brought female characters on the stage, and this was more likely to occur after the innovation of Aeschylus respecting dialogue than before it.

The acted drama ever involves the union of several arts, or draws on the resources of several; it may even be a concentration of all, and as it would appear, should then most nearly achieve its proper triumph, when it is most

---

[1] Aristoph. *Ran.* 910, 1299; *Av.* 749; *Vesp.* 220.

comprehensive and when the various elements that it unites
are united to the best effect, are so subordinated as to give
best prominence to the worthiest. Every variety of poetry
may here find place—the epic, the lyrical, the melic; every
variety of rhetoric—persuasive, declamatory, argumentative;
chorus and song bring in music; and scenery, costume, grouping, mien, and gesture are effective on the same conditions as
admit architecture, painting, sculpture. It is perfectly legitimate for an artist who is to be justified by his results, to
exclude from his accompaniments of impersonation either one
or more of the arts, to dispense with music, with scenery,
with lyric or with narrative poetry; and no less so for him to
determine, from considerations of his capacity and his theme,
to which art and to which class of its resources he will
assign the predominance. But the best attaches to the best.
The aim to give the fullest expression 'to high actions and
high passions' conducted the Attic tragedian to, not exclude,
but subordinate, the lyrical and musical elements of his
composition, as absolutely as he retained the musical and
dancing accompaniments in subjection to the lyric words
and their intelligible effect; as absolutely as he repressed
any tendency of scenic pomp and surprise of machinery to
distract attention from the main purport of the play.

In what manner another class of combinations were dealt
with it is less easy to determine. The drama has for its
general subject the entire range of human feelings, every
phase in every age and class, of hope and fear, of love and
hatred, of admiration or amusement; and there is no feeling,
however dignified, that has not its relations by over-tension
or by lapse to the mean or the ridiculous, and none so
irretrievably comic that may not glide into the serious and
severe by very moderate variation of a circumstance. The very
grandest tone of sentiment and thought can therefore scarcely
receive its full illustration unless its divergences and limits
are defined by indication at least of its controlling contrasts.

It is as open to the poet to make one tone or another predominant, as to make election among the arts that are to be its vehicle; and thus arises the grand distinction between tragedy and comedy, when most unchallengeable; and thus the various graduations of either, till in certain phases and proportions they meet and coalesce. But Socrates assumed, as a corollary of one of his most favourite general principles— that perfect apprehension of one thing implied as perfect of its opposite—that the best appreciation of tragic and of comic effect must necessarily go together; and so the perfect realisation of tragic effect seems to require concurrent presentation of at least an adumbration of its comic phase. Abundant illustration of this principle may be gathered from the plays of Shakespear; we need go no further than the clownish conundrums of the gravedigger, which are introductory to the over-curious considerings, as they seem to Horatio, of Prince Hamlet over the skull. How is this requirement satisfied, how was it satisfied, in the Attic drama? Apparently by the medium of the satyric drama—the drama with a chorus of Satyrs—which was in the time of Aeschylus, and presumably of Phrynichus, the complement of a tragic representation. More we can scarcely say; we have but one satyric play, and of that we know not the tragic accompaniments; we have the title of another and one of the three tragedies—the Persae—that it followed, to which, as we shall see, we can attach its subject as having a certain pertinence, but beyond the confirmation of a general presumption we can deduce nothing more.

The Persae of Aeschylus is the only later example even on record of tragic treatment of a contemporary subject, and was said to be copied in a degree from the Phoenissae (the Phoenician women) of Phrynichus. The Phoenissae was the second such attempt of Phrynichus; a previous, and indeed the only other on record at all, was on a theme which was as painful for the Athenians as his later was exultant—

the Capture of Miletus by the Persians, the catastrophe of Ionia (B.C. 494). So profound was the sympathy of the Athenians at that wreck of the most glorious of their colonies—manifested in other ways frequently—that when Phrynichus brought it before them ou the stage, though doubtless with no lack of sympathy, the whole theatre burst into a passion of tears, and the people resented the public exhibition of afflictions which they counted as their own by inflicting upon the poet a fine of 1000 drachmas.

The title of his later play is no doubt true indication that the chorus consisted of Phoenician girls or women. We learn from the argument of the Persae, which was said by the same authority—Glaucus—to be in some degree an imitation of it, that the scene opened by entrance of a eunuch to arrange the seats for the royal councillors; for such an assembly of dignities in due order therefore, as is described by Herodotus on the occasion of a council of [1] Xerxes, and as we see depicted around Darius on the Neapolitan vase,—a recognised display of Persian state. The eunuch prologised by relating the defeat of Salamis—a precipitate discovery that is more artfully reserved by Aeschylus. The poet would thus appear to have written the play, upon a flattering theme, in compensation of his previous offence, no less than as a gratification, a glorification of the victor of Salamis—his choragus.

The acceptance of such personal glorification was not without its dangers at Athens, but dangers that Themistocles seems to have made a point of carelessly provoking; possibly from simple want of self-control in this direction, possibly, on the other hand, from a definite notion that by persistent provocation of enviousness of a somewhat mean type he could shame it to silence or blunt its faculty of offence.

Earlier in time, and by the elder and earlier poet, the

---

[1] Herod. viii. 67.

Phoenissae of Phrynichus may be certainly assumed as characterised by more than the archaism that we usually assume as recognisable in the Persae. Whatever innovations are implied by regular dialogue, feminine interlocutor, a chorus of senators, extensive adoption of the tragic senarian, are found in the Persae; but along with these, as archaic residues, are not unfrequent adoption, for speeches, of the tetrameter that Aristotle tells us was relinquished when a measure fitted for dancing was of less consequence than one which, like the trimeter, had a natural harmony with the measure of discourse; general excess of proportion of lyrical element, its encroachment on or rather retention of place where it is afterwards missed, as in the long prologue, itself an archaism; and the protraction, though not unre-.ieved by interruptions, of the messenger's narrative.

Phrynichus therefore is an apt representative of the drama at the epoch of this Olympind, as advanced to the formal condition which is precisely anterior to that last effort of genius which carries it to perfection, a condition which it shares with several other arts.

CHAPTER XVIII.

A NOTICE is preserved by [1]Vitruvius, that a proper theatre
was first constructed at Athens by Agatharcus, who described
it in a treatise. From [2]Suidas we learn that it was erected in
place of a wooden structure that gave way with the spectators
on an occasion when Aeschylus was exhibiting in competition
with Pratinas, the reputed inventor of the satyric drama, as
early as the 70th Olympiad (499 B. C.). In the absence of
closer information, we are left to entertain the high probability that here at Athens, and in this way was originated that
type of the Greek uncovered theatre which was repeated with
only secondary variations all over Hellenic ground—of vast
capacity usually, and, in Asia Minor especially, on colossal
scale. The general characteristics that agree with such an
origin are, the solidity that was secured by basing the con-
centric lines of seats, as they rose one behind the other, immediately on the hollowed slope of, if possible, a rocky hill-side ;
and then the liberal extent which was allowed for the orchestra,
the dancing-place of the chorus, a level semicircular space
embraced by the arc of the lowest range of seats. The concession of so large and central a position is in accordance with

---

[1] Praefat. 7.   [2] s. v. Aeschylus.

the relative importance of the chorus in the earlier drama
as compared with the proper dialogue, and still more with
the traditional regard for its performance as a celebration in
honour of the god—of Dionysus, to whom the entire structure
and all its purposes were sacred. At the same time, although
the area reserved for the chorus has its name from dancing, it
is not the less certain that in the execution to music of the
beautiful and elaborately-constructed choruses of the dramatists, as of the Odes of Pindar, the dancing was but a secondary
adjunct, that, so far from superseding or even interfering with
the interest and distinctness of the poetry, was only valued
for heightening its effect.

The long transverse slip of elevated stage for the dialogue
of the actors was more remote, on the chord of the semi-
circle; the difficulty of giving effect to the voice in theatres
so large and under the open sky, for due delivery of speeches
which depended for interest and charm on refined poetical
expression, was resolved with as much ingenuity as daring.
Besides certain acoustical adjustments that are still but imperfectly understood, but were evidently directed less to
countervailing echoes than enhancing resonance, a contrivance
was employed for adding loudness to the issuing voice. The
deformity which this involved was relieved by, and perhaps
originally suggested, the adoption of a mask that completely
covered both face and head. Threatened disproportion was
again evaded by what was considered only a further propriety, the artificial exaggeration of the entire height and
bulk of the actors, sometimes representatives of gods, or in
any case of heroes who, by the convention of ancient art,
which was allowed on the frieze of the Parthenon as on the
shield of [1] Achilles, ever claimed superior magnitude. There
was thus a readily accepted contrast between the personages
on the *bema,* and the natural forms and proportions of the

---

[1] *Il.* xviii. 519.

chorus, which in the days of purer dramatic art all but invariably represented the weaker and vacillating, in fact, the generally meaner minds of ordinary mortals. The thick-soled cothurnus, the majestic costumes, and the masks were inventions of Aeschylus, and are in striking harmony with his style, with the boldness of his metaphors, the unhesitating originality of his expressions ; and we need not doubt were on the whole equally justified, equally admirable in result, though in like manner not seldom startling, even sometimes to the extent of a shock. The number and variety of characteristic masks that were required by such a fertile dramatist as Aeschylus alone, must have given a marvellous stimulus to inventive design, and it is impossible to say how much his personal influence and suggestions may not have contributed to the decision of those types of divine and heroic physiognomy that were elaborated by the sculptors. His own description of the aspect of his Furies evinces how forcibly characteristic were the types that he accepted.

As regards the temple architecture of the Greeks, we have the names of four architects of Athens who were employed on the great Olympieium under Peisistratus,—names only, not a fragment of their work, as little of the work of Rhoecus in the vast Heraeum of Samos, or of the Corinthian Spintharus at Delphi. But for our immediate epoch we happily possess remains which when closely examined discover how much careful theoretical study was devoted to the original design, and even throw back light upon certain more archaic fragments of unassignable date. The temple that was measured and published with great completeness by Mr. Cockerell, under the title of The Temple of Jupiter Panhellenius at Aegina, illustrates the architecture of this period and its sculpture also, and furnishes an intermediate example between some scanty remains of an earlier Parthenon and a temple at Corinth, and the perfected Doric temples of the age of Pericles.

The Doric may be said to have been the common style of

Hellenic architecture at the date when building first attained
with the Hellenes to the dignity of a style, a point that is
found already attained in no imperfect sense even in the very
earliest examples of which fragments are preserved. The first
that we possess betray most clearly in their details derivation
from timber originals, but not more distinctly and scarcely
more crudely than the latest ; and the moderateness of subsequent change in this respect warns us how remote the earlier
may be from the epoch of original adaptation. For all their
archaism, they exhibit the style complete in its essential
members, and with far more than the rudiments of its characteristic beauty ; most important fact of all, they betray a
consciousness of the principles on which character and expression in architecture are dependent.

The obligations of Doric to Egyptian architecture have been
recognised with a circumstantiality that is not easily gain-
said, in the details which offer for comparison in the so-called
Proto-Doric of Beni-Hassan and Philae ; among them the most
plausible, for they are in truth too specific to be ascribed to
common suggestion of natural fitness, are the abacus, echinus,
and rudimentary annulets of the capital of the column, and
the facetted shaft that prepares for the all-important flutes.
But the most important lessons that the Greek might have
learnt and probably did learn among the primeval monuments
of Egypt, were the capabilities of beauty that reside in the
column as a structural member, and in extended colonnades,—
in contrasts of columns of subordinated dimensions and proportions, and of the cylindrical column with rectangular pier
or anta,—the value of equalities of spacing and of symmetry in
elevation,—the dignity of close and massive proportions and of
consistent adherence to trabeative construction in the span of
voids by the horizontal beam. To Egypt, with all its barbaric
limitations and sophistications and affection for extravagant
mass that did but dwarf the artist, must still be allowed the
achievement both in sculpture and architecture of a very high

grade of dignity and expression, which merits recognition in
no slight degree as a grand style, and that at a time which
relatively to Greek art—carry it back as far as we reasonably
may—was remote antiquity indeed.

But whatever the Greek borrowed was first selected as the
most suitable, and then very speedily became his own by
a process equivalent to the changes of transmuting nature.
It was by his steady reliance on nature and recurrence to
nature that he had shaken himself free from many a sophistica-
tion that clung to him for a certain time from earlier forms
of Aryan language or mythology; at the utmost he retained
them as wild stocks on which to graft expression and poetry
of a perfection that goes far to reduce enquiry respecting their
ulterior origin to little more than vulgar antiquarianism. The
superseded forms may leave a certain impress, but it is as
vestiges of forms that have departed; adopted forms may still
upon scrutiny betray their prototype, but ever concurrently
with the final renunciation of allegiance to such an origin.
So the stone architecture of the Greeks, while manifestly
derived in numerous details from models constructed in
timber, as manifestly does not minutely mimic, does not
studiously imitate them, and in all most important points
adjusts itself to new conditions. The substitution of stone
for timber had early enforced contracted bearings between
open supports, the span from column to column being controlled by available scantling of materials; then the composition, which so was of necessity closed up, betrayed of itself an
elementary principle of dignity that the sensibility of the
Greek was quick to recognise and eager and able to develope.
It was here that his imagination was most affected by the
exclusively stone architecture of Egypt; but out of the
various types presented to him he selected and made chief
use of that which harmonised best with past associations
from constructions that were already in possession of his
sympathies.

R 2

The climatic difference of a stormy as contrasted with a rainless region was recognised and allowed prerogative influence over mouldings and profiles throughout; responsively to this consideration, a sloping roof, adapted to weatherfend the interior, now descended on the cornice; and to the cornice was given a bolder horizontal projection that sheltered the exterior also, and delivered rainfall clear of the members below. Even to the crowning capital of the column, in deference to the same idea, was assigned a spread that is quite independent of reference to the bearing and breadth of the architrave, the beam which it carried; but is sympathetic with the expression of ample cover to the shaft and foot below.

A solid and spreading basement, the line of regularly interspaced columns, the bracing architrave and covering and repeated triglyphs of the bonding frieze, completed the elements of the composition, and gave occasions for telling contrasts of void and solid, of vertical and horizontal, of open and enclosed. But it was by his mastery of the harmonising influence of consistent and characteristic proportion that the Greek attempered these contrasts, and by blending them in unity knew how to elevate propriety in purpose and construction to the charm of stateliness and beauty in highest perfection.

The Aeginetan temple is but small—100 feet by 50 on plan, with columns of $3\frac{1}{4}$ feet in diameter against the $5\frac{3}{4}$ feet of the Corinthian. It represents the distribution of larger structures by being divided in the interior even to inconvenience by colonnades that, upon such a reduced scale, obstruct passage; but it is in other respects elaborate in design and refined in execution and ornament, to a degree that certifies it to be an example of the best advancement of its period. As regards the architecture of the temple, its Doric style is the same that, complete in all members and details, and even in characteristic treatment and the general

proportions of the whole, had been already transported to
Italy and Sicily; it was there to be embodied on colossal
scale, but scarcely to receive any modifications that, as compared with the primary scheme, are beyond the value of
provincialisms. The architecture of Paestum and of Agri-
gentum, and other Sicilian cities even of later date, has
marked analogy with Aeginetan Doric in the specimen before
us, and separated too early from the parent stock to participate in the exactness of refinement that still remained to
be conferred by Attic genius.

In almost all its forms at all times Doric architecture is
distinguished for breadth, boldness, simplicity, majesty, and
its merits in these respects are already pronounced in the
age of Themistocles with considerable dignity; but archaism
even at its best never quite compasses perfect consistency, and
purity of style awaits the sensitiveness of a more refined and
fully practised age. Severity is usually the characteristic of
archaic art, and the remains of the Doric temple at Corinth,
of an earlier age than the Aeginetan, are in respect of some
forms more heavy, it may be said more majestic; but in the
profile of the capital they demand still more stringently that
correction of a common weakness which was afterwards to be
administered by the Athenian.

Ionic architecture, or rather the Ionic style of Greek architecture, can scarcely be traced quite up to the age of Themistocles, but must have been already in progress of developement, and may be referred to in anticipation as illustrating
by contrast the developement to which it supervened. It
stands in the same relation to Persia, from whence it derived
many suggestions for treatment of column in capital and
base, and to Assyria for ornamental details, that the Doric
style occupies to Egypt. Again, the Greek gave more than
he appropriated. Egyptian architecture was Dorised by
fusion with inventions drawn from systematic timber construction; and then this developed Doric supplied the funda-

mental forms which received enrichments of Eastern origin, but which it remained for Hellenic genius to render refined, and to distribute with unimpeachable propriety and grace.

In leading divisions and even certain subdivisions of stylobate, column, entablature, pediment, the Ionic style in the majority of instances adheres accurately to the lines and precedents of the Doric. The main differences are that the column as Ionic assumes for the first time a proper moulded base and interpolates the peculiar Eastern form of volutes below the abacus of the capital, and that the frieze becomes continuous by dispensing with the intermittent series of triglyphs. What are really more important distinctions are found in the uniform adoption of slenderer proportions, in harmony with the lightness of decoration, though still regulated on the same general principles, and above all in the characteristic profile of the order.

Pass the eye down the Ionic profile and it will be observed that every angle is tempered by an adjacent curved moulding precisely at the points—as in architrave-band and abacus, and at meeting of cornice and bed-moulding, of shaft and stylobate —where the angularity of the Doric is most unqualified; and curves of contrary flexure are admitted as frankly as the more simple. In the Doric profile, the imperceptible entasis of the column apart, it is only in the cymatium or gutter-rim of the pediment, in the echinus or the bowl-like member of the capital and the mere lip of a drip-moulding that curvature is admitted at all; all other projections are bounded by right lines at right angles, or at angles very acute or very obtuse. The cymatium at Aegina is a curve of contrary flexure, but even this indulgence was destined to be corrected in the Parthenon, for a simple curve stopped by a right line; and the curve of the echinus of the capital was also to be set there more severely upright and returned upon the abacus with greater approximation to the vertical than in the Aeginetan and in the still more abnormal Corinthian example. So the sinking

of the Aeginetan flute as a segment of a circle was afterwards
rendered more severe by the substitution of the flatter ellipse
that gives a sharper and steeper arris. At Aegina already,
the tendency to contrary flexure in a curve as continued
from the echinus to the shaft of the column, is qualified
by the deep sinkings and bold angularity of the annulets
and necking; but even here the Athenian was not satisfied
without rendering the break still more pronounced.

As regards general proportion, not only is Doric majesty
acknowledged and valuably realised at Aegina, but it was
moreover already effected by studied adjustment of exact
numerical proportion; and much progress had been made
towards discovery of the appropriate terms and appropriate
directions for the application of the principle. I have illustrated this point in detail in an Appendix to Mr. Cockerell's
work.

The Doric column, as compared with the Ionic, is shorter
relatively to its diameter, thicker relatively to its interval,
and consequently lower relatively to its spacing; but varies in
different examples in a sequence that tends directly to Ionic
proportion. A comparison of Doric examples among themselves in the last respect gives the following progressive con-
traction of arrangement on plan, and illustrates—this is not
the place for more—one application of the Greek theory of
architectural proportion :—

At Corinth—Height of Column = 2 Intercolumns + 1½ diameters of the column.
At Aègina   ,,   =   ,,   + 2   ,,
The Theseum at ⎫ ,,   =   ,,   + 2½   ,,
  Athens   ⎭
The Parthenon   ,,   =   ,,   + 3   ,,

In both the Aeginetan and Corinthian Doric columns the
upper and lower diameters of the shaft and that of the abacus
have the same relative proportions of low numbers, 3 : 4 : 5;
a sequence that occurs in like application in some Attic
examples, but in others, and especially the Parthenon, was
superseded by further refinements. The retention of like

proportions between corresponding diameters in columns that differed considerably in height introduced effects of delicate variety.

Lastly, the architect of the temple at Aegina had as yet no more than the school that carried on the art in the West, appreciated the value of giving preponderance of height to the vertical member, the column, relatively to the joint height of the horizontals—of the rest of the façade. This was a discovery still reserved for Attica, and the rational vindication of it goes far into the principles that govern architectural design of every style and age to the extent that it approaches full perfection. It was at Athens first, at Athens chiefly, that the principles of the appropriate application of proportion to architecture were discovered and exemplified; principles that even so far as already recovered await intelligent recognition.

Authentic evidence fails for instituting a comparison of the entire coloured enrichment with that of the Parthenon; for little more can be advanced without risk of controversy than that there also the stringcourses and mouldings that framed in the pediment and frieze were painted with patterns. At Aegina there is more sufficient proof of the colour applied to some plain broad surfaces, with manifest crudity and as lingering traditions from primitive usage of timber constructions.

The sculpture of the Aeginetan temple is so far in harmony with its architecture, that in hardness of forms and expressions, as distinguished from unskilfulness or rudeness, it retains much of traditional archaism, together with very high merits that evince capacities and promise of advance to any height of excellence. The various degrees of merit that are found among the figures of these compositions, attest an already established and still proceeding improvement. We cannot do them full justice as compositions, in consequence of many figures being lost from each, but fortunately enough remain to illustrate the principles of com-

position that were adopted, as well as to display the feeling
that had been acquired for truthfulness to beauty in nature
and technical mastery. The original marbles are at Munich,
restored by Thorwaldsen, and so far with a misdirected ingenuity that designedly obscures the distinction of new parts
and old.

The chief seats of sculpture in Greece at this time—and
for long before, as for long afterwards—were Aegina, Athens,
Argos, Sicyon. Each city may have had peculiarities of
school, but their artists are found working in concert, and
it would seem to follow, exercising lively reaction in style
and interchanging instruction. Synnoon and his son Ptoli-
chus of Aegina are pupils of a Sicyonian ; Simon of Aegina
works together with Dionysius of [1] Argos as Ageladas of
Argos works with the Sicyonians Canachus and Aristocles,
and has for scholars Myron and Pheidias, Athenians, as well
as Polycletus, an Argive like himself.

The early notices of Greek sculpture defy definite chronology ; allusions to particular artists are scant, confused, or
contradictory'; notices of their comparative styles are inconclusive. So many of the most distinguished Greeks, again,
lived and were active to very advanced age, that this may
well have been the case with many artists ; and we know—
it is a commonplace in the history of arts—how rapidly at
certain epochs an individual artist may advance in style, and
also how long after art generally has passed into a totally new
style one of the earlier innovators may continue, persevering
in a style at a date when, but for biography, it would be
unhesitatingly declared to have been long superseded.

Pausanias refers to Callon of Aegina as representative of
the same archaic style of art as Canachus of [2] Sicyon ; and
Latin authors, as [3] Quintilian and [4] Cicero, apply to the works
of both the same terms ' hard ' and ' rigid.'

---

[1] Paus. v 27. 1.   [2] Ib. vii. 18. 6.
[3] Quint. xii. 10.   [4] *Brut.* xviii. 70.

Of the style of Canachus we may form a certain notion, from comparison of these terms with recognised copies of his celebrated Apollo, which was carried off from Miletus by the Persians, to be restored long after by Seleucus. There can be little doubt that it is more or less accurately represented on coins, and then by the small Payne Knight bronze now in the British Museum. The date of the original work has been somewhat hastily assumed by Brunn and others as later than 479 B.C., on the assertion of both Pausanias and Strabo that it was carried off by Xerxes. But it surely is clear that all these authorities transfer to Xerxes the earlier outrages of Darius, who by testimony of [1] Herodotus plundered and burnt the temple at Didyma, and transferred captives from Miletus to Ampe on the Tigris. Brunn, in his History of Greek Artists, also confuses Ionians with Aeolians and Miletus with Miletopolis in [2] Mysia.

This statue was colossal; another at Thebes, a repetition of it in both magnitude and design, was of cedar. To Canachus is also ascribed a seated temple statue of Aphrodite of ivory and gold—chryselephantine—at Corinth; a valuable notice of the early date of this sumptuous form of art.

The Aeginetan artist Callon, who ranked with this master, could not have been unimportant.

Another Aeginetan, of whose very important works we have abundant notices in Pausanias, though strangely enough not a single mention of him occurs elsewhere, was Onatas; and here we obtain a certified date; he was in full reputation Ol. 78. 3 = 496 B.C., not long after which date one of his works was dedicated by Deinomenes, son of Hiero, at Olympia. He wrought, at least principally, in bronze, gods and heroes and victors in the games; and in the characterisation of his works by Pausanias, we find the Aeginetans

---

[1] Herod. vi. 19.   [2] Brunn, p. 76.

indicated as usually more archaic, for all their merit, than the archaic school of Attica.

A contemporary of Onatas was Glaucias of Aegina; we only read of his statues of Olympic victors; of Gelon with his chariot; of Theagenes the renowned athlete of Thasos, victor in boxing, Ol. 75=480 B.C., the year of Salamis, and as Pancratiast in the following Olympiad; and of Glaucus of Carystus, whom he represented characteristically, in the attitude of that sciamachy—sparring—in which he peculiarly excelled.

The material of all the Aeginetan sculpture of which we have literary record is metal, chiefly bronze; it was perhaps with a certain symbolical intention that the colossal Zeus— ten cubits high, erected at Plataea by the Hellenes collectively, and work of an Aeginetan, Anaxagoras, not otherwise known—was formed of [1] iron. The recovered sculptures of the Aeginetan pediments, although of marble, seem to follow a precedent or conform to a taste established by familiar use of bronze. Each figure stands freely on its legs, with no obligation for support to stump or attached drapery, or other of the usual contrivances in marble sculpture for securing against collapse by proper weight. The comparatively small scale of the figures of course renders this more easy, but still the feat is remarkable; each figure rested upon its plinth, that was let into the cornice and run with lead, and except for some ornamental adjuncts to helmets, was formed from a single piece of marble, even to the shield that in some parts did not exceed three-quarters of an inch in thickness. The parts of the figures that, as turned towards the tympanum, must have been always invisible from below, are finished with all the scrupulous care that was bestowed on the fronts.

The subject of one composition certainly, and probably of both, was a combat for possession of a slain warrior. Athene

---

[1] Paus. v. 23. 1.

stands upright in the centre, represented with only a qualification of the formality that might pertain to her archaic
statue, but still with so much as to vindicate her interest,
indeed protective interference, in the fight. This point is somewhat obscured by misarrangement of the grouped casts in the
British Museum; the feet of the goddess ought to protrude
below the knees of the prostrate warrior who lay further to
her right. The angles are occupied by extended wounded
figures, of which the correspondence is heightened into a
blunt and over-formal antithesis; the remoter arm is bent
in one case, extended in the other; the remoter leg crosses
over the nearer in one case, in the other is behind. Then
follows on either side a triplet of figures,—a kneeling archer
in each group behind an advancing protagonist and with
a kneeling spearman behind him. Here contrast is chiefly
entrusted to some difference of costume in the archers, and
then to the variety that is given by the shield arms being
necessarily next to the tympanum on one side, and the spear
arm on the other. The most marked contrast of all ensues
between the figures that answer indeed as figure for figure
on either side of the goddess, but are as different as the
prostrate in death from the enemy who crouches forward to
seize and drag him away.

In such arrangement there is recognition of the symmetry
appropriate for sculpture that is to be associated with
strictly symmetrical architecture; but at best there is only
a commencing break into that bolder rhythmical distribution that can balance group by group, of which both the
elements and arrangement are contrasted, as exemplified
beyond all rivalry in the pediments of the Parthenon.

The drapery of the Athene is stiff and formal, and none
appears elsewhere to relieve the nude; it is much if we may
say that there is a poor substitution attempted by interposing
on either side the more entirely, and closely covered and
accoutred archers.

Archaic formality is retained in the stiffly curled hair and set smile of the combatants, even of the dying, even of the spectatress goddess. One fashion however does but preserve the Doric custom of a toilette of battle, as exemplified by the Spartans preparing for battle at Thermopylae ; and Homer ascribes such a smile to Aeginetan Ajax at the very crisis of combat :—

> Τοῖος ἄρ' Αἴας ὦρτο πελώριος ἕρκος Ἀχαιῶν
> Μειδιόων βλοσυροῖσι προσώπασι· νέρθε δὲ ποσσὶν
> Ἤιε μακρὰ βιβάς, κραδάων δολιχόσκιον ἔγχος [1].

If colour was crude on the architecture, it was still more so on the sculpture, where armour and eyes and lips and wounds were certainly painted, as well as probably emblems on the shields.

The subject of the best preserved pediment is, I do not doubt, the contest over the body, not of Patroclus, but of Achilles himself, the rescue of which was the great glory of the Aeacid Ajax. Hector with Paris as an archer and a characteristic figure, are then recognised on one side, as Ajax and his constant comrade Teucer, and perhaps Ulysses, on the other. The kneeling Hercules of the other pediment, an archer as he is described in the Odyssey, gives sufficient assurance that its subject was that earlier contest with Trojans in which Telamon, as ally of Alcides, gained his bride Hesione ; a second glorification of heroes of Aegina whom Pindar lauds as unfailingly in every Aeginetan ode, and in victorious conflict in the wars against Asia, of which Herodotus himself regards that with Xerxes as a continuation.

The contrast of these works to the Pheidian pediments may not be greater than was that of a drama of Phrynichus with one of Sophocles ; certain in any case it is that very decisive archaism clung obstinately to the art. An example of how it could defend its ground is seen in a bas-relief found at Eleusis, where on the very same slab one figure of a group

---

[1] *Iliad,* vii. 211.

is in the later, another, for no discoverable reason, in the style that was all but obsolete.

The notice which has been already quoted of the statue of Glaucus in the attitude of 'sparring,' by Glaucias of Aegina, may be regarded as a link in history which connects Aeginetan art with that of Pythagoras of Rhegium and Myron of Attica, who are both celebrated as breaking through ancient rigour more or less completely, and at the same time venturing boldly upon characteristic—dramatic— attitudes and gestures. The art of the Italian colony was at this time capable of holding its own in competition with Attic, for Pythagoras was held to have surpassed Myron in a figure of a Pancratiast at [1] Delphi. Particularly cele- brated was his statue at Syracuse of a figure painfully limping from the suffering caused by an ulcer,—as I have elsewhere inferred,—a Philoctetes ; a group of great interest was ascribed to him of the Theban brothers, Eteocles and Polynices, dying by mutual blows.

Myron was of Eleutherae in Attica, a town on the road to Boeotia, a hint that criticism has sometimes too eagerly seized on to impute to his art Boeotian characteristics that would not otherwise be suspected. A vast number of his works are on record, from single and associated figures of animals as well as of men and gods, in bronze, and some colossal, to modelling and chasings in silver. Like his rival, he is one of the artists who are signalised by innovations in art together with retention of considerable archaism. By rare good fortune we have certain representations of some of his works, which are sufficient to avouch that, like Pythagoras, he was studious of 'rhythm and symmetry,' in other words, when sculpture is in question, of proportion and composition. The daring attitude of his Discobolus, who bends down and forwards and sideways preparatory to the delivery of his cast,

---

[1] Plin. *H. N.* xxxiv. 59.

is described with admiration by the ancients, and is reflected for us in various copies and repetitions,—one is in the British Museum,—which however differ too much among themselves for us to accept any one as an exact reproduction. His exhausted foot-racer, Ladas, represented as just winning, but winning only at the expense of his last breath, was almost equally celebrated. A figure in the Lateran Museum has been recognised with great plausibility as representing Marsyas, from his group of the Satyr in an attitude of astonishment at Athene as she flung away the pipes that he was to take up to be his bane. It is difficult to resist an impression, on regarding this statue, that Pheidias was under the same obligation to the original for the Poseidon of his west pediment of the Parthenon, that Michael Angelo did not disdain to owe to the Christ of Orcagna for the central figure in his Last Judgment.

How far and in what manner Ageladas of Argos showed the way by his own productions to the marvellous advances that were made by those who are assigned to him as scholars, we cannot say. Not a few of his works are recorded, but unfortunately in no instance with a characterisation of style. It is significant however that it is not to himself but to his scholar Myron that so much merit is assigned for a decisive break with archaism, from which Pheidias and Polycletus were entirely emancipated. How defective are the materials for a history of early art appears in the fact that we have not a single notice of that grand transition in the treatment of drapery which was equivalent in itself to a revolution in art. Apart from this the glory must be assigned to Myron and his competitors of occupying in ancient art the position of the Masaccios and Mantegnas in the history of modern painting.

Two Athenian artists, Critios and Nesiotes, in [1]480 B.C.

---

[1] *Marm. Par.*

made statues of Harmodius and Aristogeiton in substitution
of those which were carried off by [1] Xerxes three years previously. Some records of this group have been traced on
coins and vases, and, it is believed, even copies in sculpture.
By comparison of these it is still possible to appreciate the
skill with which the figures of the two youths rushing forward
together to an attack were so composed as to display the
action of both in effective combination from whichever side
they were regarded.

[1] Paus. i. 8. 5; Lucian, *Philops.* 18.

CHAPTER XIX.

FROM 476 down to 466 B. C. the page of Greek history presents what may seem to be a happy blank. No collisions with Persia are set down within this period, and not even any considerable dissensions among the Greeks themselves. It might be supposed that they were now enjoying the unmixed rewards of patriotic exertions and free co-operation, devoting themselves entirely to the reconstruction of their industries, the celebration of their festivals, the production and dedication of the numerous and elaborate works of art by which they commemorated their deliverance and acknowledged their gratitude to the gods for glory, for safety, and for wealth. Political feelings however, we may be sure, were not in suspended animation during this interval, nor could significant political events, however comparatively sparse and unobtrusive, be wanting; but historians neglected the tameness of the time to dissert in preference on the broader and more startling effects of Persian or Peloponnesian war, or were diverted to fill up what seemed a gap by annals of opportunely livelier events in the colonial West. Sicily and lower Italy supplied some highly exciting incidents,—tales of the courts of Hiero and Theron, the important naval victory gained by Hiero over Etruscans in the Bay of Cumae in 474 B.C., and the crushing defeat of the Dorians of Tarentum by the Iapygians 473 B.C., with its consequent supplanting of Tarentine oligarchy by a democracy.

Deserted thus by the detailed guidance that we could wish

for in central Greece, we are left to interpret a few general notices as best we may, and so elicit explanation of what contrasts are discoverable between the situation of affairs at the opening of the period and at its conclusion.

Important changes, it is certain, were gradually supervening throughout this period in the relations of Athens, not only to Sparta and the Peloponnesian states, but also to her own confederates in the alliance assumed as still subsisting for active prosecution of hostilities against the Persian. And it was impossible that differences of opinion as to the policy dictated by such changes or inducing them, should not be very decided at Athens itself, where the control of public affairs on this extended scale offered so tempting a prize to the ambitious. The value of party combination for the compassing of political power was no new discovery at Athens, and the leaders of party, now that Aristides, probably through age, had comparatively retired, were recognised distinctly enough in Themistocles and Cimon. By the circumstances of the time a large measure of popular support was enjoyed by either. Themistocles, as creator of the fleet with its fortified arsenal at the Piraeus, and leader in its prime glory at Salamis, was the proper representative of the new democracy; while Cimon, though more immediately allied with the aristocracy, had no slight popular hold, in some degree from the memory of his father Miltiades, still more from his own considerable achievements, and also from the open and liberal manners that are never so appreciated, even in the most resolute democracy, as from a born aristocrat. Influential members again of the Eupatrids—of that aristocracy of descent which comprised some who were devoted to all that was desperately oligarchical, not to say tyrannical in aspiration— were the Alcmaeonids, who knew well how to avail themselves of the connection for the sake of aid from those of less flexible principles than themselves, but had ever in view to effectuate a compromise at a favourable time, and so to acquire the guidance which by management might become equivalent to the mastery of the democracy. Of such a section Cimon would naturally receive the support, but only until it produced from itself a rival and a competitor.

On the great question of the treatment of the allies, there can be little doubt that Themistocles was disposed to carry matters with a high hand, and to forego no opportunity of making the leadership of Athens stringently imperative. Whether the synod of representatives met regularly and debated and voted at Delos or not, would not much alter the case; the preponderance of Athens would enable her easily to rule every discussion, every decision. It was therefore a consequence in the nature of things that however, as time went on, alarm at the urgency of danger from Persia might decline, there was decided indisposition to admit of any question as to reduction in the assessed contributions or of the rigour with which they were levied. Already even while apprehension was still subsisting, the same difference in respect of energy and organisation that had appeared in the resistances offered by Ionia and by Athens when they were tried independently, had begun to tell in a manner that encouraged Athenian pretensions. Already before any thought came into question on the part of the allied cities of repudiating continued assessment, there was a declared preference among many of them to compound for exemption from personal service, to furnish ships rather than their quota of men, or with still more alacrity to substitute both for men and ships a contribution in money. The Athenian population, on the other hand, had fairly taken to the sea—to public service afloat that involved remote voyages and renunciation or suspense of private occupation, and the policy of its leaders gave them every encouragement in this direction. Arrangements for money compositions therefore, which went to supply liberal pay to Athenian crews and to fit out Athenian vessels, were readily accepted. The efficiency of a war trireme depended,

from the tactics that were applicable, on discipline and training that were not speedily acquired, and so by degrees Athens
became, by the habits of her population as well as the numbers
of her ships, not so much the preponderant as the sole naval
power of the Aegean. Only the larger islands of Lesbos,
Chios, and Samos remained in the distinct condition of properly autonomous allies, and still kept up war fleets, though
comparatively inconsiderable.

The affection however for positive autonomy in even very
small Greek cities was so much a part of Greek nature, that
the sense of subordination which qualified the relief obtained by
such compositions could not before very long be otherwise
than galling. Nor were the Athenians disposed either to
indulgence or tenderness in administration; they had the
consciousness, and did not care to conceal it, of possessing
qualities themselves that were proper to a superior and
governing race; they assumed the tone and independence of
command, and took slight care to mask the fact that their
nominal allies were rapidly declining into the condition of
subjects. It is only at the conclusion of the period we are
now concerned with that we have notice of hostile collisions
induced by these growing discontents; but the expressions of
Thucydides seem to authorise the [1] inference that outbursts of
contumacy were early as well as frequent, and had been
followed up by Athens, in instances that have escaped particular record, with a severity that left the offenders thereafter
in a perfectly different relative position.

All this implies the constant exercise and cruising of the
Athenian fleet, quite apart from special expeditions. In such
operations Themistocles was at home; and the notice occurs,
among examples of his ostentation of ability and distinction,
how on one occasion of assuming command he put off the
settlement of all his matters of business, private as well as

---

[1] Thuc. i. 99.

public, for the sake of the display of his multifarious concerns
and facility of despatch, on the very day of [1] embarcation.
The ambitious views which he entertained for the city that he
had re-created were without limit; and his faculty of political insight, so celebrated by Thucydides, gave him clearest
perceptions of the openings that would conduct its present
largely extended power most directly to the limitless beyond.
The position that Persia seemed to be rapidly forfeiting, of a
vigorously organised and overwhelming empire, left a vacancy
for a successor who could profit by the opportunity and by
the examples of her glory and her decline. But for a Greek
state to be her successor or rival, the relations of the
states of Hellas could not be unchanged. The first difficulty and the last in the way of the largest organisation, was
the inveterate Hellenic tendency to mere municipal, or at
best cantonal independencies, asserting for themselves the
right of war and peace, of exclusive treaties and legislation.
To the disorders that ensued it is due that even Herodotus
refers to the conquests of Ionia by the Persians with a certain sense of relief as pacifications—pacifications, that is, of
the very internal feuds and quarrels that had disabled them
from uniting for effective self-protection. Hellas no doubt
could not have been what it was, have done what it had done,
but for the spirit of individuality of which this tendency was
an outgrowth; but its difficulties, always great, were rapidly
becoming inconsistent with the necessities of changed times,
and the true problem of politics was how to carry over the
best of its advantages; the Athenian could discern that the
option lay between succeeding to empire or succumbing to it.
For such a succession the irresistible predominance of a central
power was a condition, and thus direct constraint or the
threat of it, its equivalent, was applied without remorse to the
minor allies, who might show impatience at demands upon

[1] Plut. *Themist.*

their active services or even payments in composition. Impatience could not but spring up under such conditions among communities of which the restricted limits admitted of no interests so important as local distinction, local festivals and festivities, and the pursuit of wealth; while they fostered narrow-mindedness that would require danger to be very close to them indeed—such in all ages is the story of small confederate republics—before it roused them thoroughly, and to continue very close to them if they were to remain for long united and alert.

In the more important communities, such as Thebes or Samos, the hold of Athens upon loyalty to alliance was largely or chiefly dependent on the security given by her alliance to the possession of power by the democratical party. A firmly-planted democracy constituted an Athenian garrison, an Athenian outpost.

Against what an opposition such a party had to strengthen itself at Samos, where aristocratical traditions maintained themselves, as at Athens, by certain traditions of the pomps and indulgences of a tyranny—of the court of Polycrates—is evidenced by the convulsions that ultimately led to its overthrow and a very serious revolt. There is then nothing that should surprise us in the fullest sympathy and co-operation of democratic Samians in power with the Athenian policy, and even to the extent of being the proposers of the removal of the treasury of the confederation, and with it, as of course, the synod, from Delos to [1] Athens. The accumulation of the fund after a few years might well seem to demand that a protection of the strongest walls should be superadded to that of sanctity; Athens, as collector and disburser of the fund, could make as many difficulties and inflict as much inconvenience as she chose, while appearing, if she cared to be at the trouble, to be quite satisfied with the first arrangement, which was now finally superseded.

[1] Plut. *Aristides,* 25.

Some more ancient authority is no doubt represented by Justin when he dates this [1] transference several years later, after the dangerous sympathy of Sparta with the revolt of Thasos. But it is certain that the depth and designs of this sympathy remained secret for a year or two at least; the meditated invasion of Attica on that occasion by the Lacedaemonians, avouched by Thucydides, was secret at the time, and not notorious enough to prevent the friendly aid of Cimon's expedition to Ithome soon after. Where one authority must needs be sacrificed, I adopt in preference the record of Plutarch; there is a confirmatory sentence in Deinarchus that Aristides in this case, as in the extension of the democracy, assented to and even promoted a measure which in itself bears a certain resemblance to the less scrupulous policy of Themistocles. The transference however may easily have had full and manifest justification; and that it was passed over so slightly by the historians, rather implies its adoption with a facility that is in accordance with the universal confidence in Aristides; its consequence however could not but have been even more important morally than materially, as conclusively expressing the sanctioned right of Athens to extended metropolitan control.

It is impossible not to be struck with the abstention during all these years from any offensive operations against Persia, of sufficient importance to enforce an historical allusion; this may well have been due on the one hand to the retirement of the Persians from collisions which had so little prospered, and to the comparative insignificance, whatever their number, of those that might have taken place in restoring the independence of minor cities and territories; but indications are not wanting that it was chiefly because Athens was now more immediately concerned in extending, or preparing to extend, her influence within the limits of Hellas. There is a tale in

---

[1] Just. iii. 6.

Plutarch to which we have already adverted, inadmissible as literally told, but which cannot but be noticed once again, as involving elements which, however disarranged, are very distinctly in general harmony with the situation. Themistocles, it is said, conceived a scheme for assuring the supremacy of the Athenians by burning the Hellenic fleet when it was stationed for the winter at Pagasae after the retreat of [1] Xerxes, or generally to burn the Greek naval [2] station. That the story was current in more forms than one is proved by a version of the project quoted by Cicero as referring to Gythium, the port of the Lacedaemonians, and which was destined to be burnt by Tolmides at later date; all accounts agree that the opposition of Aristides was fatal to its entertainment. Through this haze and confusion we at least may be justified in discerning that Themistocles, who had laid out the walls of Athens so as to defy the land force of the Spartans, was prepared to put aside every scruple, should opportunity occur, to render the formation of a rival Hellenic fleet, especially by Sparta, an impossibility. Even less than the infallible faculty of divination that is ascribed to Themistocles, would apprise him that rivalry alone, still more when necessarily compounded with jealous apprehension, must sooner or later bring on a conflict to prove which of the two powers, Athenian or Spartan, Dorian or Ionian, was not merely to have superior control in Greece, but to positively check and overbear the other. That he was even prepared to take the issue at once, in his own time and the earlier the better, may not be too much to infer when we have followed his career to its catastrophe.

This conflict then, for better or worse, was deferred; but in the meantime the influence of Athens might assert a still wider range, and with Themistocles again are connected some hints that her views were already directed westward across

---

[1] Plut. *Themist.* 20.   [2] Ib *Aristid.* 22.

the Ionian sea, to Italy at least.   When Cimon, his political opponent, expressed the contrasted direction of his sympathies by naming his sons Thessalus, Eleus, and Lacedaemonius, it cannot have been without meaning that Themistocles, after adopting such self-asserting names for other children as Archeptolis, Cleophantus, and Nicomache, named two other daughters Italia and Sybaris; as the daughter of his exile afterwards was named by him Asia.   The colony to Thurium, which dates under the administration of Pericles, would thus be a fulfilment of his earlier abortive but definite project.

We are without information as to the precise relation to Athens of those states which, having a certain dependence upon her rather than on Sparta, were yet not members of the Delian confederation.   In this position was Thebes, where democracy had been installed after the suppression of Medism; and the other Boeotian towns, which the same change had released from Theban control, however much of Athenian, on whatever terms, may have taken its place.   The same remark applies to Phocis in a qualified degree, and more positively to Locris, the Medism of which would afford pretext for any amount of interference.   It is highly probable that a certain command was obtained by Athens, through her present position in relation to these regions, over the northern ports on the Corinthian gulf, the ancient outlet of colonising Ionians to Sicily, Italy, and the intermediate islands.   The Ionians of Achaia on the opposite side of the gulf were either brought under Athenian control, or, which is much the same thing, accepted the Athenian alliance at a later date ; but this event, like the interference with the Spartan control of Delphi, seems only to have given form and reality to foregone projects for broadening the basis of Athenian power, which in their mere existence as projects had a reality of their own, and which, when they came to be surmised by the rival or the enemy, had certain very serious consequences forthwith.

The policy of Themistocles to found the influence of Athens

above all things on a predominant navy, and to divert to its
formation, and to the ports and arsenals which it required, the
chief resources of the State, was carried in the first instance,
as we have seen, against the opposition of a party which urged
the advantage and necessity of reliance on a land force. A
union of the two might indeed well seem indispensable for
the support of the vast project which was now more or less
avowedly and which, it is certain, was consciously, entertained.
It was by co-operation of an army and a navy that Persia
had subjugated Ionia, its coast cities and the islands ; it was
by like concurrent action alone that the liberation commenced
in the Saronic gulf had been completed on the slopes of
Cithaeron. It was for want of a powerfully co-operating
land-force that the liberation of the Greeks of Asia could not
penetrate beyond the very fringe of the sea-coast; and if
Athens in the pursuit of her designs had to lay her account
with the possibility of a collision with Sparta, the want of a
countervailing heavy-armed force involved the surrender of
the open country of Attica to plunder and devastation.

A remnant of the old party, ever ready to take a chance for
reviving its fixed idea, might proudly vindicate the ability of
the Athenian hoplites to cope with the redoubted Spartans in
open field ; the less audacious might still be sanguine that the
support of a cavalry force would at least make the balance
even. When we weigh the impression however of the reputation and achievements of the Dorian hoplites, it becomes
quite intelligible that a politician like Cimon should patriotically and in all sincerity hold at last, that while Athens was
bound to do her best to maintain an efficient land-force—
a force as efficient as possible—her great necessity still,
whether as operating against Persia or as hoping to continue
undisturbed at home, was to persevere in a frank and cordial
alliance with Sparta. Thus would the power of Hellas be a
truly perfect organism, and ' limp neither on one leg nor the
other.' So might the action against Persia go on with fullest

effect in expeditions both lucrative and glorious, for which there were still abundant opportunities; while at home the recognised obligation to retain the sympathies of Sparta by deference to her principles, could not but operate to check the constant encroachments of democracy.

There is much in this of 'honest general thought and common good of all' the Hellenic family; but there was little that Themistocles would not denounce as obsolete, or deride as a dream. Athens was committed by circumstances first, and then by all the inducements of honour and of revenue, to a new career, and must make the most of it; must do her best no doubt to maintain power by land, but would assuredly have to rely at last upon the navy, and might safely do so, if this were only so maintained as to be crushingly preponderant.

It is difficult to say that this may not have been the only course that was now open to Athens, albeit involving of necessity a primary defect that was liable to become more and more perilous as events moved on. As the wealth and population of Athens and Attica increased, the theory of Themistocles, that the Athenians must look to their fortified port as their refuge as well as the basis of their power, could only be held to in virtue of a capital modification, the connection of the city with the Piraeus by the long walls which in a few years were to unite the earlier and later city into a single vast stronghold upon the sea. By whomsoever this extension of the original plan was first proposed, it was cordially adopted, as we shall see, with all its implications by Pericles; upon this he based his confidence that when Lacedaemonian opposition broke out into the violence which no politician believed could be postponed indefinitely, Athenian activity and power would make short work in rendering an account of it; how his hopes were falsified in result, and mainly through the catastrophe of the pestilence that decimated the over-crowded city, is the moral of the story that we read in Thucydides.

The policy therefore which the Athenian demus accepted with all its sacrifices for the maintenance of empire, in deference to the arguments and eloquence of Pericles, was the ultimate and most resolute application of the conceptions of Themistocles.

CHAPTER XX.

IT was in the archonship of Menon, 473–472 B.C., when
these contrasted policies were hardening into form and ripening for conflict, that Aeschylus produced his play of the Persae.
In subject it was at least the same, and it was said to have
some correspondence in detail, with the Phoenissae of Phrynichus, which had subserved the glorification of Themistocles
only four years earlier. The story of Salamis could scarcely
be presented again with enhanced dramatic force without
again telling to the same effect, albeit the name of Themistocles
is suppressed throughout, and no lines can be detected as introduced to give occasion for a spontaneous outburst of recognition, as little as any that tend to extenuate his merits by a
cavil. A more direct allusion is sometimes said to be made to
Aristides in the description of the exploit at the island
Psyttaleia; but this was only an episode; even so the name
of the commander is suppressed, and the poet is deferential
throughout to the jealousies of a sovereign people, who could
not endure that the victory of Marathon should be especially
connected with the name of Miltiades, or that the very inscriptions, by which as an unusual honour they commemorated
the highly valued successes and conquests of Cimon in Thrace,
should include his name.

The notion is at the same time too absurd to controvert,
though not to have been stated or adopted, that Aeschylus
in dramatising the story of Salamis, and insisting expressly

on the happy stratagem that determined Xerxes to engage, had in view to derogate from the merits of the Athenian commander, who was notoriously the author of the stratagem, and in favour of Cimon, whose name never positively occurs in connection with the battle at all.

The Persae was one play associated in a tetralogy with three others, of which we fortunately have the titles, though only scantiest fragments; and I have now to show that it is possible to recover such a drift pervading the four, as vindicates for Aeschylus the merit, which Aristophanes asserts as proper to the tragic poets, of being as much the political as the moral monitors of their [1] countrymen.   A poet who addressed a serious play to such an audience as the Athenian, that came to the theatre thrilling with all the agitated and suspended interests of the politics of the time, could scarcely hope to retain attention unless he so chose his theme and treated it, as to affect however covertly whatever sympathies were likely at the time to be most alert and sensitive; he walked amongst the hot embers of political passion, and his gait and deviations were of necessity not uninfluenced.   It was not only that he was concerned to touch their very deepest sensibilities, but that these could not be approached at random or with unconsidered directness; according to circumstances they might for the time be utterly callous to one stimulus, while susceptible, as Phrynichus had found, to exasperation in another.   Distinct allusions to current or even recent politics no doubt appear henceforward resigned to the less dignified handling of the comic poets, but even so the sense of a present or impending crisis can be recognised in many cases as controlling the treatment of a tragic theme.

At the present time, to the stimulus of home politics was added an especial revival of self-consciousness of achievements against the barbarian, from the fame of another naval victory

---

[1] Aristoph. *Ran.*

over .other barbarians at the western extremity of Hellas, achieved by Hiero of Syracuse.   His aid had been solicited by envoys from Cumae, which was threatened by the Etruscans. He appears to have embarked himself, though suffering at the time from a painful disorder, engaged the hostile fleet in the noble bay within sight of the Phlegraean fields, and inflicted a total defeat.   An iron helmet inscribed as his dedication at Olympia from the spoils is now in the British Museum.   In the same year he gained a chariot victory in the Pythian games; and the ode—one of his noblest—in which Pindar celebrates [1] this, celebrates proudly the warlike achievement also, reverts to his earlier victory at Himera over the Phoenician, the Carthaginian barbarian, and associates the rescue of Hellas here from impending slavery, with the Athenian claim to Hellenic gratitude at Salamis and the victory at Plataea, the conquest of the Dorian spear, below Cithaeron.

The occasion was most apt for reviving at Athens the memories that Athens most delighted in, and events that had so many bearings on the actually impending problems of the day.   The complete analysis of the play, and of the tetralogy, in reference to these is the subject of a special dissertation, which cannot be inserted here; but the results of the enquiry may be given; it has convinced me that the poet wrote in no party temper, but as directing enthusiasm in the purest spirit of patriotism to the maintenance of Ionian and Dorian alliance (*homaichmia*), at the same time that he furthered domestic harmony by bringing to mind the services of the politician by whom this alliance might seem to be in most danger of being jeopardised.

The play of the Persae, then, with the account of Salamis, was introduced by the 'Phineus,' and this referred to the previous and preliminary trial of Athenian strength with the Persian

---

[1] *Pyth.* i; cf. *Pyth.* 3, and *Hyporch. frag.* i. 3.

at Artemisium, and it was followed by the 'Glaucus of Potniae,' a mythical subject again, but so treated as to bear immediately on the decisive victory of Plataea, that is foretold in the Persae by the shade of Darius.   This assertion with respect to the 'Phineus' is proved by comparison of the tenor of his mythus with the story of Artemisium as told by Herodotus.   Phineus, the blind king of Salmydessus in Thrace, is the son-in-law of Boreas,—the north wind,—and of the Athenian nymph Oreithyia, whom Boreas carried off from the scene so cele- brated from Plato's description and comments in the Phaedrus. Victim of the foul and violent harpies, he is rescued by the winged sons of Boreas, Zetes and Calais, who drive away his tormentors, pursuing them through the air.   Now it was to the same agencies—to the happy interferences of Boreas, the north wind, and on the same ground of relationship— that the Athenians owned their obligation for the discomfiture of the Persian fleet off the coast of Magnesia and the head- land of Artemisium.   They averred that they had been bidden by an oracle to invoke the aid of their son-in-law Boreas, who responded with such vehement effect accordingly.   How more exactly and pointedly the two stories might be brought together by the poet it were easy to conjecture; but records fail, and having now recovered for the first time the leading import of the drama, we may be better contented to remain in inevitable ignorance of the rest.

It is much the same with the 'Glaucus of Potniae.'   The German critics, to whom we owe so much, have hitherto essayed to help themselves in their difficulties here by substituting, with perfect arbitrariness, another recorded play of Aeschylus, the 'Glaucus Pontieus,' and so have contrived an argument that after all is anything but conspicuously plausible.   The story of Glaucus of Potniae is very variously told indeed.   He ap- pears sometimes as himself a *daemon*, Taraxippus, a 'causer of horse-shying,' sometimes as a hero overthrown by such accident in a chariot race, and—for what impious offence is doubtful—

torn to pieces by his horses maddened by having been watered at a spring at Potniae. Now the Potniae of this mythus may be said to be on the very battle-field of Plataea; it was passed by the *periegetes* Pausanias on his way from that city at about ten stadia from Thebes,—the actual ground occupied by the Persian army and passed over by the pursuing Greeks. The great services of the Athenians in these encounters were against the Persian cavalry, which previous to the battle had choked and ruined the—we may safely assume—sacred fount Gargaphia; and it is at least easy to see how the fate of Masistius and Mardonius on their Nisaean chargers and the rout and carnage of the mounted Immortals may have been brought into connection with interference or desecration at the maddening waters of Potniae close to their encampment.

These combinations are clinched by the peculiar pertinence of the concluding Satyric play—the ' Prometheus, the Fire-lighter or Fire-bringer.' The advent of the element which is the type as the cause of all gladness, and purity, and health, might happily symbolise the restoration of Hellas after the dispersion of the dark barbarian cloud. It had a further specific appropriateness from the formal and ceremonious renewal of pure fire from Delphi, after the Persian evacuation and preparatory to the sacrifice to Zeus Eleutherius.

When we 'look over the single play of the trilogy that is preserved in its entirety, we find very distinct characterisation of the Asiatic Ionians and the European Greeks, especially the Dorians, and the Persians. There is then a very marked contrast effected between Xerxes as the youthful, over-confident, too-widely grasping inheritor of power, and the more wise and sober Darius. The contrast is indeed rather strangely heightened by the ascription to Darius of a moderation in conquest that belies the record of the Scythian and Thracian expeditions which he conducted in person, to say nothing of that which he despatched under Datis and Artaphernes, and was only prevented by death from following up more

T

vigorously. The suppression indeed of every allusion to Marathon by Aeschylus, who himself was a Marathonomachus, might so far be understood if he also had equal part at Salamis, but has certainly some appearance of a declining to seize an opportunity to glorify the house of Cimon. It would be in accordance with such a feeling of the poet that tradition ascribed his final departure from Athens to pique at an award of victory given by Cimon in favour of Sophocles.

The fundamental moral however that underlies the entire play, and comes forward into most definite expression over and over again, is the perilousness of excessive prosperity as provocative to fatal insolence. The catastrophe of such a frame of mind is represented as induced by the agency of a delusive daemon despatched by the gods, as if in envious grudge, to tempt the overweening to their downfall. Prosperity doubtless, even though most innocently or most honourably attained, may prove scarcely less corrupting, scarcely less deluding, than the achievement of a course of violence and guile, and its downfall came thus to be as naturally ascribed to the same grudge of Nemesis ; the warning being as useful in one case as the other. Now this sense of awe at the peril of great prosperity was a commonplace of popular philosophy ; it is the leading moral that is constantly insisted on in the history of Herodotus, and meets us again in that of Thucydides in the mouth of the pietist Nicias, who in deepest disaster has a last hope from the exhaustion of the φθόνος of the gods. So, on the one hand, it furnishes the prime motive of the drama, and, on the other, it is embodied in much later times in the paintings on the large Darius vase of Naples. In the play no doubt the moral is pointed against national enemies, but this would not blunt it in its application to the consciences of the present spectators of the play. The elevation of Athens, the extension of her sway, the swelling of her revenues, had reached such pitch so suddenly, that never could the moral of moderation be more fitly brought forward.

That the example was taken in the case of a conquered enemy served to secure a hearing for the homily, but left its purport quite as unmistakeable. Athens at the head of a confederacy of numerous allies, that varied in every degree of interestedness and loyalty, might take warning if she could from the fate of Xerxes, induced by blindfold elation to assume invincibility, only to witness his motley armament shattered and wrecked at collision with the very first obstacle,—the derision of men and gods.

In this manner the tragedian, while he gratifies to the utmost the national pride of the Athenians, appeals even more distinctly to the common Hellenic feeling in memories of all the most glorious Hellenic achievements, rewards of the united efforts of Dorian and Ionian by land and by sea; nor could this be done without reviving a sense of the merits of the commanders, however their names were passed over in silence,—of Themistocles as well as Aristides, for they had been colleagues in the war, and colleagues afterwards, or certainly not rancorous rivals, in the politics of peace; nor could some sense of sympathy have been unrevived with Pausanias—his errors notwithstanding—with the victor in the last decisive battle, who was still lingering, and doomed so long to linger, and to fret, in obscurity, inaction, and restraint.

CHAPTER XXI.

SINCERE and wise a political monitor as Aeschylus may have been for the Athenians, he was not popular with them in this [1] character; at best they left him, according to his own profession, to dedicate his tragedies to [2] Chronos—Time; they were quite capable of divorcing appreciation of the beauty and force of his poetry from acceptance of its obvious moral. So it was certainly on a later occasion, and so it appears to have been on this. His was a rugged, because a high-principled and a self-reliant nature, and his consideration for the feeling of the day was sufficient to secure attention and engage interest, but did not prevent him from risking administration of a shock. We must not be surprised therefore, if within less than two years after he had revived so gloriously for all the memory of Salamis, the Athenians were in a mood to forget to whom they chiefly owed the victory, and Themistocles was driven from the city, —the city that he had saved, and more than resuscitated,— an ostracised refugee.

The leaders of the opposed party to whom he owed this reverse were Cimon and Alcmaeon — the most important among many; while Aristides, now advanced in age, held himself honourably aloof, whether out of regard to the generosity of Themistocles in his own recall, or to his later

---

[1] Aristoph. *Ran.* 820.　　　　　[2] Athen. p. 348 E.

co-operation with him as a colleague in reform. Such an institution as ostracism—the extrusion of a citizen from the state for years by secret ballot upon no definite charge—does not carry its own justification. According to the most plausible apology, it provided a safeguard available at short notice, when the overgrown influence of an individual threatened republican institutions, and yet might countervail all ordinary legal procedure, or only give a hold for charging treasonable intent when the time had ripened for treason's fatal triumph. By such a process a vague panic, that might or might not be truly prescient, could take security with more certainty and more innocently than by fictitious charges for the occasion. In a less severe contingency the State could so relieve its active policy from the dead-lock of a nearly even balance of parties. These however were more likely to be pretexts for ostracism than the principles of its application. It offered too tempting a chance for the supremacy of faction not to encourage faction; and the need of such a contrivance was warning of constitutional defects that demanded more serious remedies. A polity strong enough to expel a mischief in this manner ought to be strong enough to control it, strong enough to keep a troublesome citizen in subjection, and also in reserve in case those who were so anxious for his expulsion might themselves, when exempt from check, become still more troublesome. Athens, that had been glad to recover the ostracised Aristides just in time, was destined at a later day to reverse another sentence, and be eager to revert after a serious disaster to the counsels and services of Cimon; and at the present time the prolonged exile of Themistocles did not enable his opponents to ward off a crisis which his foresight had anticipated, and which he of all others was most competent to grapple with.

As regards the application of ostracism in this instance, nothing more may be required to account for it than the weariness that will supervene in free communities of the

prolonged leadership of even the most able and most successful single man. This ensues no doubt in part from the
prejudice caused by ever-accumulating secondary lapses and
errors, by insolences and favouritisms, and then by misfortunes
merely unavoidable; but it is also usually due not a little to
the volatility that would have change of tone and topics;
to curiosity, especially on the part of a new generation, as to
proof of untried men of their own generation; to the concurrent impact of class cabals overbearing, each in their own,
the common interest. Full force is lent to these influences
by the eagerness of growing and excluded talent which fairly
and naturally claims an opening and an opportunity, but
of talent also, new or old, which would mount to power by
any means, and can parade the contrast between a purity
that has never had a chance of going wrong, and sagacity
that must needs be sometimes right in a course of general
denunciation; lastly comes in that jealousy, the weakness
of every sovereign power, which ever looks askance at the
exceeding prosperity of those to whom it owes its own, and
resents as an affront with all the venom of vindictiveness the
slightest hint of independence.

In the latter respect chiefly Themistocles was little likely
to escape scot-free in the state which had not been restrained
by either respect or gratitude for Miltiades and Aristides,
notwithstanding the extension of its democratical element
in favour of his most natural supporters. In the absence of
information as to how party opposition came at last to a
crisis, there is significance in the notice of the different
temper in which were regarded the displays of wealth that
were made by Cimon and Themistocles respectively at
the Olympic games. This must have been at the 77th
Olympiad (472–71 B.C.), the second recurrence after the
Medica; for it could not have been in the year of the Medica,
and it was in the immediately ensuing festival that Themistocles had been so universally popular. If we were held to

Plutarch's literal words as to the youth of Cimon at that time, we should be thrown back on another impossibility, the 74th Olympiad, too early in the life of Cimon, too near the death of his father Miltiades in indigence. The splendour of Themistocles in tents, and hospitalities, and apparatus, was carped at as the ostentation of riches, riches that there were too many to denounce, and with too much probability, as ill-acquired ; belonging moreover to a new man : while indulgence was accorded to Cimon, comparatively young and of noble descent, and lavish of wealth unimpeachable in its origin, as a recovered inheritance derived from an ancestry renowned through Hellas.

It was not of the nature, and probably not of the policy, of Themistocles to dissimulate his conception of his own merits and services out of hope to deaden the impact of enviousness. On the contrary, a tone of almost perverse bravado seems to have characterised both his private and his public expressions. At the very time that the Athenians were fretting uneasily with the sense of obligations exceeding their power of requital, he did not hesitate to twit them with their inconsistency in finding benefits burdensome only because they happened to be all conferred by the same man. He likened a grumbler at the large share of advantage that he had secured for himself to the day after a feast, that should discontentedly contrast its fare of orts and leavings with the full provision of the day of the feast itself, that day but for which the day after would have no provender of any kind, no existence at all. He likened himself to a plane-tree to which the Athenians were eager to run for shelter in a storm, but, without gratitude or forethought, despoiled of its branches at the first change to favourable weather. It is more likely to have been his observation to his own son Neocles than, as we read it, that of his father Neocles to himself, that one of his own galleys, open-ribbed and rotting on the shore, was a fair type of the ultimate regard of

Athenians for their best servants. Lastly, in days when his policy was being vigorously impugned, he gave expression to his claim to unerring political insight, by erecting close to his house a fane that he dedicated to Artemis Aristoboule,—Artemis of the most excellent counsel,—perhaps even by setting up therein that statue of himself which Plutarch saw there, in company with one of his descendants, and recognised as presenting lineaments justly expressive of his heroic nature.

The storm that he provoked—as probably as not in the conviction that come it must, and the sooner the better for his chance of dealing with it—broke heavily and with the consequence that we know. His ostracism apparently dates under the archonship of Praxiergus, [1] 471–70 B.C. Among the means by which it was brought about, we must not, out of deference to Plutarch, who is given to idealising his favourites, be induced to overlook the natural tendency of Cimon's employment of his wealth. Cimon and Themistocles are both associated with Pericles as principal contributors to the decoration of the city; but only in the case of Cimon do we hear of devotion of private fortune to such public works, the devotion apparently of spoils of war and presents of allies by which he might without positive malversation have added to his own riches. Fame at least told that he spent funds of his own on the fortifications of the Acropolis, and that he directed, on the erection of porticos, the planting of shady trees about the agora, and the reclaiming of the Academia from drought and sterility by laying it out as a well-watered grove, with cleared places of exercise and shady walks. Others of his generosities wooed popularity still more directly; he scattered coin freely among the paraders of poverty in the [2] agora, and on occasion would bid a well-clothed attendant exchange cloaks with a citizen

---

[1] Diod. xi. 54.   [2] Plut. *Cim.* 10.

encountered in a garb unworthy of his elder years and franchise. We cannot be told that he flung down the fences of his gardens and orchards in order that the indigent, whether native or strangers, might help themselves to the grapes and olives, kept open house daily where the poorer citizens, of his tribe at least if not others, might daily find a modest but welcome meal, and so be able to spare time from labour for public concerns,—this we cannot ponder and not bethink ourselves how such largesse would influence votes; especially when contrasted with the disposition of Themistocles, who insatiate in getting, was never extravagant as if from irrepressible geniality, but rather out of the ostentation that might astonish but conciliated no man. By art then or by argument, by concerted intrigue or as the result of conflict on a positive question of policy, Themistocles was ousted from his position at Athens within about eight years after the battle of Salamis, and had to consider where he would await and perhaps also would be in best position to hasten the reaction, which he surely counted on for his recall; the independent march · of events already threatening might be quickened by influences that he knew how to set well in train, when not only would his foresight be vindicated, but his promptitude of resource be again indispensable. He retired to Argos, a state not in immediate alliance with either Sparta or Athens; with Sparta it had been in such relations of enmity as were its pretext for taking no part in the resistance to Xerxes; while the grave suspicion of Medism under which it laboured was a present bar to the sympathy of Athens. Here therefore he might seem to be resident in a neutral state; he was heard of however, and necessarily with interest or apprehension, as occasionally moving about in various directions in [1] Peloponnesus.

The absence of Themistocles is naturally signalised by conspicuous activity on the part of Cimon. It is within

[1] Thuc. i. 135.

the next year—the archonship of Demotion (470–469 B.C.)—
that [1] Diodorus includes a series of his naval achievements
from Byzantium to the Eurymedon and Cyprus, and adds
to his inaccuracy a certificate in positive terms, 'Such were
the actions of this year.' We are able to correct this chronology on many points by better authorities: part of the
actions thus find their place earlier; the assumption of
command of the Byzantine fleet and the capture of Eïon,
as we have seen; and the battle of Eurymedon as certainly
occurred four years later. Nevertheless there can be little
doubt that some special activity of Cimon at this time—
the year after the exile of Themistocles left him in full power—
must have given Diodorus the hint to insert such an assemblage of his doings under the year. That it was not aggressive action against Persia seems manifest from the following
years being unmarked by any incidents pursuant to such
a present policy. But here Plutarch comes to our aid, who
states that it was in the very next year, the archonship of
Apsephion or Aphepsion, that Cimon brought back to Athens
from Scyros the relics of [2] Theseus; and of this assignment
we shall find very interesting confirmation.

The island of Scyros lies somewhat by itself off the eastern
coast of Euboea; the inhabitants, who are specified as Dolopians along with some Pelasgic [3] admixture, appear to have
been of inferior Hellenisation; even as Dolopians are included
in the Homeric realm of Achilles, but still only at its remotest
[4] outskirts. The contrast that the verdant island presents
in our days to the now dry and naked [5] Cyclades was doubtless not so marked in antiquity, but its northern portion
must always have been peculiarly susceptible of cultivation, and it had good and safe harbours. The inhabitants,
hereditarily more disposed to abuse the latter advantages than
to apply to agriculture, made the neighbouring seas unsafe

---

[1] Diod. xi. 63.   [2] Plut. *Cim.* 8.   [3] Diod. xi. 60.
    [4] *Iliad*, ii. 681; x. 480.   [5] Leake, *N. Greece*, iii. 3.

by piracy, and at last—an enormity beyond the licence of
Homeric days—did not even spare those who resorted to their
shores; and among others plundered and detained some Thessalian traders. The captives escaped and brought their re-
clamation before the Amphictyonic council which met alternately at Thermopylae and Delphi, and in which both the
Thessalians and Dolopians were represented. A fine was imposed, and contention waxed warm in the island when the
authors of the violence tried to shift the mulct from themselves on to the community at large; foreseeing failure in
this scheme, they preferred to invite the intervention of
Cimon, and fulfilled their engagement to him by betrayal
of the city.

The fleet of Cimon was probably already in the neighbourhood; the suppression of piracy was naturally among the
duties of which Athens had assumed the responsibility, and
might be prepared to prosecute quite independently of an
Amphictyonic sentence, however the occasion of this might
have brought matters to a crisis. The acceptance of help
from the traitor pirates is quite consistent with the general
piracy being the pretext or occasion of the severe measures
of the Athenian commander. He took entire possession of
the island, and disposed of the inhabitants as [1] slaves; unfortunately not in itself a proof that they were the barbarians
they are called by Plutarch, though the tribe had evidently
little hold upon public sympathies either by habits or relationship.

The clearance of the island was preparatory to a distribution of the hitherto 'ill-cultivated' lands among Athenian
citizens—cleruchs or holders of allotments; according to Plutarch, this was the second benefit of the kind that they owed
to Cimon, the first having been connected with the capture
of Eïon, which agrees with the interpretation that has been

---

[1] Thuc. i. 98.

given to the brief notice of Thucydides. At the same time
a solemn search was made through the island for the remains
of Theseus, who, according to tradition, had been treacherously
murdered at Scyros by King Lycomedes. As Plutarch relates
in his life of [1] Theseus, it was as early as the archonship of
Phaedon (476–5 B.C.) that the Delphic oracle had enjoined
the Athenians to recover these relics and deposit them
honourably in their city, a notice which has led to the conquest itself being frequently ante-dated. Thucydides has
been falsely quoted to the same effect, but his statement,
though following on a paragraph in which he blames Hel-
lanicus for inaccuracy and negligence in chronology, only
mentions the capture of Scyros as subsequent to that of Eïon,
and does not define the interval either as long or short. We
may be satisfied however with the date given by Diodorus
(470-69 B.C.), associated as it is with whatever blunders, when
we find it confirmed by Plutarch's account that the commands of the oracle, whenever asked for or given, were
fulfilled in the ensuing year (archonship of Apsephion =
469–8 B.C.).

Pausanias rather awkwardly makes the possession of the
remains the condition, not the consequence, of the [2] conquest;
but he may be credited for his agreement with the biographer
in telling how it was due to malignant concealment that the
discovery was a matter of difficulty and there was need of a
certain inspired sagacity. Such obstacles and such assistance
have never failed the resolute pietist from that time to our
own to embellish the unhoped-for recovery of sacred relics.
The mighty remains were found, of course; they were recognised by their heroic magnitude: beside them lay a spear-
head and sword, authenticated by the bronze material as of
the heroic ages. Transferred by Cimon to a trireme magnifi-
cently decorated, they were brought to Athens, with pomp

---

[1] Plut. *Thes.* 36.   [2] Paus. iii. 3. 5.

and popular rejoicing, as if for the return of the very hero himself, 'after eight hundred years;' a satire, if any cared to point the moral, on the popular ingratitude that was even yet not obsolete.

Among the various comments that have been made on these transactions, it seems worth while to signalise the following extract, though it is probably more accurately illustrative of the genius of some unpleasant passages of contemporary history, than of the career and character of Cimon.

'The whole undertaking which was so successfully accomplished by Cimon,' says a German historian, 'and which so firmly established his fame, was in every respect most opportune for him. Hence a conjecture naturally suggests itself, that the opportune occurrence of its two causes, viz. the Delphic oracle and the complaint of the Thessalians, was occasioned by a mutual agreement : in which case we should have to admire in Cimon not only the successful general, but also the statesman possessed of sagacious forethought, and capable of exerting a far-reaching influence by means of the combinations at his ¹ command.'

The sacred remains found a resting-place in the midst of the city, close to what, in Plutarch's time at least, was the site of the gymnasium. That the temple which still remains so wonderfully preserved is justly called the Theseum has never been questioned on reasonable grounds, though it is uncertain, but uncertain only, whether its erection dates quite so early. The precinct attached to it was constituted an asylum for household slaves and other meaner victims of oppression,— recognition of an heroic career of protection extended to the weakest. Pausanias indicates the locality in the same terms as Plutarch,—'the hieron of Theseus near the gymnasium of the agora ;' and the collocation was probably not uninfluenced by the national tradition that to Theseus was due the application

---

¹ Curtius, *History of Greece,* 1869 ; and compare Goethe, Reineke Fuchs, *sub fin.*

of skill to wrestling,—the proper exercise of the palaestra,—which had previously been a contest of mere brute [1] strength.

The title Theseum is fully vindicated for the structure by the agreement of the still existing external sculpture with the notice of [2] Plutarch, that at Athens the Theseia and the Heracleia were interchangeable. The metopes of the eastern front are occupied by the labours of Hercules, and those of the western with such parallel exploits of Theseus as his slaughter of the Minotaur, punishment of Skiron, capture of the Marathonian bull, and so forth.

The frieze of the posticum is sculptured in high relief with the battle against the Centaurs, in which Theseus is ever the protagonist ; the subject on the pronaos is more obscure, but a battle against rock-hurling antagonists is recognisable, and it would seem must represent a gigantomachia ; and in that case may probably be the contest of Hercules against the giants of the isthmus of [3] Pallene, and not without allusion to the exploits of Athens and Cimon in the liberation of that region after the fall of Eïon.

Pausanias mentions three paintings of Micon in the interior ; two of the subjects would be appropriate pendants on the opposite lateral walls. One was the ever-varied, ever-repeated battle of Theseus with the Centaurs, in which Theseus had already killed his Centaur, while between the other combatants victory was still in suspense ; the other, the battle of the Athenians and Amazons, doubtless included again an exploit of the hero as antagonist of Antiopa or [4] Hippolyta. The third subject, which would be the principal, as occupying the end wall opposite the entrance, was partly unfinished by the painter, and partly obliterated beyond recognition. The subject of it—so I read my author—appears to have been the adventure by which Theseus vindicated his descent from the sea-god Poseidon from the aspersions of Minos, and ap-

[1] Paus. i. 39. 3.
[2] Plut. *Thes.* 35.
[3] Apollod. i. 6. 1.
[4] Plut. *Thes.*

parently in the presence of the youths and maidens whom he
had led to Crete.   He brought back from the depths a ring
that the Cretan had thrown in to test him, and returned
crowned with a coral wreath, the gift of Amphitrite.

It was fully in the manner of the Greeks to assume that
the mythical death of Theseus at the hands of King Lycomedes
of Scyros was a quite available indictment against successors,
their own contemporaries, even apart from the late convictions
for piracy; but Cimon had no indirect personal interest in
this ceremonial re-establishment of Theseus in his city.   To
Theseus was ascribed a most important part in his father's
victory of Marathon; the legend of the hero told how he had
mastered and bound the destructive bull of Marathon;
in origin probably it is a physical legend of the regulation of
the torrent that still breaks its bonds—a bull being the
accepted type of a rushing torrent—and damages agriculture
so far as it is at present carried [1] on.   The legend may all the
same have reflected at another time the conclusion of a contest
between Attica and the Marathonian tetrapolis.   In the [2] Poecile
Stoa, in a great picture of the battle of Marathon, Theseus
was shown rising out of the earth in the very scene of his
traditional exploit to take part in the fight along with
Hercules, whose fane was on the battle-field, Athena herself,
and the eponymus hero Marathon.

In virtue of such familiar associations it was that this
dedication and pompous translation of relics revived the glory
of the earlier and more peculiar triumph of the Athenians over
the barbarians, almost as if in rejoinder to the trilogy of the
Persae; and yet the son of Miltiades, well warned, and with
something more than the affected modesty of Shakespear's
Henry V, evaded the grudge that attached to the self-
asserting inscription of his father.

It can only be thrown out as a vague conjecture that

---

[1] Leake, *Top. Att.*   [2] Paus. i. 15. 3.

Lycomedes of Scyros may have been connected, traditionally
or invidiously, with the gens of Athenian Lycomidae, or
Lycomedae, to whom Themistocles claimed to be related.
They were a priestly race who administered peculiar initiations of the Great goddesses,—of Ge or Earth, of Kouré
Protogoné,—and sung at their celebrations hymns of Pamphus
and Orpheus; the latter few and short, and if we were disposed to take the word of Pausanias, only inferior as poems to
Homer's, in sanctity far [1] above.   Themistocles rebuilt the
telesterion of the Lycomidae at the demus Phlya which had
been burnt by the Medes, and adorned it with paintings.
We learn from a fragment of Plutarch preserved by Hippolytus
on Heresies, that the mysteries of the Great goddesses at
Phlya were at least claimed as even more ancient than those
of the same goddesses under other names at [2] Eleusis.

In this year the Parian marble, in accordance with Plutarch,
dates the first tragic victory gained by Sophocles, and Plutarch
says over Aeschylus, though he grossly antedates the retirement of the latter to Sicily in final disgust with Athens as
taking place upon this occasion.   The audience we are told
were balanced in preference, and the archon Aphepsion, with
whom it rested to determine judges by lot, remitted the
decision instead to Cimon and his fellow generals, who, by
coincidence or otherwise, were present in the theatre to make
the formal libations to the gods; 'and so the custom originated of judges of tragedies being ten in number, one from
each tribe like the generals, and so the decision passed in
favour of Sophocles.'   The generals seem to have entered
when the plays were over; their judgment must in this case
therefore have applied to an estimate of voices.

Without committing ourselves to accept the details of this
story in full, we need not doubt that the name of Cimon was
associated in some remarkable manner with this tragic victory

---

[1] Paus. i. 22. 7; i. 31. 4; iv. 1. 8; ix. 27. 2; ix. 30. 12.
[2] Welcker, *Götterlehre*, i. 322.

of a new poet, and not without some understanding of a party feeling.

The presidency of the Archon eponymus determines the representation for the greater Dionysia in his ninth month (Elaphebolion), the spring of 468 B.C. The date corresponds · with that recorded for the Triptolemus of [1] Sophocles, a drama the few surviving lines of which form part of a geographical excursus in the antique style of those in the Prometheus, Persae, and Supplicants of Aeschylus. In this extant passage Demeter is describing to the hero the various countries he is to visit on his beneficent errand of spreading the culture of bread-corn. There is a passage in the life of Cimon by Plutarch, which reads much as if it echoed some earlier comparison of him to Triptolemus, and it is open to conjecture that the original praise referred less directly to his home liberalities than to the colonies that had just been settled by him in what are emphatically called the hitherto ' ill-cultivated ' fields of Scyros. ' The lavish liberality of Cimon,' he says, ' exceeded even the antique hospitality and philanthropy of the Athenians ; for they communicated to the Greeks, what the city justly is proud of, the seed (corn) of food, and taught mankind the use of spring water and the art of lighting fire ; but he made his house a common prytaneum for the citizens, and by free communication of the best and rarest produce of his land seemed to bring back in a manner the fabled communistic state of the time of [2] Cronus.'

It seems characteristic of the prompt succession of genius in these Athenian years, that the date of the first entrance of Pericles into politics is calculated to be almost coincident with the death of Aristides. It is only by such reckoning, not by any historical record of his earlier participation in in affairs, that the fact is known. His father Xanthippus has been missed from story since the victory of Mycale. It was

---

[1] Plin. *H. N.* xviii. 7.   [2] Plut. *Cim.* 10.

probably another member of his family, Alcmaeon, who along
with Cimon pressed forward the ostracism of [1]Themistocles;
and it was the son of Alcmaeon, Leobotes, who in concert with
the Laconising party and agents, would afterwards have substituted for admonitory ostracism either the severer penalty
of exile and consequent forfeiture of estate, or, even more
eagerly, that of death. Eleven years had elapsed since
Salamis, and a generation was come to maturity which had
grown up in an atmosphere of enthusiasm, and regarded
national progress as a law of nature. Some great names of
the past were still remaining, vigorous and even progressive
still both in politics and arts; but the men who were now
coming into prominence had purposes and projects of their
own, for which all that had been done was mere preparation,
and were urged by an unresting consciousness of power within
to claim an immediate share in the guidance of national
energies worthy of and demanding their best services.

It must have been about this time, possibly this year,
that the death of Aristides occurred; at a time when, for
whatever cause, he appears to have so far withdrawn from
active politics that his departure involved no such change
as to make a record of it inevitable. Later writers, whilst
recording the fact that he left neither portions for his
daughters nor enough money for his funeral expenses, contrast
this so-called honourable poverty, and the sordid poverty of
his descendants, with the worldly wisdom of Themistocles,
the appropriate rewards of which were enjoyed by himself
to the last, and transmitted to his descendants through long
generations. 'The Seven against Thebes' of Aeschylus is
dated as produced under the next archon, Theagenides,
and an anecdote exists to the effect that the line in which
the poet characterises Amphiaraus as 'one who seeks not to
seem but to be really just' was greeted enthusiastically by

---

[1] Plut. *Aristid.* 25.

the audience as applicable to Aristides. The story comes off
but haltingly unless the application can be understood as
extending to the general context, which would distinctly
imply that the merits of Aristides were in marked contrast to
the unworthiness and unpopularity of his recent colleagues.
An Athenian audience is not to be lightly charged with the
inept perversity of catching at the terms of a single expression without completely apprehending its drift and purport.
If we are to accept the anecdote at all, we must take it as an
expression of regretful condemnation of a once esteemed and
even venerated favourite who had recently been found on the
wrong, that is on the then unpopular, side. This may well
have been the case if, during the recent unpopularity of
Themistocles which resulted in his ostracism, Aristides had
held aloof from the persecution,—still more if he had loyally
remained by the side of one with whose character his own was
so contrasted, but with whom, though once in rivalry, he had
co-operated frankly in imperial organisation and domestic
[1] reform.

Concurrent possibly with these transactions, but certainly
concluded later, was a war with Carystus in Euboea—under
conduct of what commander is not mentioned. Carystus was
Dryopian, and it is therefore fair to conjecture that the quarrel
was connected with the arbitrary treatment of Scyros. When
Datis and Artaphernes had moved from Delos upon Athens
and Eretria, Carystus had gallantly refused to surrender
hostages or to take part in hostilities against her neighbour
cities, but was forced to give way to positive pressure. It
was probably due to the continued influence of a Medising
party then placed in power that the city became liable to the
penalties for which, as we have seen, it had already in vain
attempted to compound by bribes to Themistocles. Strength
of position that enabled it to resist [2] then, as it had previously

[1] Plutarch; *Comparison of Aristides and Cato*, iii. 5.   [2] Hes. viii. 112.

encouraged resistance to the Mede, enabled it to hold out
again, although unsupported by other Euboean cities even
of the same Dryopian kinship. The besiegers had to lament
some losses; here died Hermolycus, who deserved best of
all the Athenians at [1] Mycale; but the defence, however
prolonged by [2] obstinacy, was hopeless of ultimate success;
·it ended in a capitulation, and the story brings us upon the
Carystians later [3] on as duly contributory to the *phoros.*

---

[1] Herod. ix. 105.   [2] Thuc. i. 99.   [3] Ib. vii. 57.

CHAPTER XXII.

It is not easy to believe that the art of painting had not as worthy and as remote an antiquity among the Greeks as sculpture; yet the almost entire absence of record of great works in this art, and of great names anterior to the age of Cimon and his friend Polygnotus, is in striking contrast both to the traditional and the authenticated records respecting works in metal and marble. Such difference no doubt does but represent in a general way the relative unimportance of painting throughout the whole development of Greek art. There is no account of the production by Greek painting, even when at its highest technical perfection, of works that could range in dignity and scope with the great compositions of Alcamenes and Polycletus, not to say of Pheidias; the pictures in fact that come nearest to this standard are those of Polygnotus, almost the very first of which we have any distinct account, and these are too near the transition from earliest rudimentary forms to have a chance of reaching it. It is possible that the application of colour to the great chryselephantine statues of gods and goddesses and to their ornamental accompaniments had in a certain degree the effect of superseding the rivalry of painting; as indeed the very perfection of sculpture might seem to render such rivalry hopeless. The conditions were the reverse of those which controlled the great development of Italian art, when even

Buonarroti, the greatest modern genius for sculpture, renounced the chisel under the force of circumstances, in order
to embody his sublimest conceptions by what was to him the
less congenial pencil. The principle of the variegation of
sculpture may be recognised even on the Homeric shield
of Achilles, where many figures and objects which were
wrought in metal, and, as must be supposed, in relief, are
distinguished either by symbolical or by apt local colours.
The gods Pallas and Ares are golden and clad in golden
armour; and Fate, as she drags along the bodies of the
slaughtered, has a garment dabbled with the gore of men;
the furrows are represented, 'a marvel of art,' as black-
ening behind the ploughs; black clusters of grapes hang
from vines supported by silver props; the watery moat of
the vineyard is azure, the fence that encloses it is of tin;
the colours of the oxen are diversified by gold and tin, and
the dancing youths, dressed in delicate glistening chitons,
have swords of gold pendent from silver baldrics. For
other distinct applications of colour in Homer, there is
little to refer to, beyond the ships' sides painted red, and
the ornamental staining of ivory by Carian women; but
there can be little hesitation in inferring that the battles
of Greeks and Trojans, that Helen occupies herself in
working, were conceived, and intended to be conceived, as
made out in diversified and appropriate colours. The em-
broideries of Phoenicia, Babylon, or Assyria are of a far
remoter date, and in fact allusion is made to the possession
of Sidonian [1] specimens.

In times far earlier than Greek legend even pretends to
refer to, drawing in outline and painting in flat tints at
least had been in vogue both in Assyria and Egypt, and
some of their advanced applications might have been first
borrowed directly from those sources by the Greeks at any

---

[1] *Iliad,* vi. 289.

time, and taken as starting-points for further progress and improvement.   It is however quite consistent with historical experience, that a nation which is endowed with capacity for an independent start, will not easily resign a first intention even for the benefit of something better that is to be obtained by borrowing, but rather pursues pertinaciously its own first idea; and when it borrows at all, and even when it borrows freely, does so less by adopting what is alien, than by associating and assimilating it almost beyond recognition.   Even at the present time, for all the ease and rapidity of travel and transport and communication, the thought of modern Europe developes for the most part in parallel lines; and not only art and philosophy, but even the sciences, struggle in every country to continue national, and would fain assert hereditary rather than theoretical succession.   The Greeks, especially, loved to consider all arts and sciences as having originated independently amongst themselves; in their case, if ever, a very excusable mistake and not unnatural boast, for never was there a race that more positively subjected all borrowings to their individual genius.

Certain incidents and epochs of the art of painting occur in scattered mention as anterior to Polygnotus; and some such, even many such, there doubtless must have been; but the notices are vague and questionable, and wanting in detailed individuality and historical certitude, and seem for the most part merely contrived to eke out the customary statement of progressive development by a succession of inventors.   A list, however full, of names of unknown or uncharacterised artists, goes for nothing; and it is much if we can occasionally identify agreement of the traditions with something more than mere general probabilities, and connect them consistently with seats of the art in later days.

The black figures upon red ground of the earliest vases represent the *skiagraphia*, the production of monochrome drawings by the aid of shadows; and this is given as the earliest form of the art of painting as practised at Sicyon and Corinth and Samos. So Saurias of Samos was said to have delineated a horse after the shadow cast by sunlight, and the daughter of Dibutades at Corinth the profile of her lover after the shadow thrown by artificial light. On the vases the delineation of figures in black on lighter ground is helped by interior lines scratched with a sharp point through the dark paint, and it is noted as a further advance when interior lines were introduced in the monochrome paintings. The incised line is sometimes employed to give exactness of definition even to the proper outlines or contours of the black figures. With this aid and no more, groups of very considerable complication are rendered perfectly distinct,—as for instance the four horses of a chariot very slightly advanced beyond each other, the attendants beside and beyond them, the warrior in the chariot; at the same time very considerable taste is exercised in securing so much definition of the forms by free outline, as not to throw the main balance of responsibility on the interior incised lines. The practice of some of the earlier vase-painters, of inscribing not only the names of persons represented,—'Achilles' or 'Ajax,'—but also of objects that perfectly and even excellently explain themselves, such as 'a fountain,' 'a hydria,' 'a seat,' at least explains the origin of the tradition that the earliest paintings were so rude, that man or horse or tree were undistinguishable without such written hint and aid. That such aid was ever really required, and thence survived by habit after the necessity had gone by, is hard to think; the application of determinatives in hieroglyphics is a proof how, in the earliest times, it was painting that came to the aid of syllabic writing rather than the reverse.

In the next stage of vase-painting, the figures are red upon a black ground; or rather they are made out by the proper red ground of the vase being left untouched

within their outlines and painted black without and around
them; the incised line, being no longer applicable for the
interior, is now superseded by painted black lines; the colour
of the vase supplies a certain resemblance to the local
colour of the nude. So Dibutades of Corinth was said to
have modelled in clay the face of his daughter's lover, upon
the outline she had drawn, and added artificial red to the
material; and Cleophantus of Corinth to have filled up
outline drawings with a red colour obtained by pounding
terra cotta.

When the vase-painter laid down the pointed tool to take
to the brush exclusively, he had already acquired command
of hand in drawing; and very refined delineation and beautiful lines are often found associated, however strangely at
variance, with the rude principle of the process. The new
process was soon eager to prove its own independent powers;
and preferred to continue even more strictly monochrome
than that which it superseded, renouncing some approaches
that had already been made with the black figures to the
application of local colour, in arms and ornaments. The
distinguishing of female figures by white faces and flesh,
which had been in truth less an advance to proper local
colour than a supplement in the way of symbolism, was
given up along with irrational inscriptions, as not only
unnecessary, but obsolete. At this stage the Greek was
well content for ceramic painting to make a long halt,
until it had perfected a style appropriate to its application
and opportunities; it is simple, free, and refined, but with
no affectation of an exactness which must invariably have
failed in a process by its nature excluding not only palliation
of *pentimenti*, but, much more, their correction.

Eumarus of Athens and Cimon of Cleonae are names
associated by Pliny with improved skill and daring in
draughtsmanship,—both of uncertain, but by manifest implication of very early dates; for to Eumarus is assigned

renown for his success in distinguishing male and female
figures, as well as his bold imitation of varied [1] attitudes.
Cimon is credited with the further advancement of these
feats, by venturing to represent foreshortened [2] figures, and
presentations of the countenance in varied aspects—looking
back, upwards, or downwards; the expression of joints and
veins, more probably muscles; and, very important indeed,
the folds and waves, the arranged or accidental convolutions,
of drapery. Here again we may trace upon the vases a
parallel advance in the direction of elegance and nature,
from the stiff and formal draperies of the archaic style,
neither swayed by air nor swung by movement, nor indi-
cating, by apparent capacity to sink or swell, the natural
modelling of the limbs [3] beneath. If these innovations could
really be brought home to the name, Cimon of Cleonae—an
Homeric dependency of Mycenae—would justly rank as one
of the best deserving masters in the history of art.

The historical notices thus far refer less to painting proper
than to simple draughtsmanship, which has however, at least
in the case of bas-relief, an equally direct application to
sculpture. It is only when we reach Polygnotus that we
encounter hints of the proper glories of painting, for even·
his father Aglaophon has no verified claim beyond standing
on the record as instructor of his son.

Polygnotus was of the wealthy island of Thasos, and his
date is fixed generally by his known relations to Cimon
and to Elpinice, before she was quite so old as Pericles
thought her in 463-2 B.C. The inscription for his Delphic
picture is ascribed to Simonides, who died four years earlier,
Ol. 78. 2 = 467-6 B.C., and gives perhaps a more precise
date. The picture was executed by him for the Cnidians;
his friend Cimon was at Cnidus before the battle of the Eurymedon 466-5 B.C., but as this was in the next year after the

---

[1] *Figurae omnes.* Pliny, xxxv. 34.   [2] *Catagrapha, obliquae imagines.* Ib.
[3] Cf. Aelian, *V. H.* viii. 8.

death of Simonides, the inference appears to be that this dedication of the Cnidians was anterior to their participation in the spoils of Eurymedon. We are thus thrown upon an earlier date for the motive and occasion of the picture,—to the days immediately after the liberation of the Ionian cities and of Thasos from the Persians, and the time of the transactions of Cimon with the Amphictyons at Thermopylae, relatively to Scyros, 476 B.C.

Again, Polygnotus decorated with paintings the Theseum, which received the bones of the hero about 469–8 B.C. As regards the style, modes, and manner of Polygnotus, Pliny states that he painted the drapery of his female figures as transparent; and Lucian has a reference to the delicacy with which he depicted it as either gathered naturally in folds or fluttering in the wind; Aelian is another authority to the same effect. [1] Cicero names him as one of the painters who employed only four colours, of which one was [2] black; a simplicity for which, as it seemed to Quintilian, it could only be affectation to profess admiration. Criticism therefore it seems was already known in antiquity, to be given to assert peculiar insight, to be jealous of the claims of beauty that condescended to be manifest to unsophisticated taste, or even that reposed on the best judgments of the past, and preferred to announce a revelation of it where it must needs be a mystery to the rest of the world. The better critics however, it is most certain, did not err in their lofty estimate of the art of Polygnotus, restricted as were his appliances. Nor were his resources in respect of colour too narrow to admit of great variety. That he was liberal in the variegation of feminine head-dresses is an unimportant matter; more to the purpose are the notices that he did not content himself with flat uniform tints, but compassed gradations both of tints and

---

[1] *Brut.* 18.　　　　　[2] Plin. xxxiii. 12; xxxv. 6.

tone, and so made the first and all-important advance beyond
monochrome. He painted fishes as seen indistinctly in the
dark waters of Acheron; the vast and mutilated form of
Tityus in Hades was mysteriously obscure; the daemon
Eurynomus was coloured like the flesh-flies; the wrecked
Oïlian Ajax was recognised with his sea stains about him;
the cheeks of the abused Cassandra bore the tender blush
of her situation.

As regards expression, the blush of Cassandra was in
harmony with the beauty of her [1] brows. And his Polyxena
was praised still more enthusiastically; he gave movement
to lips, exposed teeth, relieved physiognomy from archaic
rigidity; he represented the tender, the pathetic, the impulsive, the reserved, the heroic.

Hence Polygnotus is to Aristotle the ethical [2] painter,—
the ethical artist indeed as compared either with sculptors
or painters, especially as compared in his own art with
Pauson and [3] Zeuxis. Polygnotus, says Aristotle, exceeded
reality in his representation of man, Pauson fell below it,
Dionysius was on the same level.

We have most happily a detailed description by Pausanias of his great paintings in the Lesche, or public apartment for conversation, at Delphi, the work already referred
to which he executed for the citizens of Cnidus. Like so
many of the early Italian painters, and under the same
influence of requirement to cover large architectural spaces
with subjects that could not appropriately be disconnected
with each other, he had very large views of composition,
both as within each separate picture and as demanding
certain connections and contrasts of one picture with another.
In such early combinations we constantly find a well-marked
gradation in associated dignities, so that a subordinate subject supports a principal, whether the secondary subject be

---

[1] Lucian, *Imagg.* 7. [2] Arist. *Poet.* vi. 15; *Polit.* viii. 5. [3] Ib. *Poet.* ii. 2.

introductory or, as more frequently, a sequel, or as, perhaps with equal frequency, with no pragmatical interdependence, but an ideal antitype.

The subjects, disposed on opposite walls, to right and left of the entrance, were the Capture of Troy and Departure of the Greeks on the right; and on the other side, scenes in Hades, including the descent of Ulysses to consult Teiresias. The figures in each were very numerous—as many indeed as seventy—but disposed in groups of considerable independence, so that the picture might seem made up of a system of groups in separate though not harshly disconnected scenes. Names were inscribed in archaic fashion, in one case even a collective description is added—'The Uninitiated.' I have given [1] elsewhere a detailed exposition of these pictures, group by group and indeed figure by figure, with illustrative restorations for which the account of Pausanias gives inviting opportunity. The aim at symmetry is very marked in particular groups, and still more so in their general correspondence with each other; in one degree less formally than in the Aeginetan pediments, but still as decidedly in intention. In each case we see that grace and variety are superinduced upon a sublying arrangement as orderly as a pattern, and always more or less discernible, but not least happy in effect when least conspicuous; even as the disorder of fluttering drapery owes its gracefulness considerably to the occult but still regulative fact that it is order in disturbance.

Disconnected as the several groups might be in action, a very considerable breadth of effect was compassed in general composition, and that in spite of the still further difficulty that the groups were in rows, two, three, or even more, one above another, and—at least so far as appears—without either perspective diminution or continuous landscape. The practice of the Apulian vase-painters, although at a considerably later

---

[1] Falkener's *Museum of Classical Antiquities.*

date, may be taken as exemplifying the conventions of this
style of painting, where disgrace of failure was precluded by
limitation of what was attempted ; the vase-painters judi-
ciously recognising the need of the limitation in their own
case long after painting in the larger sense had as wisely
asserted its emancipation.   In the Capture of Troy the
central portion exhibited the ruthless prosecution of the
slaughter by Neoptolemus, the demolition of the walls, and
the Greek chiefs in council on the subject of an act of
sacrilegious violence by one of their number during the
sack.   These groups were flanked on one side by the heaps
of slain, the burials in progress, the spared Trojans preparing
for retirement inland ; on the other by more important groups
of wounded and captives, and Greeks preparing to embark
with recaptured Helen and spoil.

The groups of this wing of the composition are more
weighty and numerous than those of the other, and were
made so not without artistic design ; it is thus intimated
that the first long composition is not complete in itself but
demands a sequel,—found in fact in the opposite picture,—
which concludes, as this commences, with a more impressive
mass of groups.   The subjects are thus not only paired anti-
thetically, but knit together as one in general intention by
common reference to terminal inclusions, commencing the
first, concluding the last.

In the second subject, the general scene is indicated most
emphatically, no longer by the central but by the terminal
groups ; giving correlative representations of the punishment
of the irreligious and impious—Tantalus, the Danaids, Sisyphus
at one end ; Tityus, the parricidal and sacrilegious man, at the
other.   The intermediate space, in contrast to the first picture,
has no central compartment, but is divided by a comparatively
blank central space between two lateral systems, each in symmetry at once independent and contrasted.   These intermediate
combinations are formed of groups of heroes and heroines, of

the Homeric period chiefly, represented as occupants of the underworld.

It was by an oversight that, in rearranging the groups of Riepenhausen, I missed the necessity for another capital modification, and failed to reverse the sequence of groups in the second picture. Pausanias goes through the subjects in order, beginning on his right as he entered the building; but when he reached the end of one wall he naturally and properly enough passed over to the corresponding end of the opposite wall, and so worked back towards the entrance. The relative collocation of figures as opposite to each other is therefore represented falsely by a drawing which follows the enumeration as if both series commenced at the same end of the building.

It surprises us at first to find that pictures dedicated at Delphi can be so entirely without allusion to Apollo, the peculiar god of this most sacred locality; but the solution of the difficulty, though it carries us into remote associations, is complete, and is a most remarkable exemplification of the retentiveness of Hellenic memory for tribal connections. Religious allusion is not and could not be omitted, but it refers to the worship not of Apollo, but of divinities whom his splendour might have obscured but was powerless to obliterate,—to the Pelasgic worship of the powers of earth and of the underworld, whose seat he invaded, and only occupied at last by a compromise and alliance such as he himself afterwards had to concede to Dionysus. The Amphictyons who met at Delphi also assembled on alternate occasions at Thermopylae, at the temple of Demeter; and the worship of Demeter was most affected by those earlier colonists of Cnidus who, starting from the neighbouring coasts, had again transmitted the worship from their new seats to new colonies, and to times far later than those we are now dealing with.

I have pursued this subject in detail in my historical illustrations of Pindar's Sicilian Odes.

Thus is accounted for the introduction, that might otherwise seem intrusive here, of reference by typical incidents and
inscriptions to the rites and initiations of Demeter. The
Danaids are inscribed as contemners of her mysteries, and her
Thasian priestess Cleoboia crosses the Acheron holding her
sacred cista.

The episode of Ulysses, who consults Teiresias as to his safe
.return to Ithaca, connects the subject of this picture with that
of the sack of Troy and departure of the Greeks. The successful issue of the Trojan war meets us again and again at
this time, as an adopted mythical prototype of the recent
victories over the Asiatic host of Xerxes, and was probably
intended to be understood so here. At the same time the
predominant sentiment of the designs is the inculcation of
moderation in victory, especially in the matter of respect for
sanctities and sanctuaries. Neoptolemus, who had a traditional ill-name for sacrilege at Delphi, is conspicuous here for
regardless blood-thirst; and the central subject of all is the
reprobation by the Hellenic kings of the unholy violence of
Locrian Ajax.

The recovery of Aethra, the mother of Theseus, supplies an
Athenian allusion which might be gratifying to Cimon.

The Peisianactian, afterwards called the Poecile Stoa, at
Athens was decorated with paintings, partly at least by
Polygnotus, and partly by Micon, who appears as his colleague in another instance, and partly, as it seems, though at
a later date, by Panaenus, brother of Pheidias.

Pausanias, who gives no names of painters, enumerates—

(1) Battle of Athenians and Lacedaemonians at Oenöe in
Argolis; the battle and the painter are alike unrecorded.

(2) The battle of Theseus and Athenians with the Amazons;
distinctly ascribed to [1] Micon.

(3) The third, which [2] Plutarch ascribes to Polygnotus, was

---

[1] Aristoph. *Lysist.* 678 ff.   [2] *Cimon,* 4.

at least a repetition of the subject that he painted at Delphi,—
the Capture of Troy and debate on the sacrilege of the Locrian
Ajax. This latter incident was painted again by an Athenian
at Olympia, and must have been recommended by some
specific application to current feelings, apparently as repro-
bating the sacrilege of the northern Greeks, who had abetted
that of the Persians. It was in this that a portrait of Elpinice
was introduced as Laodice, the most beautiful of the daughters
of Priam.

(4) And the most celebrated—the battle of Marathon, which
authorities ascribe variously to Micon and to Panaenus.

The subjects chosen indicate the prevailing influence of
Cimon, the son of the victor at Marathon.

In the temple of the Dioscuri at Athens, Polygnotus painted
their marriage with the daughters of Leucippus,—how treated
the text does not enable us even to conjecture. Micon painted
here the Argonauts,—including, no doubt, the Dioscuri,—
though the picture was chiefly admired for the horses of
Acastus.

In the Pinacotheca, at the entrance of the Propylaea,
Pausanias saw six pictures among others of which he gives the
subjects, and seems to ascribe them all—the more probably as
they seem to constitute a set—to Polygnotus.

(1) Diomedes carrying off the Palladium from Ilion.

(2) Ulysses obtaining the bow of Philoctetes in Lemnos.
Here we have manifestly a pair; and the common theme of
fraudulent capture of a charm involving the fate of a city
may be taken as an appropriate warning to wardens of an
Acropolis.

(3) Orestes slaying Aegisthus, and Pylades the sons of
Nauplius, who come to his rescue.

(4) Polyxena on the point of being sacrificed at the tomb of
Achilles. This was no doubt the Polyxena that we have
found cited with admiration.

These two subjects have this at least in common, that they

x

are parallel examples of revenge, retributive or superstitious, for the death of a father.

(5) Achilles among the virgins at Scyros,—whether at the moment of his discovery by Ulysses as represented in many ancient works of art, especially in a very remarkable Pompeian picture, does not appear.

(6) Ulysses himself, and the maidens along with Nausicaa, at the river.

Here again a parallelism is palpable,—in each picture a discovered hero and scared maidens,—but not so any definite reference to the place or to the companion pictures.

Lastly may be noticed the pictures in the pronaos of the temple raised by the Plataeans to Athene Areia,—the Warrior Athene,—Pausanias says from their share of the spoils of the victory at Marathon.

(1) By Polygnotus,—Ulysses immediately after the slaughter of the suitors.

(2) By Onasias, a painter otherwise unknown,—the first expedition of the Argives against Thebes.

The date of this temple, no doubt, can scarcely but have been later than the demolition of Plataea and its sanctuaries by the Persians, but even so, as peculiarly commemorative of the battle of Marathon, it would be considered as built from the spoils, while it might all the same receive dedications in memorial of later victories.

The paintings at least have much more obvious reference to Plataea than to Marathon. Plataeans restored to home and territory after prolonged exile, and recovering all and more than all after decisive victory and a general slaughter of their enemies at their very gates, might fairly look through Homer and find and wish no fairer antitype of their triumph than Ulysses standing in blood amidst the heaped bodies of his enemies in his own recovered palace hall. But otherwise I am much disposed to question the ascription of the picture to Polygnotus, and to connect the subject with the much later

incident of the slaughter by the Plataeans of the treacherously
intrusive Thebans, the opening incident of the Peloponnesian
war.

The selection of the other subject as appropriately typical
of the position of Plataea at this time has peculiar interest,
because it explains how the Athenians also may have been
consistently disposed to read off the significance of the same
subject as it was treated at this time by Aeschylus in the
Seven against Thebes. The discomfiture of the Argives might
seem to represent a triumph for Thebes; but it was evidently
not so regarded. The assailant himself was a Theban, and he
fell, like the Theban allies of Persia, while inciting and leading
on a host of foreign allies against those most closely united
with him in blood. The whole story was one of fratricidal and
parricidal horrors, and began and ended in the disgrace and
desolation of Thebes, the direst and most inveterate, but at
this time the disarmed enemy of Plataea and Athens.

CHAPTER XXIII.

WHILE the Athenians during these years were actively exercising their own powers, and arrogating more and more independent control over their allies, the Spartans would appear as strangely inert; but the hints which we gather from Herodotus are found confirmed in general terms by Thucydides, of collisions with their immediate neighbours, so serious that they might well concur with certain domestic embarrassments to hamper wider action. Brilliant as had been the achievements of Leotychides and Pausanias, their misconduct in foreign commands was more than sufficient to confirm the national maxim of abstention from remote enterprises; and a jealous oligarchy was on its guard against indulging the enthusiastic emulation of the young, or affording unnecessarily a dangerous relaxation of that galling restraint by which peace at home was systematically made for the Spartan more irksome than war in the field. And Pausanias was still among them, humiliated and kept in check he might be, but yet no inconsiderable power. He seems to have had some sympathetic partisans even among the ephors; but that he was not driven into exile like so many of his predecessors was probably due less to his personal influence as a Heracleid, or respect for the victor of Plataea, than to the proof which he had already given of his powers for formidable mischief when remote from direct control. In the meantime uneasy feelings of danger were gathering strength in connection with his discontent, and even obscure suspicions of intrigue among the helots.

Under such circumstances it might well be thought advisable by the ephors to withdraw for a time from active interference in extra-Peloponnesian politics, and to be satisfied with watching the movements of party at Athens and promoting as they might so welcome a result as the extrusion of the mistrusted, or certainly inimical, Themistocles, and the establishment in power of the more ingenuous and ever friendly Cimon.

But the Lacedaemonians were soon to discover that Themistocles ostracised might be scarcely less troublesome than Themistocles supreme at Athens; in no short time their views and interests within Peloponnesus itself were thwarted in a variety of transactions that had much appearance of proceeding in concert. We owe to an incidental notice by [1]Herodotus of the official services of the seer Tisamenus, our only information, that at some time between the battle of Plataea (Ol. 75. 2; 479 B.C.) and the siege of Ithome (Ol. 78. 4; 465 B.C.) two victories were gained by Sparta which imply two distinct wars; the first was over the Tegeans in their own territory supported by the Argives, and the second at Dipaea in the Maenalian [2]district over all the Arcadians in alliance, except the Mantineans. The exception is important, but conflict with such a league must still have been serious. That the Mantineans stood aloof may be probably accounted for less by present sympathy with Sparta than by jealousy of an alliance between Argos and Tegea, their neighbours on either side, or even among the general Arcadian cities. Only a few years later they are found annexing territory and asserting control over other

---

[1] Herod. ix. 35.   [2] Paus. iii. 11. 6.

Arcadians, and then the course of politics turns them back towards an Argive alliance for security against the jealousy of [1] Sparta. Unless some other equally uncited authority is relied on, it seems to be by misreading Strabo that Curtius dates at this time the fortification of Mantinea under Argive influence.

We are left in ignorance as to the interval that may have separated these victories, but may fairly assume that each was led up to by a series of considerable disputes and difficulties. We are equally left to conjecture, but not unsupported by strong presumptions, as to how these complications may have been dependent on some others of which Argos was the centre.

Argos was the usual residence of Themistocles, and it is impossible not to connect the notice of Thucydides that he was in frequent movement about Peloponnesus, with the changes that followed on rapidly in various directions,—all inimical to the influence of Sparta over even her immediate neighbours or most constant allies,—all tending to strengthen individual states, and to dispose them to independence in the choice of their alliances.

It was something, though it might not be very much, that the scattered populations of Elis were now gathered from smaller townships into one city. This process was always justly recognised in Greece as endowing a nation with the first condition of vigour and independence. There is every appearance that it was by promoting such a policy, at Mantinea especially, and then at other cities that became afterwards of chief importance in both Arcadia and Achaia, that Argos had in past centuries averted the entire absorption of the Peloponnesus by the Dorian conquerors of [2] Sparta.

At Elis, which, protected by the universally recognised consecration of its territory, dispensed with fortifications,

---

[1] Thuc. v. 29. 81.   [2] Strabo, 337. Cf. 348-356.

the chief motive may have been consciousness of enhanced importance from the great accession of valuable dedications after the Persian war, of which more were already preparing : at the same time it must be observed, that susceptibilities are developed in the future relations of Elis and Sparta which could not have been unaffected by this present self-assertion. The present agitations are premonitory of the occasion when Elis, Argos, and Mantinea were to present a bold front to Sparta, by concluding a joint alliance with Athens, offensive and defensive, for one hundred [1]years. A like movement of concentration, but carried through with violence under circumstances peculiarly offensive to Sparta, was now commenced at Argos,—at Argos the refuge of the restless Athenian, and bearing marks of being prompted by the genius who prided himself on skill to raise a small city into the position of a great one. In working for the advancement in power of the most jealous enemy of Sparta in Peloponnesus, he was but following out in exile the policy that he had consistently advocated at home. Argos certainly had rejected his proposals heretofore; had held aloof from the alliance against Persia,—had, as Herodotus avers, positively Medised ; not only sent no force to Thermopylae, to Salamis or Plataea, but promised Mardonius aid, though more than she was able or could dream of being able to perform, to detain the Lacedaemonians within the Isthmus, and had at least given promptest and repeated notice of their movements. Such were the sins of her policy against Hellas ; but Themistocles, apart from a politician's usual tenderness towards any policy that succeeds, could only witness with pleasure dispositions that might be turned to the ultimate advantage of Athens. Argos had avowedly spared her resources during the Persian struggle, from the necessity of recovering population which a defeat—a massacre—by the

---

[1] Thuc. v. 47.

Lacedaemonians had seriously and dangerously reduced, and this policy now looked for its reward. In the time of her weakness her authority had been contemned by the adjacent towns,—far inferior now, whatever their proud rivalry in poetry and mythology,—of Tiryns, Hysiae, Orneae, Mideia, and above all [1] Mycenae. Pausanias tells the same story as Diodorus, that the pride of Argos was wounded to the quick by the Mycenians having presumed,—in contravention of her decree of neutrality,—to despatch even eighty men to Thermopylae, and the offence had been repeated, in company with the other towns, at Plataea. Their anticipation that they would thus engage the protection of Sparta against Argos was frustrate. Argos seized an opportunity when Sparta was either fully occupied nearer home, or in one of her calculated periods of seeming inaction but secret discipline and drill, to attack them with all her force and with the aid of [2] Cleonae, a town which had a quarrel on its own account respecting precedence at the Nemean games, and of the Tegeans, who were ever too jealous of Spartan power to be mindful at this opportunity of their solemn oath never to subvert the city of a confederate against Persia.

Diodorus dates these events in the archonship of Theagenides (B.C. 468–7), and, with his habitual inexactness, as if commenced and concluded within the year; while at the same time he ascribes the abstention of the Spartans from interference, to difficulties consequent on the great earthquake, which certainly did not occur till three years later. Mycenae offered considerable resistance, but how prolonged before its final catastrophe there is no means of deciding. It is most natural to suppose that it was at a later and not earlier date that the Spartans were roused to activity at last, or chose to resume it with effective suddenness, when, under the auspices of Tisamenus, they inflicted the defeat upon the

<hr>

[1] Paus. ii. 16. 5; viii. 27. 1; Diod. Sic. xi. 65.   [2] Strabo, 377.

Tegeans and Argives together. The defeat of the united
Arcadians was still later, but it is probable that the Arcadian
alliance was threatening trouble previously, and even that
it was this embarrassment that cut off the Spartans from
coming to the rescue of Mycenae.

Diodorus states that the inhabitants of Mycenae were
reduced to slavery; but this is a mistake, or his word is
employed loosely as it may be on other like occasions, a
not unimportant warning. Pausanias informs us that it
was after a siege, prolonged by the strength of their
primaeval Cyclopean fortifications till provisions failed, that
some of the Mycenians—it is implied but few, who were
probably the anti-national leaders—retired to Cleonae, the
very ally of Argos; so considerable a number settled at
Ceryneia in Achaia as to enhance its strength and importance; and more than half took refuge with Alexander of
Macedon. Their attraction to Ceryneia and reception there,
seem explained sufficiently by traces of some traditional connection with the city of Agamemnon, which reflect, there
can be little doubt, a true connection with the ancient centre
of Achaian power. [1] Pausanias saw there a fane of the
Eumenides which was said to be a foundation of Orestes;
the temple statues were of wood, but well executed marble
statues of priestesses were about the entrance; for those stained
with murder or other pollution, or sacrilege, to enter the
sacred precinct, involved the risk of raving madness. The
style of the monuments and the tone of the traditions alike
refer us to times long gone by for their origin.

The Alexander of Macedon who received the fugitives is
the same of whom Herodotus relates as within his own
knowledge that he presented himself as a competitor at the
Olympic games, was met by an objection of un-Hellenic
origin, but established his claim to the satisfaction of the

[1] Paus. vii. 25. 6.

Hellanodicae, and was admitted and matched in the contest of the stadium. It was not merely as Hellenic but as Heracleid, as descendant of the Temenid kings of Argos, that the Macedonian protected refugees from the antique metropolis of the realm of Danaus and Pelops and Agamemnon; so he vindicated again his semi-mythical claim of descent, and afforded an example that was not lost upon his successors, when the time was ripe for turning it to true political account in more active interferences. It is very probable that the appearance of Alexander at Olympia was at that second recurrence after the Medica (Ol. 77 = 472-71 B.C.) when Hiero and Theron were also competitors, and Themistocles and Cimon rivals in hospitality and display. Such congresses of the ' great ones' do not occur without the pretext of peaceful amusement being made the opportunity for conferences of which results are apt to become apparent within a year or two on the course of politics. The interests of Athens and of Macedon, the scenes of action of Alexander and of Cimon, were in close proximity in Thrace and on the Strymon; and remembrance of the amenities of Olympia may easily have encouraged the Athenian demus a few years later in their jealousy of Cimon's tenderness towards a regal guest when an opportunity was neglected of gaining a political advantage for Athens by despoiling [1] him.

The resistance and treatment of the Mycenians were alike exceptional. The occupants of the other suppressed towns and of numerous scattered villages were incorporated as citizens at [2] Argos, of which we are left to infer that the fortifications were at the same time correspondingly extended.

---

[1] Plut. *Cimon*, 14.   [2] Pausan. ii. 25. 5.

CHAPTER XXIV.

IT was in the spring of 467 B.C., the year after the victory of Sophocles with his Triptolemus, that Aeschylus is now known to have obtained the first prize with his Oedipodeia, a tetralogy or system of four dramas,—consisting of a tragic trilogy, Laïus, Oedipus, The Seven against Thebes, and a satyric play, The Sphinx,—which had for their subject the crimes and fate of the house of Laïus of Thebes. The titles of the tragedies show that, like those of the Oresteia, they followed on in historical sequence of subjects, although, in the tetralogy that comprised the Persae, the poet had already either set or followed the example of a broader principle of combination. The second prize was gained by Aristias with plays of which we have only the titles, Perseus, Tantalus, and The Wrestlers; the last apparently a satyric drama of his father Pratinas of Phlius, who in these compositions was accounted inferior to Aeschylus [1] alone. The third place only was granted to a tetralogy on the Thracian subject of Lycurgus—the Lycurgeia of Polyphradmon.

It was to the great surprise of very confident theorisers that the discovery of the didascalia by Franz, in 1850, proved The Seven against Thebes, concluding as it does with the announcement of the new dispute that gave Sophocles the

---

[1] Paus. ii. 13. 5.

subject for his Antigone, to be not the intermediate, but the
final play of a trilogy. Disconcerted criticism however finds
consolation in the promise that as a final play it may point
more unequivocally to the main drift and purport of what
went before, and has been lost.

. Far back in the story of the first drama, as reported in the
argument, lie the weakness and intemperance of Theban
Laius, who thrice warned by Apollo that the salvation of
his country depends on his dying childless, gives in to false
counsels of friends and—commencement of mischief that is to
be propagated to the third [1] generation—perishes by the
hands of his own son. Oedipus, whose deed is unconsciously
parricide, contracts an incestuous marriage, ignorantly still,
but by [2] mad folly (παράνοια), a term of which the import in
this place could only be explained by the preceding lost drama.
Maddened and humiliated by the discovery and then by the
undutifulness of his sons, he utters a hasty and fearful curse ;
it is with steel that they shall share their common kingdom
between them. Fraternal hatred continues horrors that parricide and incest have not exhausted, to the third generation.
Eteocles in possession is assailed by his brother Polyneices
with six allies from Argos, each of whom advances against one
gate of Thebes ; he assigns opponents at six several gates,
elects to oppose his own brother at the seventh himself, and
briefly, the brothers fall, each on the spear-point of the
other.

Notwithstanding the nature of such a subject there is in
truth very little in the treatment of it by Aeschylus to assist
a theory which has obtained so strange an acceptation, that
blind immoral Fate is supreme in the tragedy of the Greeks.
The enunciation of this principle may be carried up to the
Oedipus of Seneca, which has had extraordinary influence on
the developement of a modern school of classical drama, but

---

[1] Aesch. *Sept. c. Theb.* 740–763.　　　　　[2] Ib. 756.

scarcely further.   To affiliate it to Athenian poetry were as
gross an outrage as to make Aristotle answerable for the
three unities of the French drama.   What Greek tragedy
does no doubt harp on, and with an impressiveness that
awes us now, and now engages our compassion, is the natural
truth that the sins of fathers are painfully visited on the
children; but it sets forth, not obscurely withal, that this
is in no slight degree because the dispositions that produce and repeat the sins are inherited by the children, who
therefore aby the consequences not more of their father's
nature than of their own.   Familiar alike to the experience of
all men, and to the records of history—of the Tudors and the
Stuarts as of the Claudian gens—is the persistence of family
characteristics and the tendency for the mischief of one
generation, when happy interposition fails, to be aggravated
in the next, till it ends by natural exhaustion ; for cumulative
wrong, unless stayed at favourable [1] moment by self-sacrifice
and self-restraint, to hurry on ruin and annihilation.

The story of Oedipus, however treated, could scarcely but
involve such aspersions upon Theban national characteristics
as were always welcome to Athenians ; and it is even possible that some of those intestine quarrels in Thebes which are
speedily to become declared in political results, might already
be sufficiently malignant to remind men of the unnatural hostilities of the sons of Oedipus.   We have one hint of a certain
movement at Thebes at this time which cannot be without
significance, however difficult it may be to interpret it fully.
Herodotus tells us that it was twenty years after the invasion
of Datis and Artaphernes (490 B.C.), and therefore, allowing
for the round number, within a year or two of the date of the
Oedipodeia (467 B.C.), that the Thebans, in obedience to an
oracle, restored to Delium, close upon the Attic boundary, a
statue of Apollo that had been carried off by the fleet of

---

[1] Aesch. *Sept. c. Theb.* 705-708.

Datis, and afterwards deposited by him, in consequence of a dream, at the sacred island of Delos. This solemn reparation of a Median outrage can scarcely but have had some bearing on the opprobrium of Medism which one party at Thebes had an interest in keeping alive. The incident may well have had a party import as distinct as the recovery of the relics of Theseus, which may indeed have suggested it. Still it must be said that the tone of the poet is not such as to turn our thoughts with distinct intention towards contemporary Boeotia. What then was the crisis that at this time chiefly engaged the attention of Athenians in the larger range of politics?

There is this unexampled peculiarity in the situation of affairs. From this year, 467 B.C., the Greek could look back to about 475, over a happy blank, a period of about two Olympiads, during which, after the subsidence of troubles due to the Persian invasion, the internal peace of Hellas had had no interruption by conflicts of sufficient gravity to occupy a brief page of the chronicles. But an ominous change had supervened, 'the noise of battle hurtles in the air,' Sparta is embroiled with Tegea, ever the harbour and resort of her exiled kings, and with Argives in [1] alliance. A victory is gained, but a battle has again to be fought, if again victoriously, against all Arcadia in alliance except the Mantineans. The struggle is still sustained when Argos, her youthful vigour now recovered from the blow of Cleomenes, can seize an opportunity to consolidate her power by the incorporation of several smaller territories, and then by the siege and ultimate capture and razing of Mycenae, her rival in traditional—in poetical—claims that were of no slight value for political purposes.

Thus the Hellas of the days of united glory was harshly roused from a dream of tranquillity by revival of dire inter-

---

[1] Herod. ix. 35.

necine quarrel; war desperate and vindictive was again
afoot extending its designs to the extrusion of nearest neighbours, the extirpation of seats of most ancient mythical
renown.

The story of Thebes furnished a fable that brought into
visible action all the passions and excitements of this crisis;
hereditary violence and crime, with Argive ambition to aid,
are found to reproduce themselves with ineradicable persistency; and even at last, when the brothers fall together,
it seems that from their very burial is to spring a new root
of domestic dissension and political misery. The warlike spirit
of the champion of Marathon is indulged by a welcome outlet
in his verse;—in the words assigned to him by Aristophanes,
'it is a drama brimful of the war-god, and every beholder of
it would fain be a warrior himself;' but it is on a long wail
that the story draws to an end; the pomp and the clatter of
war have passed away together; the pride in the infliction
and the endurance of horrors that ever tend to reproduce more
crime than they destroy, leave us to make the best of the
moral at last, that unnatural and vindictive warfare between
either princes or nations allied in blood has its happiest ending
when both parties suffer alike, and yet even then is apt to do
little more effectually than enforce a pause for the maturing of
the dragon's teeth that it has sown anew.

The story of Oedipus was not likely to be treated by an
Athenian poet, and at Athens, without being turned in some
degree to the disparagement of Thebes; but the mythus itself
has a distinct appearance of being of genuine Theban origin.
The story which connects Laïus with Elis by his rape of a
beautiful youth, corresponds with the evil report that associated Elis and [1]Boeotia in the coarse abuse of a form of
friendship which Homer exhibits in a still unsuspected purity,
and which, faintly surviving in historical times, was at least

[1] Plato, *Symph.* p. 182, et citat.

believed by Plato to be even yet recoverable. The oracle which Laïus disobeys in obtaining offspring, points to the difficulty of surplus population, so unhesitatingly countervailed throughout Hellas by exposure of the newly-born; and the consequences of his disobedience seem to embody an exemplar of the confusions which had ultimately led at Thebes to very remarkable and exceptional legislation. The so-called Thetic laws of Thebes were ascribed to a lawgiver who came like Oedipus from [1] Corinth. They forbade the exposure or desertion of infants,—the practice which the case of Oedipus exhibits as liable to bring about the pollution of the country, however unconsciously, by incestuous unions, certain to provoke the direst visitations of the wrath of the gods. The babe that otherwise would have had to take its chance of death or of rescue to an unidentified life, was, in accordance with these enactments, to be brought immediately on birth, and under heavy penalties, to the authorities, who consigned it to whoever offered a price, however small, and was willing to look to its future services as a slave as remuneration for cost and tending in the [2] meantime.

---

[1] Aristot. *Pol.* xi. 9.   [2] Aelian, *V. H.* ii. 7.

CHAPTER XXV.

SPARTA then had been disabled by whatever embarrassments from interposing in time to arrest the progress of Argos
to an aggrandizement which threatened to furnish, when time
should be ripe, a valuable ally to Athens; but she clearly
vindicated her power at the first opportunity, and in the
double victories over Tegea and Argos first, and then over
the united Arcadians, the impact of her disciplined hoplites
told with its usual effect. It shattered opposition now as
effectually as when in after years Alcibiades, with diplomacy
rivalling that of Themistocles, at least succeeded—but like his
predecessor no more than succeeded—in forcing her to imperil
her supremacy upon a single field against almost the same
[1] antagonists. Spartan influence in Peloponnesus was at once
fully restored, and as a valued consequence she was in a
position to free herself once for all from the dreaded ma-
chinations of Themistocles, though the opportunity only came
about in the course of events that involved a domestic crisis
of danger and disorder.

Sharply as the designs of Pausanias had been checked, he
had never renounced them, and when he became aware that
Themistocles, fallen like himself into home disgrace, was

---

[1] Thucyd. vi. 16.

Y

fretting in his exile with impatience and discontent, he counted
at once on sympathetic rancour as well as ancient friendship
to aid him in the revolution that he was still plotting against
ungrateful and unworthy Hellenes.   Such had before been
the revenge of Demaratus against one city, and of the son
of Peisistratus against the other; and Leotychides, who was
only just dead and succeeded formally by his son Archidamus, had at least been in a position to be not more
patriotically employed while protected in his suspicious
refuge at hostile Tegea.   Party was not unknown at Sparta,
and Pausanias may have found, if not sympathy for a project which some ascribed to [1] him,—the abolition of the
ephorate,—more probably encouragement for general innovation, among ancient comrades and ambitious spirits who
were ill content with the renunciation of larger Hellenic
hegemony, and with the elevation and pride of Athens.
Even the Persians are certainly found within a year or two
well informed of this latter root of jealousy, and prompt to
negotiate on the assumption of its bitterness.

Interpreting the feelings of Themistocles by his own—of
the ill-requited victor of Salamis by his own memories of
Plataea and Byzantium—he had communicated to him the
Great King's [2] letter, which seems so completely to have turned
his own head, and no doubt also his correspondence, which was
still active with Artabanus, though without the effect he hoped
for and relied on.   Themistocles, as we might expect, shook
off the application, and declined to have anything to do with
the partnership, but as he declared afterwards, in admitting
the communication so far, he held it nevertheless to be no
part of his to denounce a friend; quite as little might he
think it to be his part as an Athenian, not out of hope of
resuming his place at Athens, to put a stop prematurely to
transactions that, conducted as they were, could only help to

---

[1] Arist. *Polit.* v. 1.   [2] Plut. *Themist.* 23.

embarrass and weaken if not to ruin Sparta, and might probably enough put events in motion that would hasten his own recall. Whether Themistocles was made acquainted with the domestic development of the scheme of Pausanias does not appear; the plan for the intervention of Persia was combined with a plot for raising the helots in rebellion; he could count on their memory of the spoils and exploits of Plataea, and he held out to them the prospect of freedom and of citizenship, which in later Spartan history is recognised as a natural reward for their services in arms. What progress he had made in both directions is avouched by the reappearance before long, and in formidable muster, of a Perso-Phoenician fleet, and then by the still more dangerous revolt of the helots that was speedily to occur, though not before his own career, which would have added so much to the peril, had closed for ever.

In the meantime rumours of his intrigues reached the Ephors; the helots themselves, slaves as they were, had not failed to furnish even direct information; but the maxim was imperative, not to recognise obligation to such a source alone in a serious charge against any Spartiat; they could only be watchful until evidence more available arrived. And this was not long delayed. Pausanias had already transmitted a series of communications to the satrap Artabanus, before the time came for him to entrust one, the most important of all, addressed to the king and intended to be conclusive, to the hands of a dependent—there is no reason to suppose a slave—a native of Argilus in Thrace, who had been his confidential favourite and even something more. When thus entrusted, the Argilian called to mind, if he had not cared to dwell on his suspicions earlier, that no single bearer of the numerous messages of which he had been cognisant had ever reappeared. He opened the packet, after having prepared himself to reclose it with a counterfeit seal in case all was well, but found, as he foreboded, that it con-

tained an instruction to put the messenger to death as usual.
Desperate and indignant he carried the letter at once to the
ephors, with whatever other information he could furnish.
Yet even so, action had still to wait on hesitation, and was
suspended for further confirmation of the evidence of a
foreigner, and of a letter which however damning in purport
had still been opened intermediately. Arrangements however were made at once for procuring this.

Pausanias was presently allowed to hear, and he heard with
alarm, that his messenger whom he supposed to be on his
way to death, had taken refuge as a suppliant in a hut
within the sacred precinct of Poseidon at the promontory of
Taenaron. Thither he hurried to seek an explanation, and
was greeted by the man with reproaches for his cruel
treachery, for having held him—him whom he might have
safely trusted to take his share in any danger in the negotiations to which he referred in detail—in no better honour
and esteem than to consign him to death like the rest whom
he had sent on the service before him. Pausanias made every
effort to soothe and satisfy him, and, admitting the past, could
so far flatter himself, desperate as was the case, that he had
worked upon the man, between protests of regret and promise
of vast rewards, as to urge him to quit the protecting sanctuary with confidence, and undertake the journey without
delay, and so not frustrate what was now on the point of
conclusion.

The confidence of the Spartan king in his success could
scarcely under such circumstances be very assured, and it is
not surprising that when the ephors approached him after
his return to the city he read the tokens of danger in their
looks ; they had in fact, by prearrangement of a double wall
in the hut of the suppliant, been witnesses of the entire interview. A covert sign from one ephor who was his friend gave
warning of peril, and he ran at the instant, and just in time,
to gain the sanctuary of Athene Chalcioecus—Athene of the

bronze house—and took refuge in a small outbuilding within the sacred precinct. The pursuers paused at the entrance, but only to beset it. A story was current in later times, that while the ephors were considering what should next be done, the aged mother of the traitor came, bearing a brick, which she laid down on the threshold without a word, and then turned and went to her home.

We have the authority of Thucydides that the ephors did in fact build up the entrance, unroof the refuge of the suppliant of the goddess, and set a watch to await the moment when famine and exposure should bring him to the last gasp; then, in deference or subjection to the base logic of superstition—which however was afterwards to fail to satisfy themselves—they drew him forth just in time to prevent the desecration by his death of a holy place that was not held to be desecrated by any cruelty in bringing it about. It was only due to some protest that they did not cast the body into the chasm Caiadas, the place of shame for malefactors, but it still was put away in ground adjacent. It seems to have been in unworthy imitation of this insult that Athens afterwards, with less justifying provocation, assigned a spot close to the proud dedication of Themistocles to Artemis Aristoboule, for the bodies and instruments of death of malefactors and [1] suicides. In time ensuing, the Pythia, concerned for the pretensions and immunities of sanctities, appended to every oracle that she delivered to Lacedaemonians, on whatever subject, a command to give back her suppliant to the goddess. In formal compliance with the injunction they then transferred his remains to the precinct—particularly to the *protemenisma* of the temple—and erected two statues of him within it. Even so their enemies held themselves entitled to refer to the repeated oracles as imputing an ever unexpiated [2] sacrilege, and associated it with a still less

---

[1] Plut. *Themist.* 22.   [2] Thucyd. i. 128.

ceremonious treatment of Helot suppliants at Taenaron,—
very probably among the implicated in the intrigues of
Pausanias,—who were forcibly dragged from the sanctuary
to execution. For this sacrilegious outrage the Lacedaemonians themselves could recognise divine retribution in
their sufferings by a desolating earthquake—manifest expression of the anger of the god of Taenaron.

In the meantime the correspondence of Pausanias was
seized, and, besides the letters of the Persian king, some
documents were found that promised a colourable pretext
for implicating Themistocles in the crime of Medism; and
these it was determined to make use of forthwith for completing if possible the ruin of their ever-dreaded enemy, together with the forfeiture by Athens of the services of her most
gifted and best deserving citizen. Envoys were accordingly
sent to Athens, where he had enemies enough to second them,
to urge on his condemnation; he was charged in his absence
at Argos, and, though acquitted upon his transmitted defence,
the accusation was renewed at the instance of the Lacedaemonians, and a proposal submitted to the Athenians, that
the enquiry should be referred to the common synedrion of
Hellas to be assembled at Sparta. Diodorus speaks of
an earlier accusation, rebutted by Themistocles before his
ostracism; but this is inconsistent with his own account,
that the charge was promoted by the Lacedaemonians, as
cognizant, which at that time they were not, of the secret
correspondence. Plutarch, who says that he replied to the
Athenians by letter from Argos, 'respecting the earlier accusations chiefly,' specifies a formal accusation by Leobotes,
son of Alcmaeon, which was also posterior to the ostracism,
and to which such letter must have had [1] reference. His
reply was in the unsubmissive unconciliatory style that the
Athenian demus had now unfortunately for itself to listen to

---

[1] Plut. *Themist.* 23.

nearly for the last time ; 'his ambition remained what it ever had been, to govern, and it was as little in his nature as his desire to be subjected to rule, or therefore to surrender up himself along with Hellas, to the barbarians who were their common enemies.' Notwithstanding this first acquittal, such a reaction occurred as the great Athenian historian is given to adverting to as characteristic of a popular assembly, and the proposal of the Lacedaemonians gained acceptance, whether as Diodorus says by aid of bribes, or not. It admitted of plausible advocacy; it gave the hostility of Cimon another chance, and was flattering to his leading idea, that the action of united Hellas might continue to be secured by a perfectly practicable cordial alliance with Sparta. It was tempting to essay to controvert the Argive policy which Themistocles had been working for, by a revival of the authority of the Doro-Ionian congress, expressly to his personal ruin. A joint party was at once despatched—the Lacedaemonians had their men ready—with authority to attach him wherever he could be found ; and the implication that he might have been seized even at Argos may be ac-counted for by the ascendancy there of the friends of Sparta, after the defeat of the allied Argives and Tegeans, as well as of the united Arcadians. He knew his enemies, however, and even their intentions and their movements too well, and was not to be found easily. Argos was void, and when next heard of he was at Corcyra; he had personal claims on the Corcyraeans for public services rendered to them, and that he should have such is again characteristic of the man. He had evidently already discerned that Corcyra westward was as fitted to be an advantageous ally for Athens as Argos in Peloponnesus ; and if we may trust Plutarch, the obligation that Thucydides refers to was an award in their favour in respect of money and jurisdiction over Leucas, a joint colony, as against Corinth. To weaken Corinth by the encourage-ment of its contumacious colony, Corcyra, was a policy in harmony with the consolidation of the power of Argos—a policy that Athens was to adopt at a future momentous crisis of her rivalry with Sparta. The islanders however, whatever their good-will, could not afford to provoke both the great Hellenic powers, though they had held themselves proudly aloof from alliance with either, and could only speed him on his way in advance of the keen pursuit.

CHAPTER XXVI.

THE Prometheus Bound of Aeschylus is of all his extant dramas most characteristic of the poet, and stands alone moreover in the mysteriousness and elevation of its theme among all the works of the Greek tragedians of which we have remains or record. The subject goes back even to the very commencements of human civilisation, not to say of settled cosmical order; and all the actors, even the Chorus with the rest, are superhuman — nature-powers, gods, or Titans, with the exception of Io, who in her strange transformation is scarcely an exception. In this play Aeschylus treats of the divine economy with all the epic freedom of Homer, and combines, at the same time that he elevates, some elements of sublimity that might have given Hesiod, but for his crudity of treatment, a dignity to which even Homer himself did not attain.

We have no information whatever as to the date when the Prometheus was produced, though presumably from its style it must have been later than both the Persae and The Seven against Thebes. I now advance a further presumption with some confidence; it appears strange that the drama should have been so constantly read, its passion so sedulously scanned, and not have recalled the character of Themistocles and his position as ostracised and at Argos; the agreement is such as to argue strongly that Aeschylus, with daring all his own, brought home to the Athenians the characteristics of their rejected hero even more directly than when he was among them at the height of popularity and power.   Sagacity, versatility, daring, unrivalled and combined, have conducted the Titan, as the Athenian, to the highest power and alliances in a career which nevertheless is suddenly arrested by a terrible reverse; but the reverse, though in either case unforeseen in its severity and unprepared for, is endured by the victims, if not without indignation and impatience, yet in abiding self-confidence that sooner or later reaction must come round, and their qualifications be again indispensable, and the exacted reparation be at their own discretion.

Prometheus is addressed at the very commencement of the [1] play, in terms that seem to indicate Themistocles almost by name; the phrase and epithet of the line,

τῆς ὀρθοβούλου Θέμιδος αἰπυμῆτα παῖ,

ascribe the faculty of sagacious divination for which he was most renowned, recall his vaunt of it in his dedication to Artemis Aristoboule, and though another goddess is named, it is Themis—an equivalent, as said distinctly by Prometheus, of Gaia, the [2] Earth, and 'known by many another name,'—the goddess of the Lycomidae, to whom Themistocles most probably owed his own.   There is a pertinence here which confirms my rejection of a criticism that condemns the line as spurious chiefly because too significant.

I am even inclined to recover from the story of Prometheus a hint for history, that as the Titan deserted his original and natural party, alarmed and disgusted by their inability to recognise the new tactics—of craft not violence—required in a new contest against younger [3] powers, so Themistocles may have entered politics like many a new man

---

[1] Aesch. *Prom. V.* 18.   [2] Ib. 209, 210; Welcker, *Aesch. Trilogie,* p. 40.
[3] Aesch. *Prom. V.* 206.

since, by attaching himself to a party from which he ultimately
slipped away as unmanageably wrong-headed, or when it had
served his purpose.   And the parallel goes on; the original
spirit finds his energies cramped in the new connection as in
the old.   Those who conquered power by the aid of forethought [1] personified, turning incontinently to the distribution
amongst relatives, of functions and offices, the government of
the upper and the under world, the land and sea, neglected
—would even gladly have destroyed—poor human-kind, the
unprovided, miserable [2] demus.   Prometheus alone opposed; he
secured for low mortals a share of higher privileges, especially
the use of fire, a franchise that finally assured them from
annihilation, though it made their benefactor an object of
oligarchical and tyrannous vindictiveness.   /

It would be a mistake in this, as indeed in any case of the
kind, to ascribe to the poet an intention to run an exact and
proper parallel : it would be enough for him to set in action
before his audience all the motives that they themselves were
most familiar with, all the passions they had recently excited
or indulged.   Themistocles had as much cause as Prometheus
to declaim, and it is consistent with his character that declaim
he did, against the ingratitude of the political organism which
he had reconstructed, whether chargeable on his own particular party or not; and we might think it was the Athenian
himself whom we hear speaking with the proud and contemptuous tones that resound from the mask of the fettered
Titan.   When Prometheus tells of his services to men in
instituting the arts, we are reminded how in the earlier
Satyric play of Aeschylus, the boon of fire brought by Prometheus had already once been made directly the symbol of
the restoration of sacred and domestic hearths, and the
reappearance of civilised society after the barbaric desolation
left behind by the Mede.   In Athens and at the Piraeus, by

[1] Aesch. *Prom. V.* 440.   [2] Ib. 228-240.

land and sea, Themistocles had been the main agent and leading spirit in these restorations; he if any man might claim to represent a new Prometheus, as his wise counsels had given him pretensions to such title in the war. The Athens that rose up under the superintendence of Themistocles, might well be asserted as such an improvement on the city destroyed by the Persians, as could only be paralleled by the change which Prometheus asserts that he introduced in the habitations of previously exposed and squalid humanity; and the creation by him of a new port and improvement of the war ships, might as readily be called to mind by the assertion for himself by Prometheus, of the invention of sailing [1] vessels.

The younger gods, insolent, ungrateful, encroaching, are contrasted here, as in the Eumenides, with the elder Titanic powers; whether we care to approximate them to the newly established demus,—already betraying the tendencies of absolute power in an extreme democracy, as distinctly as they were to be recognised by Aristotle, indeed avowed by Cleon and the Athenians [2] themselves,—or to the younger generation of aristocrats who had discovered the secret of acquiring mastery over the demus. Prometheus, Themistocles-like, provoked the catastrophe that he risked at least if he did not fully [3] anticipate, and confident in his prescience, master of a secret that is all his [4] own, cares not, now that it has come, to avoid provoking its further violence. He has seen two revolutions, two catastrophes of powers in highest places already, and he knows that, but for his besought intervention, a third must follow, more shameful still, and more suddenly precipitate than either. Jove himself, for all his thunders, is helpless against [5] necessity, of which the course is cognisable if not guided, not by him, but by elder more mysterious powers, by ' the Triform Fates and daemonian

---

[1] Aesch. *Prom. V.* 467-70.   [2] Thucyd. ii. 63; iii. 37; v. 89.
[3] Aesch. *Prom. V.* 268.   [4] Ib. 206.   [5] Ib. 518.

'Erinnyes,'—whose plans and purposes, communicated in preference to Themis-Gaia, the Titanian mother of the ²sufferer, only come to Jove at second-hand.

There is no doubt ample vindication in the theme, the fable dramatised, for the episode, which is indeed not strictly an episode, of Io; Io, ancestress of Hercules, of whom it is prophesied that he is to be the liberator of Prometheus, and thus the main instrument of ultimate conciliation; Io, whose frenzied wanderings under the persecution of ³Hera demonstrate, like the enforced servitude of Hercules afterwards, the limitation of the power of Jove her lover, as distinctly as does his ignorance of the secret that is in the keeping of Prometheus, his enemy and victim. But the sympathy of Prometheus with the persecuted Argive heroine, and his prospect of aid from her demi-god descendant, coincide so markedly with the Argive connections and interests of Themistocles, that we seem reduced to choose between inferences; either that Aeschylus at an early date was cognisant of the advocacy by Themistocles of the Argive alliance, or at a later date, after the alliance had become a fact, was disposed to credit him with having anticipated and prepared for it.

Prometheus effected his main stroke of policy by theft, by such craft as Themistocles was ever ready and dexterous to resort to; and both relied too confidently on their capacity to sustain, or re-establish at least, as strong a position as ever after discovery. The Titan pays a penalty unexpectedly severe; but to him an immortal, with a secular term before him, the ages are destined to bring back his opportunity. Mortal man fallen of necessity if he lays out plans that are on a scale disproportionate to the conditions of his being; events might come round in a decade or two that would vindicate the sagacious policy recommended by Themistocles, and did so, but by that time all hopes of restitution for himself,

---

¹ *Aesch. Prom. V.* 511–517.   ² Ib. 874.   ³ Ib. 710.

chances of his being seen again with his strong hand on the helm of the Athenian state, were past and over.

We are unfortunately destitute of direct information as to the dramas that were associated and composed with the Prometheus Bound, no less than of the date of its production, and the field is open for speculations that have proved usually but vague and unfruitful, as to the moral or metaphysical solution that was finally worked out by the poet. The play as we have it breaks off upon a suspense as declared as the first part of Faust. In the German play, however, a difficulty is mainly constituted by the poet's declared intention—it admitted of but lame execution—to exhibit how deliberate seduction, followed by careless desertion for coarse debauchery and what he does not seem to perceive was brutal assassination, could contribute naturally to the development of a gifted but chiefly intellectual, into a perfect character. We might be well content to leave Faust, whose reappearance in a second part is an impertinence, to his companion Mephistopheles, but scarcely Prometheus to the vulture. We are fain, therefore, to make the most of what hints we can gather as to the further design of Aeschylus, from some fragments and notices of the presumed sequel, his drama of 'Prometheus Released.' When all the fragments and notices are taken together, the outcome is not inconsiderable as compared with our disappointment in other cases.

The Chorus consisted of Titans, who visit their relative, now suffering under the secular torture of the 'winged hound of Zeus,' that daily descends to tear his still renewing liver. But time has brought round the contingency on which the victim of sympathy with the wretchedness of humanity in unprovided life, relied prophetically for deliverance. The destined liberator, Hercules, of mingled divine and human origin, descendant of Io in the thirteenth generation, and son of Zeus himself, appears at last; the series of labours by which he is to initiate the relief of struggling humanity is

foretold, and his shooting the ravening bird brings on in conclusion a general reconciliation, of Prometheus with Zeus, of
Zeus with the preservation of the once doomed and despised
race of mankind. A further hard and apparently hopeless
condition of which Hermes had given [1] warning, the voluntary renunciation of the privilege of immortality, is fulfilled
by the vicarious acceptance of death by the centaur Chiron;
the sentence of the eternal chain is satisfied by the assumption by Prometheus either of a ring set with a fragment of
the rock, or of a verdant crown. Conceding now to clemency
what he refused to compulsion, he discloses his secret—that the
threatened fatality awaited Zeus in case he yielded to his
passion and married Thetis, who was fated to bear a son superior to his sire. The permanence of Olympic, of cosmical
order, is assured, when the restored Titan in festive chaplet
joins the assemblage of the gods at the nuptials of the sea-
goddess with the father of Achilles.

Whether the [2] tradition of the marriage of Zeus himself
with primaeval Themis was combined with this fable, as critics
have fondly assumed, remains more than uncertain, for information fails entirely. In any case, it must be insisted on that the
dignity of Zeus, relatively either to Titans or to man, cannot
by any ingenuity be rescued as the ideal of supreme divinity.
Aeschylus, even like Homer before him, whom he owned as
his great exemplar, treats the lord of Olympus but as a
representative of humanity with powers inconceivably enhanced, yet only in respect of death exempt from the inherent weakness of humanity. In passion and in ignorance, in
hesitation and indiscretion, in his liability to be vexed and
thwarted by powers not only superior but inferior, the conditions and qualities of humanity are mirrored, and even of
necessity exaggerated by scale and contrast. To Zeus himself,
as to the demigod and Titan, is assigned the same invincible

---

[1] Aesch. *Prom. V.* 1029.   [2] Pindar, *Hymn.* 2.

consciousness of freedom of will that is part of human nature, but withal the same half-acknowledged and contradictory sense of its exercise under permission; the relation of this consciousness to the ever-intrusive conviction of a power existent somewhere that must guide—in any case how mysteriously!—what seems an independent or a drifting [1]bark, is withdrawn, and surely with no unreverential feeling, with no unreasonable humility, from the ken and scrutiny of preciser definition.

In Aeschylus we find the consciousness above all, and frequently the unequivocal expression, of the noblest ideal of divine attributes, of the Divinity as the supreme creative and controlling energy, the centre of all material forces, and no less of the highest moral power and of presiding intelligence, which gives the rule of justice as the single norm of reward and punishment, and yet with an ultimate appeal to indulgence and mercifulness. That this loftier ideal is from time to time confused with the agencies of a plurality of gods, or with such a defective personality as the poetic Zeus, is an inconsistency that runs through all Greek poetry, and was not easily escaped even by Greek philosophers; but the inconsistency tended to become gradually less obtrusive, and it did not hinder the development of that sense of the unity of providential control of the world of matter, of life, of intelligence, of conscience, which is the essence of monotheism, and towards which the poetry of Aeschylus still doubtless marks a most important stage of advance.

That this drama, then, must needs have been suggestive to the original Athenian audience, of recurring applications to party conflicts and impending political difficulties, it seems to me impossible to doubt; it is equally clear that the poet elevated his theme far above the dignity of the most pregnant embodiment of contemporary passion, by touching sympathies

---

[1] *Aesch. Prom. V.* 513.

that are common to all reflecting mankind. The exciting
interests of a day are partly attached to and partly absorbed
in a larger reference that is true for all men, true for all time,
and that is found accordingly to be conspicuously paralleled
in literature of far other genius among very contrasted populations. The Prometheus of Aeschylus is still in the main
the Titan of Hesiod, of the poet who confronts the most
salient and perplexing contrasts of life in the simplicity of
earlier days, and embodies in mythus the cruder explanation
of men upon whom they came with the surprise of novelty.
In Hesiod also we have an equivalent in forms of Hellenic
mythology, of those opening chapters of Hebrew story which,
before it narrows down to the fortunes of a family or a tribe,
regard humanity under its largest aspects, and with a scope
as wide as it was destined to recur to and resume at last before
its canon closed. That man should be so low and yet so high
is the fundamental perplexity in both narratives; so seem-
ingly neglected or deserted, and withal so manifestly highly
endowed; possessed of faculties which in their limitless capacity of development are godlike, and yet exposed by this very
possession to evils from which the lower animals, who have so
much of life in common with him, seem happily exempt.
'Unaccommodated man' is below the level of the brutes in
equipment for commonest self-preservation; his existence is
only endurable, or indeed entirely possible, by the opportunity
of art and knowledge; these save him, but only save him at
first as the veriest wretch; and are themselves dependent on
that faculty of looking before and after which distinguishes
him from the brutes indeed, and how gloriously! but at the
same time gives opening for the most poignant of sufferings,
for all the agonies of fear and doubt, from which the brutes
are exempt. Endowments which however dignified are still
the main conditions of human labour and human grief,
seemed to declare themselves as no rightful apanage, and
their consequences too closely resembled penalties and punish-

ments, not to have been acquired at first only by breach of
law; and if so, how not then by aid and suggestion of some
ally of intellectual subtlety superior to primeval man.

The Greek mythus ascribes the rescue of foredoomed man to
Prometheus, the genius of Forecast, to whom he owed the
command of fire, chief instrument of the useful arts; who
even qualified the direst consequence of the power of anticipating evil, by implanting in his breast the germ of Hope
independent of, and even indestructible by [1] reason. But such
wresting of a privilege for man from a grudging divinity,
involved difficulty in the first instance as to the attributes
of the divinity, and then as to a reconciliation consistently
with man's retention of the illicitly obtained advantage. Of
a problem accepted in so crude a form the solution could
scarcely be less crude, and the mythologist only escapes
from his self-made dilemma by resort to a quibble, or a
metaphor, or a symbol. Poetical purpose demanded that these
should be clothed in graceful poetical forms, and so the tragedian soothes at last by a pleasing apology for satisfaction, the
distress that he had taken in the first instance little pains to
moderate; even when wilder agitation subsides, he of necessity and not unwillingly leaves over some natural awe at the
still abiding enigma of human life; but awe not unallied
with hope from the intimation that beyond these contradictions and controversies there exists in the order of the uni-
verse a remoter but a comprehensive and an over-ruling
influence that will bring all right at last.

[1] Aesch. *Prom. V.* 250.

CHAPTER XXVII.

THE adventures of Themistocles, from the commencement
of his flight till he found safety, protection, and honour at
the court of the Great King, are related with a fulness of
romantic details that enticed the attention of the historians
from larger public affairs, and cover pages it must be said,
somewhat disproportionately, when we consider what has
been omitted. The story to the extent that it is unquestionable is so extraordinary, that we are scarcely entitled to
challenge embellishment on the score of mere marvellousness,
and for once the cheap criticism, which in its keen pursuit of
the 'unhistorical' so willingly erases the unlikely from history, must own itself foiled. Read it how we will, only when
we stumble over a positive contradiction can we be certain
that one version must be false; and even then no mere
balance of general probabilities will determine with certainty
which ought to give way. The tale seems to have been told
and retold, like that of Charles the Second fugitive from
Worcester, or of the young Pretender after Culloden, and
listened to, if not with sympathy of the same kind, with all
that Greeks were so capable of feeling for dexterity and
courage.

Even Thucydides quits larger history and condensed reflection for personal anecdote, when he relates how the most

brilliant of Greek careers came to an end only one degree less unhappily and disgracefully for Greece than that of Pausanias.

There was one tradition that told how, when it was no longer safe for him to remain at Corcyra, the victor of Xerxes crossed over to Sicily, to Hiero, and there parodied the mad schemes of Pausanias, with a proposal to marry a daughter of the Syracusan tyrant, and help him to the subjugation of central Greece. Such a story only represents the conjectures of later time as to the meaning of the direction of his flight, and a likely field for employment of his talents and resources. Hiero was already dead (467 B.C.), and his dynasty was dropping to ruin; otherwise Themistocles might not have shunned his court out of apprehension as to lingering rancour for his opposition at the Olympic festival. His political friends had failed in power at least, if not good-will, to protect him from their common enemies; he was now wound up to throw himself into the arms of his personal or political enemies, and to appeal to their credulousness, or generosity or interests, to refuse to sacrifice him even to friends of their own. Doubling on his pursuers he passed over to Epirus, to the seat of Admetus, king of the Molossians, whose nobler nature he was prepared to confide in, though in his day of power he had opposed him also in some negotiations,—very probably connected with the dissensions of Corcyra and Corinth as to territories on the mainland,—which had been referred to arbitration at Athens. His residence here seems to have continued for some months; and here he may have had hope to remain unmolested, if it be true that at this time he was joined by his wife and children from [1] Athens. But again the strongest pressure of demands and threats was applied by the Lacedaemonians upon his generous-minded host, through envoys of high distinction. Admetus, however,

[1] Plut. *Them.*

declared himself bound to protect his guest by the most stringent national sanctions of hospitality; for Themistocles had
claimed and appealed to them in a form which in that region
admitted of no denial—prostrate on his hearth as a suppliant,
and holding in his arms the child of the house. Whatever
might be said or thought,—that Phthia the wife of Admetus
had really in the absence of her husband compassionated the
persuasive Athenian, whose command over the sympathies
of women seems always assumed to be unfailing, and in-
structed him in the formula and ministered the opportunity,
or that Admetus himself had suggested the ceremony to
supply the pretext,—the difficulty was the same; there was
still no sign of it yielding to any increased urgency, when it
was found that Themistocles had again disappeared, and the
clue to the course of his retirement was broken.

In the meantime the untiring and unresisted activity by
which Athens was gradually wearying her confederates into
willingness to commute maritime service and even equipment
for money payments, the rigour with which these were exacted, and the general imperiousness with which she comported herself in administration by assumptions injurious to
the dignity of autonomy, were on the point of inducing collisions premonitory of a change in history. Her authority was
to be almost simultaneously repudiated by the two important
islands, north and south, of Thasos and Naxos. These are
the first assertions of a right of secession of confederates from
a qualified union, which might now seem from the inactivity
of Persia to have answered its purpose, and to be maintained
for little else than to aggrandise a power which threatened to
be quite as oppressive, or certainly more arbitrary than under
the changed circumstances would be quietly endured.

The discontent of Thasos was brought to a head by an
extension which was given about this time to the establishment on the Strymon, that had been maintained by the Athenians ever since they wrested Eïon from the Persians, after a

difficult siege. They despatched a colony (465 B.C.) consisting
of 10,000 settlers, Athenians and general volunteers, for the
purpose of taking into occupation a very favourable position
about five-and-twenty stadia up the river, where it issues
from a lake, and which at the time was in the possession of
the Edonian Thracians. The name of the site, the Nine Ways,
—Ennea Hodoi,—indicates its importance as commanding the
communications between the fertile plains of Thrace, the district Phyllis to the east, and Macedonia and the Chalcidic
peninsulas westward. It was here that Aristagoras, thirty-
two years before, had endeavoured to found an independent
settlement, and had come to the end of his turbulent and mischievous life. A main temptation for the Athenians consisted
in the riches of the adjacent gold mines, which after being
worked for centuries remained still unexhausted, and were to
continue so to reward still more richly the energetic administration of Philip of Macedon. The precise form of these gold
deposits does not seem to be recorded or explored in modern
times; but the Athenians had appetising experience of the
profitableness of silver mines as worked at Laurium by slave
labour—the machinery of the ancients—for these had been to
her the equivalents as a basis of prosperity of the coal and
iron deposits of England. Thrace also had its silver mines,
and no bait for industry or for adventurous rapine is more
stimulative of popular greed than pure metallic riches. The
Thasians seem to have shared the advantages of these mines,
in harmony if not in regulated partnership, with the Thracians,
before the Persians interfered, and not unnaturally expected
and claimed to re-enter upon all their privileges after their
expulsion. It was not so however that the Athenians interpreted their rights; the right of conquest has been willingly
substituted many a time since and down to our own days,
for the more modest claims of reward for rescue, after
honourable rescue has served its purpose as a pretext for
interference. If the protests of Thasos were disregarded, the

Thracians who were ousted at Ennea Hodoi were not likely
to be treated with more delicacy in further operations, and it
was not long before the smouldering enmities burst out into
flame on both sides.

At the same time, as if in sympathy and probably not
without some intercommunication, discontent was coming to
a head at another centre. Naxos, the largest of the Cyclades,
and renowned for its productiveness, especially of wine,—as
appropriately expressed in the mythic encounter on its shores
of Dionysus and Ariadne,—had early connection with Athens
and a political story in many respects similar. Here again, as
so often elsewhere, the circumstances of unquestioned later
intercourse go some way to vindicate a much earlier mythus
as springing from a radical fact; and the visit of the truant
Theseus on his return from Crete matches with the notice of
Herodotus, that the natives of Naxos, as also of Ceos, were
Ionians of Athenian descent. Aristotle quotes Lygdamis of
[1] Naxos as an example of the oligarch who becomes a tyrant
by taking up the cause of a demus, glad of any leader, against
his own [2] class. His rule seems to have been shaken off like
that of Peisistratus at Athens, by whom on his recovery of
power, and after a victory over the Naxians, he was reinstated,
and whom he requited afterwards by aid in men and money
to accomplish his own third and final [3] restoration.

A parallel fate still attends the Naxian tyrant when the
Spartans, after expelling the Peisistratids from Athens, put an
end to his authority also, and re-established their favourite
and avowed form of government, an [4] oligarchy.

About 500 B.C. the demus of Naxos gains the ascendant
and expels the leaders of the party of the so-called 'Substantial' men ([5] ἄνδρες τῶν παχέων), who apply forthwith to
Aristagoras, the despot under Persia at Miletus, and in
concert with him invite the interference of the Persians.

---

[1] Pol. v. 5. 1.   [2] Athenaeus, 348.   [3] Herod. i. 64.
[4] Plut. *de Malig.* 21.   [5] Herod. v. 30.

We hear on this occasion a glowing and somewhat marvellous account of the power and prosperity of the island;
Paros, Andros, and others of the Cyclades, are dependent on
it; it is wealthy in money and slaves, has a considerable fleet
of long vessels, and can muster 8,000 heavy-armed men, as
large a force as Athens sent to Plataea. Such a representation of power corresponds with the magnitude of the
armament, 200 vessels with a large force of Persians and
Ionians, which we read was assigned by the satrap Artaphernes for the expedition. A surprise was intended but
failed; the Naxians were found to have withdrawn, with all
their transportable property and abundant victual, within
their walls, prepared to stand a prolonged siege. They had,
in fact, received timely warning by contrivance of the Persian
commander himself, the same Megabates whom Pausanias
afterwards and as it seems in consequence mistrusted, who
had quarrelled with Aristagoras on a point of discipline and
authority in the conduct of the [1] expedition. A siege of
four months' duration consumed the funds of both the Persians and the Greek adventurers, and was then given up,
the exiles being left behind to do the best they might, with
the aid of some fortifications constructed for them.

The repulse was remembered and revenged by Datis and
Artaphernes, who on their way to Euboea and Marathon,
490 B.C., burnt the city and its temples, and carried off
as captives all who had not taken timely refuge in the
mountains. After this warning all the Cyclades except the
westernmost, Cythnus, Seriphus, Siphnus, gave earth and
water, and contributed to the fleet of Xerxes, the Parians
only holding aloof from both sides to watch the result;
Naxos was controlled by a Medising faction, but could now
only make the poor contribution of four ships, and these were
carried over to the Greeks by their commander Democritus.

---

[1] Herod. v. 34.

It is probable enough that the island nevertheless did not escape some severity when visited afterwards by the fleet of the victors.

Still it is scarcely conceivable that any treatment could have goaded the islanders into defying the power of Athens as now developed, and with all the confederation at command, unless they had encouragement to look further for support. It is scarcely to be doubted, in fact, that the ancient leaven of oligarchical Medism insensibly recovering was again at work, and that the expected aid was to come from the Persian fleet, which now after a long interval appears again reinforced and reorganised. We are thus conducted to the further inference that the plans which had been just matured by Pausanias in concert with Persia, when his treason was discovered, had been arranged to take effect by a combination at this very point.

Whatever was the offence, declared contumacy in respect of subsidies or suspected intrigue with the barbarians, Naxos was attacked by the Athenians as in revolt, besieged and ultimately taken, after what length of resistance is not stated, perhaps by surprise or [1] storm. This, says Thucydides, was the first of the allied cities that were successively reduced to subjection in contravention of compact (παρὰ τὸ καθεστηκὸς), —as if in his opinion the punishment was unfairly strained beyond the provocation—a result ensuing for the most part on refusals of assessed quotas of money or ships, or in certain instances, of crews for service. The forfeiture of autonomy by the Naxians probably involved in the same penalty the smaller of the Cyclades that had retained connection with them; and signs of eagerness on the part of Athens to make the most of a welcome opportunity may have alarmed communities who had otherwise little sympathy with Naxos.

Whatever the progress of the siege, the presence of a large

---

[1] Aristoph. *Vesp.* 354.

fleet was not required after the investment was completed ; and though Cimon may have commenced the siege, he would be at liberty during its progress to proceed in search of the Persian fleet, respecting which information had been received, and which it must be supposed the Naxians were still expecting.

The brilliant exploit that followed is thus related in the summary of [1] Thucydides. 'After this attack on Naxos, occurred the land fight and naval fight of the Athenians and allies against the Medes, at the river Eurymedon in Pamphylia, when the Athenians under command of Cimon, son of Miltiades, gained a victory in both on the same day, and captured and destroyed Phoenician triremes to the number of 200 in all.' Another authority which, if genuine as it appears to be, is still closer to the time, is a metrical inscription—of dedicated spoils, says Diodorus, but apparently sepulchral—that has come down to us in several copies with but slight variation. The double achievement is here described as the slaughter of many Medes on land, and the capture or victorious destruction of 100 Phoenician ships with their full complement of men in the open sea ($\dot{\epsilon}\nu$ $\pi\epsilon\lambda\acute{a}\gamma\epsilon\iota$).

In both these statements it will be observed that the land victory is mentioned first; this is of importance when we come to examine and compare the more detailed statements of Plutarch and Diodorus, both of which, but the latter especially, seem made up out of earlier conflicting narratives.

The original fleet of Cimon consisted of 200 Athenian triremes, constructed with all the latest improvements and most efficiently manned. To Themistocles were due the changes that had increased their speed on the one hand, and then the important qualification of handiness in evolutions, facility in turning, dependent partly on form, partly on

[1] Thuc. i. 100.

drill of the rowers, that were together essential to advantageous manœuvring in action. Cimon himself had endeavoured to combine with these a more ample accommodation for a fighting crew by a greater breadth of beam, and the addition of a certain gangway to the decks, apparently to afford passage for hoplites from one end of the vessel to the other without interfering with the [1] oarsmen. With this armament he proceeded along the coast from Ionia southward and eastward, expelling Persian garrisons wherever he found them established in the maritime cities of Caria and Lycia; some of these were purely Greek and others of mixed population, or at least bilingual, from commerce and intercourse with such surrounding alien populations, however Hellenised in manners, as the Lycian Tramilae. Every new city thus acquired for the confederacy brought in of course an addition to the φόρος—an apportioned rate of subsidy. According to Plutarch his immediate starting-place was Cnidus, on the Triopian promontory, but that the Cnidians did not now for the first time join the confederacy is proved, interestingly, as we have seen by their dedication at Delphi. The only resistance in the course of these operations that we read of as of any importance, occurred at Phaselis, a Lycian city on the western shore of the great Pamphylian gulf. The citizens were chiefly Greek, but nevertheless well content with the share of quiet and prosperity that they were in possession of under Persia, and declined either to revolt or to give reception to the fleet of Cimon. After the usual preliminary of plunder and devastation inflicted on the open country, a serious attack was at once commenced upon the fortified city. Extremities, which from the temper of Cimon on the occasion—impatient as he was for action elsewhere—would have been severe, were prevented by the intervention of the Chian allies, who had friendly relations with the city

[1] Plut. *Cim.* 12.

from of old, an interest sufficiently explained by concern in
the constant flow of commerce to and from Phoenicia, as well
as inland, which its harbour accommodated. They mollified
Cimon, and by shooting missives attached to arrows over the
walls succeeded in opening negotiations, which ended in the
wealthy Phaselitans agreeing to pay ten talents and to
commit themselves to a breach of former connections by
joining actively in the enterprise against the barbarian.
With a fleet increased by these and other allies to 250 or
300 vessels, so Diodorus contradicts himself, Cimon now
sailed direct for the mouth of the river Eurymedon, which
flowing southwards enters the sea at the head of the gulf,
where both the fleet and army of the Persians were stationed. Aryomandes, son of Gobryes, is named as chief in
command, though the fleet was under Tithraustes, a base-
born son of Xerxes, and the army under Pherendates his
nephew. Of the number of their vessels there is no account
to be relied on, they were 350 in the history of Ephorus, and
increased to 600 in later authorities; both appear to be
grossly in excess, as collated with Thucydides and the inscription, perhaps even with the notice that a squadron of
eighty Phoenician vessels was still expected.

It was the object of Cimon to force an engagement before
these could join from Cyprus, and he pressed forward to the
attack; the Persians were equally anxious to evade it and
retired into the river, but finding that conflict was unavoidable even there, were fain at last to essay a sally in considerable force. It is probable that only a proportion of
their vessels were afloat, and in any case the restricted space
put numbers at a disadvantage; in a very short time they
lost heart and made for shore in order to disembark and gain
protection of the land army. The retreating vessels that
were nearest inshore discharged their crews, but of those
behind large numbers were either captured or sunk with all
hands on board. In this instance as so many others, from

the dependence of an ancient fleet upon a camp ashore, the battle repeats many circumstances of that at Mycale, which no doubt furnished a model for emulation ; Cornelius Nepos indeed confounds one with the other. The easy victory so far only excited the enthusiasm of the Greeks, and Cimon, now encouraged by success and the spirit of his troops, disembarked his large force of hoplites and boldly attacked the army. The contest however here was vigorously sustained by the Persians, who again vindicated the courage that Herodotus credits them with in the battles in Greece ; though again it was no match for the Athenian combination of superior arms with courage and discipline. The victory of Cimon was at last decisive and crowned by that valuable reward, the capture of the Persian camp, replete as usual with riches, in addition to prisoners who were little less valuable for ransom. Plutarch agrees with the inscription as to a large capture of prisoners; Diodorus records the exaggerations — 340 ships taken and over 20,000 men slain.

This compound conflict was, according to Plutarch, the double victory by sea and on land on the self-same day which was celebrated as having a point of advantage in comparison with Salamis or with Plataea. He adds that the expected Phoenician reinforcement did not escape. Cimon had information of their rendezvous at Hydrus (? Idyrus or Cyprus), and was upon them before they had certain news of the disaster of the main force. To this occasion, if anywhere, we must assign the stratagem by which Diodorus relates that Cimon drew the enemy into the toils, approaching them in the captured vessels of their friends and with crews disguised in barbaric costume. This is, in fact, the order in which Polyaenus introduces the stratagem. Such a later engagement may have been the fight in open sea of the inscription, as distinguished from that which is localised by Thucydides at the embouchure of the Eurymedon, and with which, as so closely ensuing, it would afterwards easily and not unnaturally be confused and combined.

Diodorus garnishes his narrative of these events with a wealth of details that would be valuable indeed, but that they are hopelessly discredited by his blunders in geography and time. He places the expedition to the Eurymedon years before events that we know from Thucydides preceded it, and transfers the first battle by sea to the coast of Cyprus, as also does Frontinus, following it up with a night attack on the Persian camp by the Eurymedon, which is aided by a double delusion on the part of the barbarians, who mistaking their assailants for Pisidians fly for refuge to the falsely seeming Phoenician fleet, only to perish miserably.

He appears to have been misled in part by a false reading of a line of the inscription, which as he gives it specifies the destruction of 'multitudes of Medes,' not 'on the land' simply, as in other copies, but 'in Cyprus.' This however clears up but a small part of the confusion. Broken fragments of history may be involved amongst it, but certainly, if we make an attempt to disengage it as a merely 'tangled chain nothing impaired but all disordered,' we shall fail entirely.

Victories so gained we might expect to find followed up energetically, and Cyprus is at hand, which before and afterwards invited attempts to swell Athenian power and revenue at the expense of Persia; operations however cease here suddenly; a new danger recalls the fleet and the commander northwards, a disaster of the Strymonian colonists and the open defection of Thasos. The colony of 10,000 settlers, Athenian and foreign volunteers, represents an enterprise on an enormous scale at its commencement, and probable plans for still further extension. Pausanias reckons it as a third Athenian expedition that ranges with their mythical adventure with Iolaus to Sardinia, and their colonisation of Ionia, and we find it rated along with the vast armament with which Pericles reduced Samos, and the still vaster Syracusan expedition. The Thasians were threatened with interference in their Continental emporia and [1] mines, and not only were the Edonian Thracians ejected from Nine Ways but an advance was made inland as far as Drabescus. The effect of this boldness, however, was to alarm and unite a number of tribes, who set upon the intruders unexpectedly; a storm seems to have been taken advantage of to cover the [2] surprise, and with such success as to be fatal to nearly the entire force. Then perished Sophanes, son of Eutychides, who had deserved best of all the Athenians at Plataea, and was here in joint command with Leogrus, son of Glaucon. This crushing catastrophe raised the enthusiastic hopes of the Thasians, discontented as they were and plotting already, for the recovery of lost ground of their own. The opportunity was the more inviting, as they had already been encouraged to count upon that active sympathy at Sparta with the repression of Athens which was to develope afterwards with such momentous results. In preceding generations Sparta had won the confidence of Hellas by her readiness to interpose for the suppression of governments whose genius was absolutely opposed to her own, and the same zeal with which her oligarchy was credited in opposition to individual [3] tyranny, was now looked to with confidence as available against an arbitrary democracy that threatened still more seriously to become her enemy and rival.

The policy that Athens would apply to such an emergency was already exemplified in the case of Naxos; no failure of loyal adherence to the confederacy as Athens chose to administer it would be admitted; and an attempt to vindicate infringed liberties was to be visited by their entire forfeiture. Cimon, as might be expected, had no difficulty in defeating the Thasians at sea. He captured or destroyed their

---

[1] Thuc. i. 100.   [2] Paus. i. 29. 4.   [3] Herod. v. 92.

fleet of thirty-three [1] ships, and then, probably after a land engagement also, as Thucydides mentions battles, commenced a blockade, the usual process of reducing a strongly-fortified city ; and its three years' duration in this case argues not only the resoluteness of the besieged, but the well-furnished premeditation of the revolt.

[1] Plut. *Cim.* 14.

CHAPTER XXVIII.

IN the meantime if Persia, in consequence of this with-drawal of Cimon, was indulged with a respite from annoy-ance on the Greek frontier, her recent defeats had a reaction at the centre that filled her palaces with.discord and blood-shed, and the life and reign of Xerxes came to an end under circumstances that affected the relations of East and West for a considerable time. Three of his sons are named, of whom Darius is called the heir and still but a youth or a young man, though Hystaspes, two years younger (Ctesias), is old enough to be entrusted, according to Diodorus, with the satrapy of Bactria ; he makes, however, no further appearance by name in history, and Artaxerxes, the youngest, of an age to be referred to as a boy, is assumed as the next heir after Darius. Against the dynasty so represented, a plot is formed by an Hyrcanian, Artabanus, commander of the royal guards, himself the father of seven sons of power and ability. His immediate confederate is Spamitres (Ctesias), or Mithridates (Diodorus), his friend, and, though his relative, a eunuch, who was at the head of the domestic establishment of the palace. Possible apprehensions apart, of which hints occur in a various account of the catastrophe that was known to [1] Aristotle, there was suggestion enough for an ambitious man in the

---

[1] *Polit.* v. 8.

A a

observation of the declining energy of a self-indulgent monarch and the declining reverence for a reign that had been marked by a constantly recurring series of military disgraces, and had lost in their course so many of its most devoted supporters. In a night of horror and confusion, Xerxes was murdered in his bed, and the young Artaxerxes, roused from sleep to hear that the crime was due to the impatient ambition of his elder brother Darius, beheld him dragged forth, vainly protesting as he was taxed with guiltily simulating sleep, and hastily despatched on the spot. For seven months thereafter, Artabanus, as regent, governed so absolutely as to be admitted by [1] chronologists for that term into the series of Persian monarchs.

Even so soon he was prepared to take the last step to undisguised possession by the removal of the youthful Artaxerxes, relying especially on having secured, as he believed, the adherence of some malcontent connections of the royal house in support of his own and his sons' influence with the army.

Xerxes had been considerably indebted to Megabyzus for the recovery of Babylon, and had rewarded him not only with the golden [2] plinth—or flat cylinder according to [3] Ctesias and as represented on the Naples vase—of ten talents, with which Persian kings recompensed the accepted responsibility of bold and successful advice, but also with the hand of his daughter Amytis. The dignity of the alliance was, however, seriously qualified by the laxity of her manners; and the admonitions of Xerxes, when appealed to by the exasperated husband, had been as futile as might be expected, considering the shamelessness of his own intrigues. Even this check was removed by his death, and the brooding jealousy of the brother-in-law of Artaxerxes marked him out to Oriental sympathies as prepared for any extremity of revenge, even

---

[1] Manetho ap. Syncell. Cf. Clinton, p. 314 g.   [2] Aelian, *V. H.* xii. 62.
[3] Ctesias, p. 117.

though it ruined the dynasty that had exalted him only to
more conspicuous disgrace. Megabyzus, however, Oriental
husband as he was, was still a politician, and a politician of
insight and experience ; he could estimate at their true value
the oaths by which a double traitor professed to bind himself, and set no more on whatever he was invited to give in
exchange. On the other hand he was not himself without
military following and influence, in aid of the traditions
of loyalty and the prestige of the house of Darius, which
the misconduct of only one successor and an interval of
twenty years had by no means cancelled.   He formed a
just appreciation of the fundamental strength of character
of Artaxerxes, young as he was ; and for the rest, the risk
was great either way, and he could trust to his own courage
and promptitude to turn the balance on the side where he
cast in his fortunes.   Artaxerxes justified his confidence, and
was equal to taking part in a counterplot which, by resolutely
suspending its execution until the very moment chosen by
Artabanus for the crisis of his own, brought all the leading
conspirators within reach together.   The occasion was a
grand military muster, at which not only the Regent but
three of his sons were present,—present in arms and with
their adherents, but ignorant of the feelings with which
they were watched by an associated force.   A tumult, not
in itself surprising to many, suddenly arose in the group
around the person of Artaxerxes.   The details of the incident
of course were variously related ; it was even said that it
began by the king complaining of the tightness of his body
armour, and proposing to try on that of Artabanus, who
proceeded to divest himself (Justin), and unarmed or embarrassed in disarming was stabbed there and then by Artaxerxes himself. Artaxerxes was slightly wounded, and Megabyzus much more seriously, before the general conflict that
ensued ended in the complete suppression of the conspiracy
and the deaths of the three sons of Artabanus.   In the

investigation that followed, the particulars of the first plot came to light, and the eunuch Spamitres expiated his complicity in the murders of Xerxes and his eldest son by a death of prolonged and disgusting [1] torture.

The date of the death of Xerxes is one of the most happily certified points in the chronology of these times, and supplies a limit for the dates of several events in Greek history proper. Diodorus assigns it to the archonship of Lysitheus (July 465 B.C. to July 464 B.C.), after a reign of over twenty years. It is shown by [2] Clinton, on comparison of the canons of the Persian kings, that it would fall about the first month of that archon, and the proper accession of Artaxerxes seven months later, about February, B.C. 464.

It was, according to Plutarch, within this interval, while Artabanus was still in power, that Themistocles arrived at Susa; an assignment which is in accordance with the siege of Naxos being in progress when he passed into Asia, and with the revolt of Thasos, which was proceeding in the fourth year of King Archidamus of [3] Sparta (464 B.C.), being still later, as stated by Thucydides.

But many of the details inserted by Plutarch as to the reception and demeanour of Themistocles at the Persian court and his intercourse with Artabanus are manifestly late inventions or hopeless exaggerations, connected as they are with the untrustworthy accounts that told not only of his arrival at Susa but even of his death at Magnesia, during the life of Xerxes. The combination most in harmony with the brief note of Thucydides, is that he arrived in Asia during the power or usurpation of Artabanus, but did not reach the Persian court until after the revolution that overthrew him.

Such a gap as intervened between his disappearance from Molottis and his reception at Susa, is the very playground of

---

[1] Ctes. *Pers.*; Plut. *Artax.* ii. 16.   [2] Clinton, p. 314, note b.
[3] Plut. *Cim.* 16.

conjecture, but of curiosity also, which may be trusted to
have gathered many facts that are worth the gleaning of
history. The conclusion of his story is warning to historical criticism not to reject fairly authorised tradition, on
the mere ground of its inconsistency with antecedent probability; if such a principle sufficed to guide through the
uncertainties of the past, there need be little mystery for
us even about the future. He had known how to conciliate
the warm zeal of two young men of Lyncestis, a district
between Macedonia and Epirus, who from their engagement
in inland trade were fully acquainted with the obscure passes
and by-roads of the continent to which he might trust to
baffle the most vindictive pursuit. By aid of their untiring
guidance he made his way from sea to sea, not neglecting, as
it seems, to obtain a useful oracle at Dodona on his [1] way,
and arrived at Pydna in the Macedonian territory of Alexander, where he took passage, in a false name, on board a
merchant ship bound for the coast of Asia Minor. Stress
of weather carried the vessel direct upon Naxos, where the
Athenians were engaged on the siege, and where to run in
would have involved fatal recognition, while it would require
much to induce a Greek skipper to forego even the rest
and refreshment offered by such an opportunity, to say
nothing of shelter from really dangerous weather. Themistocles put himself at once so far in the man's power as to
declare who he was and what was his jeopardy, but appealed
to him at the same time in a manner to compel him to
the required decision. He overawed him in the first instance
by the distinct intimation, that to betray him would be
fatal to himself, as the Athenians would be given to
understand that his intention had been to assist the escape
of their enemy for a bribe; his only chance of avoiding this
catastrophe was to keep the sea at any inconvenience and
any risk, and to permit no soul to land till the voyage

[1] Plut. *Them.* 28.

could be continued. When it was quite clear that intimidation had done its work, it was time enough to clinch it by a promise of rich reward, which was afterwards honourably performed. After battling with the weather and privations for a whole day and night, the vessel resumed its course and reached Ephesus. Asia had dangers of its own for the fugitive, and he was now nearer to those who could claim, it is said, an immense reward of 200 talents proclaimed by the Persian king for the capture of his most mischievous enemy. Plutarch refers to the 'following of Ergoteles and Pythodorus,' as to men notorious and on the lookout for him; and about Cumae, the old station of the Persian fleet after Salamis, as if it were still in Persian occupation. Xenophon long [1] after finds the adjacent towns under the control of descendants of Demaratus and Gongylus, to whom the Persian had granted them in reward for treachery to Greece. He was in this neighbourhood when he moved, in disguise, inland to Aegae, where he had a host Nicogenes, a man of vast possessions in Aeolis; so vast indeed that Diodorus seems to confound him in consequence, under the name of [2] Lysitheides, with the magnificent and ill-requited host of Xerxes,— he may have been a descendant,—whose tale is told by [3] Herodotus. With resolution that astonished and alarmed his friend, he proposed to avail himself of his intimacy with Persians of position, to prosecute the plan of presenting himself at Susa; and accordingly, in company with his [4] friend, he started on the journey in a litter, which was closely curtained and jealously watched as the conveyance of an Ionian female destined for the harem of a Persian magnate. Besides hints of direct personal introductions, we have in Thucydides notes of a missive said to be addressed by him to the Great King, which reappear in Plutarch paraphrased as a [5] speech. He represents that he had strictly limited all the mischief

[1] Xen. *Hell.* iii. 1. 4.   [2] Diod. xi. 56.   [3] Herod. vii. 29–38.
[4] Thucyd. i. 137; Diod. xi. 56.   [5] Plut. *Them.* 28.

that he had wrought against his father, Xerxes, to the requirements of self-defence; and as soon as these were satisfied had seized the earliest opportunities to do him all the service in his power. He claimed a balance of gratitude as due to him for secret information at Salamis, and for his hindrance —which Thucydides takes occasion to say was none of his— of the disruption of the Hellespont bridge. It is on this same account of friendly disposition to Persia, that he has now been driven into exile; he comes prepared and able to render signal service, and only solicits the suspense of a year, that by the acquisition of the Persian language he may be enabled to do full justice to his plans.

The reception of Greek fugitives was the common policy of the Persian court, on the usual principle of all powers that seek for pretexts, or not hesitating about pretexts desire only instruments, for interfering in the politics of conterminal states with a view to ultimate conquest and appropriation. There might seem to be somewhat of barbaric hebetude in the readiness with which the subtle refugee was entertained, notwithstanding experiences of double dealing, in the cases of Histiaeus, or Aristagoras; but to a certain extent such traitors were indispensable to Persia for administration of Greek cities and districts, if they were to continue to yield the tribute that was the chief reason for holding them: and there were always abundant instances of able men who were rendering most valuable services to Persia, and proved to be quite content to advantage themselves at no greater sacrifice than desertion or even betrayal of national and party connections. His reputation for wisdom—how could it be otherwise?—was at Susa before him, and his arrival could not have been more opportune. The young king, who had himself just emerged from a sea of perils, was struck with surprise and admiration at his daring and dexterity. He seemed to hold in his hand a solution of those difficulties of dealing with the Greek frontier which had been fatal to his father, and even it may be of others that were still surrounding him at home. It is perfectly credible that, as is told, his elation found vent in unusual festivity, and even his sleep was interrupted as he broke out at midnight into exclamations, 'I have got Themistocles the [1] Athenian.'

Notwithstanding his years, Themistocles mastered the new language with incredible facility, and as readily acquiring and accommodating himself to the customs of the nation, came more than safely through all the jealousies or animosities of the palace and court. The sister of Xerxes, and aunt therefore of the king, was fain to renounce or suppress her feelings against the enemy of her sons who had perished at Salamis : he was received to greater favour than ever was Greek refugee before him ; admitted to the royal huntings, to the private amusements, and even the domestic relaxations of the king, and was taken into confidence in his most important councils. At this time, says Plutarch,— and it may well be believed after the revolutions and violence that had just passed over,—there were many innovations and changes in progress with respect to the court and the royal friends, and considerable jealousy was felt towards Themistocles on the part of men of dignity, as presuming to make free observations respecting them to the king. It was on such an occasion that the Athenian, who is characterised for us by Thucydides, was in his proper element ; and the characteristics indeed that are specified by the historian are given as explanatory of the influence that he acquired with Artaxerxes. ' For Themistocles,' he says, ' displayed most absolutely what is the force of natural endowment, and was in this respect conspicuously more than another worthy of admiration. For by native intelligence, and independently of either previous or occasional information to assist it, he formed on briefest deliberation the soundest judgment respecting

---

[1] Plut. *Them.* 28.

affairs as they occurred at the instant, and no less with respect to the future was most excellent in forecasting what was likeliest to ensue. He was capable of giving account of any business he had in hand, and did not fail of an apt judgment as to what he was without experience in; and as to a matter that was still in a state of obscurity, he, at least, foresaw what would be for the better and what for the worse. To sum the whole, by the force of his genius and by rapidity of study he was the ablest of men to decide on a sudden what was necessary to be [1]done.'

How complete were the confidence and admiration he commanded was proved by his dismissal ultimately to comparative independence, as governor of Magnesia on the Maeander, and of its district, which extended, as it surprises us to find,—but perhaps only because the Persian chose to assume so,—even to Myus, intermediate on the seaboard between revolted Miletus and adjacent Mycale. In barbaric formula, Magnesia, with its revenue of fifty talents in the year, was assigned to supply him with bread, and Myus, on a gulf abounding in fish, with condiment,—that is, with salt relish,—Lampsacus on the Hellespont with wine, for which Thucydides implies that it was more preeminently celebrated in that day than his own, scarcely a generation later,—Perkote in the same neighbourhood with bedding, and Palaeskepsis in Aeolis with wardrobe.

There would seem to have been some particular purpose in furnishing him with occasions for authoritative visits at widely separated points on the frontier. Mention occurs of some ill-feeling on the part of a Persian, Epixyes, Satrap of Upper Phrygia, abutting on these northern grants, of such rancour and so dangerous that Themistocles ascribed his escape to divine favour, and founded in acknowledgment at Magnesia a fane of Dindymene, mother of the Gods, of which he made

---

[1] Thucyd. i. 139.

his daughter Mnesiptolema priestess. On another occasion he was in peril at Sardis; in the temple of the Great Mother there he came upon a bronze figure of a maiden with a pitcher —a Kore hydrophorus—two cubits high, spoil taken from Athens, where he himself had dedicated it when he presided over the water supply, from the fines of fraudulent abstractors. His suggestion, prompted by whatever motive,—an interesting one however interpreted,—that he should be allowed to restore it, aroused indignation which he only pacified by conciliating with the aid of bribes the indirect interposition of the occupants, probably Ionian, of a Persian harem. At Magnesia he remained in wealth and dignity, amidst a numerous family. Much of his property in Greece had been saved by timely transfer to Argos, and some was even transmitted to him from Athens by his friends, in evasion of the general confiscation of all that could be attached there—still an enormous sum. Such friendship was perilous, and it is disagreeable to find on record that Epicrates the Acharnian was even put to death, and that too at the instance of Cimon, for having aided the escape of his wife and children. It would be a poor extenuation that they were regarded and retained as hostages for the dangerous exile. Political rancour of this stamp was of bad example, and bore fatal fruits at a later time, when the resentment of such an exile as Alcibiades was envenomed by the execution of his adherents and friends.

So long as Themistocles was known to survive, his life and possible action could scarcely be left out of political consideration at Athens; it is observable, however, that whatever promises he may once have held out at Susa, there is no hint or slightest indication, between his arrival there and his death, of any renewal of Persian aggressiveness, or preparation for it, against Greece. The persistence of his favour notwithstanding, would almost of necessity imply that his counsels had been given and had weight in favour of a purely defensive policy on this frontier, where attempts to recover full command of the coasts and islands were manifestly futile, unless all the consequences were to be accepted of reviving the disastrous projects of Xerxes, not to say of Darius, against Europe. Apart from such designs, which in any case demanded reconstruction of a powerful fleet, there was no better frontier for Persia after all than an interior line of Hellenic and semi-Hellenic towns contented, as we have found was the case with Phaselis, to be at peace and to pay tribute, whether through Persian or Hellenic satraps. It was by such representations that Alcibiades at a later date reconciled Tissaphernes to favouring the Athenians against the Lacedaemonians—on the ground that if they were allowed to have their way with the cities on the coast they would even help the Great King to his with the inland Greeks, and might be trusted to have no designs to penetrate [1] further.

His countrymen may be considered to have made some reparation to Themistocles, when, despite his equivocal position, they never brought themselves to credit him, whether ostracised at Argos or exiled and proscribed in Asia, with any really treasonable activity against either Athens or Hellas. His death, at the age of sixty-five, is assigned to about 460 B. C., at a time when Athens was again resuming active hostilities at Cyprus and in Egypt, and it was thought to have occurred too opportunely for his honour not to have been voluntary. Thucydides concludes for his death in course of nature, but still records the report that he destroyed himself in despair of being able to perform what he had promised to the Great King against the Greeks. Another report that he places on record at the same time, that it was by Themistocles' own command that his relatives secretly transported his bones to the soil of Attica, harmonises better with those versions of his death that ascribe it, not to inability, but to unwillingness to injure his [2] country. The

---

[1] Thuc. viii. 46.   [2] Diod. xi. 57.

story that the mode of his death was by a draught of bull's blood at a solemn sacrifice seems derived in some recondite manner from a traditional rite of his tribe of Lycomidae. Such a draught was the test of the priestess of Ge (=Gaia-Themis of the Prometheus Vinctus) at Gaius in [1] Arcadia, where it seems implied that death ensued on a false oath. Compare, however, another Persian instance, but [2]compulsory. With Aristophanes, who alludes to this form of his catastrophe, ' to die like Themistocles' is to imitate the noblest of [3]models.

That even at Magnesia he had not been inactive in his boasted faculty of making cities prosperous, is intimated by the magnificent monument raised for him by the citizens in the midst of the agora, as if to a second founder, and by the honours which were continued there to his descendants through long generations.

[1] Paus. vii. 25. 8.   [2] Herod. iii. 15, and Creuzer's note.
[3] Arist. *Equit.* 84.

CHAPTER XXIX.

THE year after the death of Xerxes—the second of the
Thasian War—brought round at midsummer (464 B. C.) the
seventy-ninth Olympic festival, and of some of its incidents
we have authentic illustrations that most happily supply certain
social characteristics which are all-important for the appreciation of the period. For two of the victors on this occasion,
Diogoras of Rhodes and Xenophon of Corinth, Pindar composed epinician odes that have come down to us entire, and
for the latter a scolion of which the fragments—all that are
left—are even more important and interesting.

Xenophon, of the noble family of Oligaethadae, gained—a
success unprecedented—the double victory of the stadium and
the pentathlon ; his father forty years before had been victor
in the foot race, and Pindar opens his ode with the proud
epithet for the family 'Thrice-Olympian-victoried.' This
instance furnishes a conspicuous example—but only one among
abundance of others in all parts of Hellas proper and even
in Sicily—of hereditary distinction in the games, in the case
of families of high social and even political importance. But
it is still more interesting as preserving intimations of the
interior characteristics of Corinth at this time, of which we
know too little ; as indeed how little do we know of the
endlessly varied characteristics of the inner life of any of the

numberless Greek cities except Athens. Corinth was always
the most influential of the Peloponnesian allies of Sparta, by
true sympathy of Dorian race, though most contrasted in
manners and pursuits; she was very soon to be the most
active of the agitators against the power of Athens—to a
very great extent in consequence of points of agreement
unfortunately diverted to irritating contact and collision.
A gleam of light is flashed for a moment by Pindar into
the deep obscurity of a busy, energetic, and luxurious social
system, and we are bound to make the most of its revelations
in the interests of history. In his two poems for the same
victories at different celebrations, two sides of Corinthian life
are presented to our view—two aspects that are in more than
Doric and Ionic contrast.

Corinth was still at this time, as of yore, aristocratic, and
in the enjoyment of the prolonged tranquillity which Pindar
was ever disposed to associate with the predominance of 'the
Best.' Justice, Order, and Peace are the characteristics that
he asserts for her under presidency of the Seasons, the Horae,
which are personified by him, as they had already been by
Hesiod, under ethical titles—Dike, Eunomia, Eirene—though
still without forfeiting their epithet of the 'many-flowered.'
To the influence of these goddesses are due the wealth of the
city, the virtues that triumph in the games, and the ingenuity
that originates novelty alike in the aesthetic and the useful
arts. The poet cites as examples of Corinthian inventiveness,
such as her citizens assert the value of in their taunts to
the stationary [1] Spartans, the dithyramb which Arion had
commenced when in favour at the Court of Periander; improvements in the harness of horses, and the decoration of the
expanded wing-like pediment—the aëtoma—of the temples
of the Gods. Thucydides credits them with the invention of
the [2] trireme. Intellectual, poetical, warlike, gymnic distinc-

---

[1] Thuc. i. 70.   [2] Ib. i. 13.

tions are all ascribed to the inspired prompting of the goddesses of all established order and beauteous development. The Seasons in their conjoint natural and ethical aspects are interchanged by the Greeks not unfrequently with the Moirai, the Fates, or are associated with them as correlative expressions of the ultimate energies of all change and movement; and it is therefore highly probable that they are to be identified with the Moirai whom Pausanias finds associated with the nature goddesses Demeter and Kore in their temple on Acrocorinthus, where the priestesses had a faculty of divination by dreams.

The usual mythical example of the qualities that are celebrated in the victor is in this case Bellerophon, son of the god of the Isthmus. It was he who invented the bridle, or rather the bit—the very condition of any effective horsemanship; which in his hands was equal to controlling even the winged Pegasus, the favourite type of Corinthian coins, with the head of Athene on the obverse; this knowledge came to him in a dream which he invited by couching near the altar of Athene—the Athene Chalinitis doubtless of the fane known to Pausanias on this spot. This mode of consulting the gods was chiefly resorted to for suggestion of cures for diseases, and hence the poet calls the bridle 'a mild medicament,' 'an equestrian philtre.' After recounting the achievements and then the fate of Bellerophon, Pindar recurs to the catalogue of victories of the family of Xenophon, and ends with a gracefully covert injunction—itself a flattery—to moderation and modesty.

But even so we should still miss the point—as it has been missed—of the parallel of Bellerophon, but for regard to indications that survive in the fragmentary scolion. From these it appears that Xenophon, like his heroic antitype, ascribed his victory to suggestions of a goddess, and like him acknowledged the favour by a sacred celebration; while that the goddess was not Athene, but Aphrodite, explains a reticence that befits Epinician dignity, though the circumstances could not but be notorious to the audience of the ode and be recognised as pointing the aptness of its allusions.

Corinth was wealthy above all through the advantage of her situation, where in closest connection between two seas she held between East and West the gates of commerce, which willingly avoided, even at the cost of some land carriage, the long and dangerous sea route round Cape [1] Malea. The influx of strangers, of mariners, of wealth on travel, of 'wayfaring licentiousness,' brought into importance in this Dorian city an institution which is not paralleled even at Athens—the attachment of vast numbers of female hierodules to the temple of Aphrodite as consecrated ministers and contributaries to her revenues. To the prayers of such a tribe to their patroness did the Corinthian State resort, and not shrink from admitting obligation for the repulse of the Mede. Their intercession and their participation at a solemn sacrifice were represented in a dedicated picture, and Simonides—the most renowned contemporary poet in this quality—furnished the elegiac inscription that has come down to us. To this goddess had Xenophon addressed himself, and now with his double Olympic crowns evinced his gratitude by a festive sacrifice, and therewith the dedicated services of one hundred of these ministrants. Pindar, who is only taking the place of Simonides, writes the scolion for the occasion; not, however, be it said, without introducing very decided expressions to the effect that, after all allowance made for those who have to accept a necessity gracefully, the task he had himself undertaken was embarrassing and incongruous enough, and craved almost equal indulgence.

These were the contingencies that, according to Strabo, explained the Greek metrical proverb,—more familiar in Horace,—that Corinth was not a city to be visited by every

---

[1] Strabo.

man. With what persistency such characteristics clung to the locality, even after the desolating Roman had passed over it, is well known from the injunctions and warnings which were most urgently demanded by Corinth [1]Christianised.

The victory of the Rhodian Diagoras at the same festival was gained in the pugilism of men; he was son, father, and grandfather of Olympian victors—his son Dorieus was even victor, as pancratiast, in three successive Olympiads. Thucydides introduces a reference to the occasion of his second victory as useful for defining a date.

Diagoras belonged to the Heracleid families that had once ruled at Rhodes with kingly power, and still retained certain political predominance. His father Damagetus is alluded to as in a leading position, and Dorieus is found in a military command in the Peloponnesian war after the island had joined the enemies of Athens. When fortune of war threw him into the power of the exasperated and seldom lenient Athenians, he owed his life—so at least it was said—as much to the admiration of his magnificent frame in presence before them as to the glory of his [2] deeds.

It is only among Dorians, as of Corinth, Rhodes, or Aegina, that we still meet with men of birth, position, and power taking this personal concernment in contests of physical strength and skill, which seems out of place at the stage of civilisation now attained by Hellas, whatever might be the case in the simplicity of antiquity, in the contests at the funeral games of Patroclus, or at the court of Alcinous. In one respect the civilisation of Homer seems even a degree more refined, for we observe that he is careful to commit to the rough hazards of the pugilism in which Diagoras excelled, only personages so utterly unimportant or secondary as Epeius and Euryalus. The prizes of this contest are the most insignificant of all—the victor has only a mule; and

---

[1] *1 Cor.* vi. 13, 20.   [2] Paus. vi. 7. 5.

in this contest alone does the poet allow sympathies to be seriously disappointed, as if in rebuke for their engagement about so coarse a conflict—the victory being given, with a certain contemptuousness, to a boaster and a bully.

Pausanias found the statue of Diagoras at Olympia, by a leading sculptor, Callicles of Megara, and with it an entire group of victors all of his family. Pindar composed for him the beautiful seventh Olympic Ode, which was afterwards seen set up in letters of gold in the temple of Athene at Lindus in Rhodes.

Although at present not only popularly, but by Herodotus as well as by Pindar, the cultured perfection of the bodily frame could be taken as presumption of all the virtues and all refinement, voices had already been raised in Greece— that of Xenophanes particularly — against the excessive glorification of athletic prowess. Training became, as on the modern race-course, too much valued for the sake of the particular contest to have regard to any purpose beyond, and the primary justification of the system fell out of view and was frustrate. Euripides, who was of such age as to have been born at Salamis sixteen years before our date, on the very day of the battle in which Aeschylus was a warrior, and for which Sophocles, as a beautiful youth, sang the pæan to the lyre, was soon to denounce the pride of the athlete in terms as sour and severe as those which were echoed afterwards by philosophers, statesmen, and [1]physicians.

---

[1] Eurip. frag. *Autolyc.*; Plato *de Rep.* iii. 410; Arist. *Pol.* viii. 3; Galen *de val. tuend.*

CHAPTER XXX.

THE brilliant victories of Cimon, the additional subsidies that he brought in from new confederates, to contribute, together with the spoils of enemies, to the riches and embellishment of the city, went far to complete an influence already fostered by his popular manners and lavish employment of his own great wealth. So it was that he threatened to ' [1] out-demagogue' his political rivals; and among those who were driven in consequence on new demagogic arts, were some who would perhaps have preferred to aid the conservation of whatever aristocratical elements the constitution still retained, might this only be done consistently with their own emergence to power. Such was especially the position of Pericles, of distinguished birth, but who as son of Xanthippus, the prosecutor of Miltiades, might find himself of necessity on the side of the opponents of his son. He was at present only gradually coming to the front, but working meanwhile influentially in the councils of a party of which he was content for a time to leave to others the ostensible and perhaps invidious guidance. It was his policy, indeed,

---

[1] Plut. *Pericles,* 9.

B b 2

even after his eminence was declared, and partly it was believed from his apprehension of the catastrophe of ostracism
which ever threatened an Athenian statesman, to work in association with others and hold himself in reserve for special
occasions.　Political management had now become more than
ever a task of delicacy and danger also.　The Athenian
demus had assumed a self-consciousness and a self-will which
made it a necessity for one who hoped to rise to political
power to reckon with it as a personal entity of special
character, having its own passions, and aims that were ever
acquiring more positive and resolute definition.　Still more
urgently than in the case of Solon did it now behove the
aspirant to legislative influence to consider what proportion
of the best he might venture to go for as possible; it was
well if he combined with administrative ability such true
political insight as to extend this proportion by the force
of his own character, and were spared the weak descent
into assentation, the lazy adoption of only so much of
the desirable as was easiest, or unprincipled furtherance of
whatever would carry most favour at the hour.

　　Cimon, on his part, seems to have trusted too much to the
power of popularity when opposed to a popular movement,
and to have been little disposed to pursue the example which
had been set by his master and colleague, Aristides, of conceding a change which had become inevitable, and so at least
gaining an opportunity to qualify if not to control it.　Encouraged by his successes and personal favour, he stood firm
on his political lines, and prepared to defend a policy which
was the reverse of popular, and a political theory that the
consequences of his own proceedings were naturally tending
to discredit.　At this very time he was engaged as a commander in promoting a change of relations between Athens
and her allies which gradually impaired the cordial understanding with Sparta which he had most at heart, and at
the same time so stimulated the pride of the demus as to

make them ever more and more restive under restrictions which he would himself have preferred rather to tighten than relax.

As fear of the barbarian declined, the confederates began to find, first the obligations and then the burdens of the assessment of Aristides, the price of their rescue and continued safety, intolerably irksome; those who were bound to personal service on shipboard, to supply crews to their own or Athenian ships, were especially recalcitrant, and became ever more unwilling to give up the ease of life on land, and the tranquil pursuit of wealth, in industries never so profitable as on a recovery of security after war. To Cimon Plutarch assigns the origination of the policy of accepting composition for personal service, first in unmanned ships and then in money payments which would always provide crews, and those more entirely under Athenian control. Crews were, in fact, taken in rotation from among the Athenians themselves, who thus with liberal pay acquired maritime habits and warlike discipline, in every way at the expense of allies who sunk unawares into the position and experienced the treatment of subjects and servants. Disputes as to the money payments before long involved state prosecutions, and compulsion which was sometimes so severely administered as to aggravate the already serious discontents. In the meantime every Athenian oarsman, every artisan in the dockyards of the Peiraeus was acquiring the self-consciousness of a unit in an imperial state; and every trireme that left the national port carried men who had risen with the extension of the[1] marine, and indulged, as the new men of new empires will and sometimes brutally, in the demeanour of superiority.

The reaction on home politics at Athens of this constantly advancing spirit of pride and independence, soon led to

---

[1] Xen. *Rep. Athen.*

agitation not merely to shake off restraints, but to share in
the immediate control of affairs and in its appropriate rewards.
The efficiency of administration might be liable to become
impaired by the changes so induced, but in this case, from
the temper of the times, even any corrective policy could
scarcely but involve a further concession to democracy. It
seems to have been a conflict on some of the questions which
were soon to induce capital constitutional changes, that first
seriously affected the position which Cimon had gained by
his liberalities as well as his services, and so rendered a
single reverse in his conduct of external politics for him
an irretrievable disaster.

Tribute and the commutations for service were already
accumulating at Athens the surplus treasure which was afterwards to supply a fund for her magnificent public monuments, and Pericles, now acting in conjunction with Ephialtes,
was the first to declare that it might be fairly drawn upon
to contribute to the enjoyments of her so well-deserving
citizens. It was apparently by the institution of the *theoricon,*
—of the payment to poorer citizens to enable them to participate in the national festivities of the Panathenaea and the
Dionysia,—that a system was commenced which had the
most important and gravest results, and in the meantime
at least countervailed the private donations of Cimon, and
probably committed him to unpopular opposition. Since
the erection of a costly stone theatre in place of earlier and
more simple accommodation, a charge of two obols had been
made for seats, which, small as it may seem, was sufficient to
shut out many on occasions when as members of the ruling
body they seemed to have every right to be present. The
periodical theatrical entertainments were a chief part of a
public celebration at a sacred Dionysiac festival: whether in
their comic or tragic manifestations, they were addressed
most immediately to the same public sympathies and interests
that agitated the political assembly, and the democratic spirit

required that the audience should be the same. A payment by the state of the admission money of the poor was in reality but a circuitous form of public subvention to the expenses of the theatre,—the condition which in modern times has too certainly proved indispensable for the prolonged maintenance of either the poetical or the musical drama at the highest standard. The poor citizens by this assistance were in effect admitted free to the theatre, on the same principle that they might participate in the sight of a costly national procession through the open streets, or in the enjoyment of public parks, or gardens, or porticoes, of which the expense had been defrayed out of either foreign tribute or the home taxation which only touched classes above them. That the multitude should be allowed such an enjoyment at a reduced cost, or even gratis, is in itself no more of an anomaly than that they should walk cost free past a noble building or through a gallery of pictures.

We are destitute of precise information as to the dates of successive extensions of this principle; but Plutarch, right or wrong, distinctly states that it furnished one of the instruments by which Pericles and Ephialtes were enabled to make head against Cimon, and the *theoricon* appears to be the example of its application which has least connection with movements that occurred after the party victory was decided. This victory was not long to be delayed, and was due at last to the collapse of Cimon's policy of a close alliance with Sparta; events were already in progress to vindicate the sagacity of those who mistrusted it all along as a delusion and a snare. The Thasians were not reduced till 463 B.C.; in the previous year, the fourth of King Archidamus, they were still sanguine of relief, on the ground, according to Thucydides, that the Spartans had distinctly promised to render it by the invasion of Attica, which it was believed would infallibly cause the siege to be raised. The tradition was still in force and was to continue for some time longer, that the delivery of one strong blow by Sparta in a short expedition in the interval of her festivals would suffice to redress a grievance and assert the respect due to her authority; even considerably later a mere threat, or certainly a demonstration of an intention to invade, was expected to constrain a reversal of Athenian policy. The relations of Sparta and Athens for still a year or two onward agree with the statement of the historian, that if not the negotiations, the results of them certainly, were very successfully kept secret.

Whatever may have been the precise form of their promise or the value of their intention now, the collision that was to come more furiously, and fatally, hereafter, was deferred by a catastrophe which gave the Spartans full occupation at home, and which, by involving them as one of its consequences in a ten years' war, within their own borders and for very existence, was to accustom them perforce to sustained efforts. Their country was wrecked by an earthquake more terrible than had ever been known, and the city of Sparta itself was the centre of the convulsion: chasms opened in the valley, vast masses were detached from the impending summits of Taygetus; of the city shaken down or overwhelmed by landslips, five houses at most were left standing,—such is the record; large numbers perished, and by one peculiarly destructive and lamentable accident a great assemblage of youths were crushed to death by the fall of the building in which they were exercising. Even in the midst of this distress and disorder, the apprehensions of the ruling class were turned to a peril which was always with them, and never more threateningly than of late since the treason of Pausanias— the helots. And with good reason: when Archidamus hastened to give the signal by trumpet that withdrew the citizens at once from all occupation in salvage of lives or goods, and they mustered instantly under arms, it was not a moment too soon; the helots were already collecting in the surrounding country, and preparing to surprise their tyrannous masters in the midst of their trouble and confusion. By the promptitude of the king they were foiled and had to retire, but it was only to commence a struggle that was to last for ten years.

The helot class were for the most part descendants of the Messenians, whom the Dorian conquest had reduced to [1] slavery; chiefly, it is possible, of the lower and inferior classes of the Messenians, who may not have enjoyed full privileges even before the conquest, while ages of studied repression since had imbruted them still further : but strength was infused into their cause by the sympathy and accession of Messenians and the perioeci of Thouriae and Anthea especially. This class enjoyed a restricted franchise in their several townships, but was subordinated in every respect to the Spartiats, and had oppressions of its own to complain of; what was most important now, they had experience and discipline from having served in the Persian war not only as light-armed but as hoplites. First or last the war, stamped with the character of a helot insurrection as it might be in origin, became a revival of the lost cause of Aristodemus, a struggle for the recovery of Messenian nationality : the old Messenian acropolis—the precipitous hill of Ithome—crowned by the temple of Zeus Ithomatas, was seized and obstinately maintained ; and later history, following Thucydides, relates the vicissitudes of the third Messenian war. The courage of the insurgents was roused and sustained by a confidence in divine support, which even the Spartans could not pretend to disallow as unnatural and unauthorised. An earthquake was the appropriate sign of the power and anger of Poseidon, the earth-shaking god of Homer, and of this god the most venerated sanctuary, at Taenaron, had been grossly violated by them in the persons of vainly suppliant helots. His severe visitation of the indignity was recognised through-

[1] Thuc. i. 101.

out Hellas, and while it roused the insurgents to enthusiasm, was not without effect in unnerving even Spartan
confidence.

To provoke the hostility of Athens at such a time was
out of the question; it was much if the secret treaty could
be kept a secret, and the Thasians in consequence were left
to their fate. In 463 B.C. they surrendered on hard conditions; their navy was given up, their walls demolished,
a large immediate payment was exacted, decided probably
by an estimate of inability to pay, without the irony, not
exclusively modern, of reference to formally calculated expenses of the war; and a future annual subsidy—now rather
a tribute—was assessed: lastly, the islanders had to cede the
mines which were the immediate origin of the dispute, and
their possessions on the mainland. Of these [1] Thucydides
mentions Galepsus and Oesyme as Thasian, and [2] Herodotus
Stryme further eastward on the coast; and Scapte Hyle,—
renowned for all time as the retirement of Thucydides in
exile,—is noted as especially valuable for productive gold
mines. Festus mentions its silver mines also, and observes the
derivation of the local name from mining. The exact situation
of Scapte Hyle, or Scaptensula of Roman writers, is uncertain;
but the influence which Thucydides speaks of as possessed by
himself in the neighbourhood of Amphipolis, implies that his
gold works were not remote from the Strymon. Another
important station on this coast was Daton, more directly
over against Thasos, and which, according to Leake, commands an eastern pass only second in importance to that
westward at Nine Ways (Amphipolis). A fragment of
[3] Strabo ascribes to it advantages of which some are perhaps
transferred in error from Nine Ways, and Eïon,—its lake,
and rivers, and docks,—made peculiarly valuable by the ship
timber available at hand, in addition to fertile plains and

---

[1] Thuc. iv. 107.   [2] Herod. vii. 108.   [3] Strabo, 331. 36.

lucrative gold mines. The expedition to the Strymon, which had come to ruin so disastrous at Drabescus, is connected by Herodotus with Daton, and probably made this its immediate base of operations in advancing inland; for it is precisely between Daton and Drabescus that were situated the mines which Philip of Macedon found afterwards so profitable, and which gave occasion to his founding his city, so celebrated in story sacred and profane, of Philippi.

It seems therefore ascertained that the Athenian scheme extended to taking possession of these mines also, and gaining command of the entire district between the Strymon and Daton, including the beautiful and fertile valley of Phyllis. The defeat at Drabescus had not only checked encroachments in this direction, but crippled, if it did not for the time defeat, the intended settlement at Ennea Hodoi; and the Athenians, disappointed by the failure of Leogrus at Daton, were in a temper to be discontented with Cimon that he had not made up for it by acquisitions in the neighbourhood of the Strymon, at the expense not merely of Thracians but of Macedonia. Whatever gains he might have brought home from the subjection of Thasos, the popular greed for mines was comparatively disappointed; it was objected to him that he had neglected an opportunity of wresting from Alexander of Macedon some metalliferous districts — the same doubtless that Herodotus speaks of as adjacent to Lake Pratinas above Nine Ways. A pretext would not be wanting if it need be waited for, were it only in imputed consequential damage by permitted if not open aid to rebels: that he had foregone such an opportunity was ascribed to his reception of bribes from the Macedonian king, and upon this very serious, and indeed [1] capital charge, he was put upon his defence. At Athens then, no less than at Lacedaemon, a grudge against even a successful commander found a convenient opening in

. Plut. *Pericles*, 10.

the accusation that he had held his hand too soon, and in ascribing the lapse, whether truly such or not, to the influence of corruption rather than of prudent moderation, or at most to the astuter diplomacy of his opponents. The recoil of this injustice was apt to be serious: no inconsiderable proportion of the Athenian demus was in after years to be detained by Nicias before Syracuse, against his own better judgment, and to a miserable catastrophe, from his conviction that most of those who were then loudest for the necessity of retirement would, at home, be clamorous in ascribing it to his acceptance of bribes from the enemy.

Pericles was at least popularly regarded as attached to the party of the accusers of Cimon, if, as Plutarch records, he was one of the publicly appointed prosecutors; but we may safely set down as a mere inference of the biographer—convicted moreover on his own showing—that he was the most violent; for Plutarch himself has a tale of the not ineffectual intercession of Elpinice, sister of Cimon, who made a personal appeal to him. She is one of the few Athenian ladies whose names come up in anecdotes of any kind, much less of public affairs. Her distinguished beauty and perhaps her own manners, along with the notorious youthful laxity of Cimon, were sufficient to set afloat the scandal, which the comedian Eupolis found amusing, that there was more than fraternal love between them: she was however only his half sister, and several examples in Greek history of the time,—an instance comes before us in the royal family of Sparta,—prove that such relationship did not preclude lawful marriage, which is one recorded version of the connection. The Thasian painter Polygnotus, whose attachment to Cimon left many traces in his art, introduced her portrait among the captive Trojan women, in the picture with which he gratuitously decorated the Poecile stoa. She was his model for Laodice, 'the most beautiful,' says Homer, 'of the daughters of Priam,' though certainly he pays the same compliment elsewhere to Cassandra; but it were hard indeed if such a compliment from an admiring painter is to be urged as even the support, much less the ground, of a disparaging imputation. Pericles set aside the appeal with a verse of rather obscure pertinence, which it is to be hoped was intended and understood as a compliment, though it scarcely sounds so.

CHAPTER XXXI.

EPHIALTES AND THE DEMOCRACY.—ATHENIANS BEFORE ITHOME.—
CIMON OSTRACISED.

B.C. 461.

THE indictment failed and Cimon was acquitted. Pericles
was more indulgent than Elpinice had perhaps anticipated
from her reception; he supported the accusers, but by a
single and that a markedly perfunctory speech. What we
read of the defence of Cimon himself seems to imply that he
had had some personal intercourse with Alexander. He
appealed to the dicasts whether it was his known way to
attach to himself wealthy foreign hosts—Ionians or Thessalians—as was the manner of others who found their recompense in services and gifts, and not rather to the simpler and
self-restrained Lacedaemonians; the riches which he valued
were spoils captured from an enemy,—their application, to
contribute to the adornment of the city. The latter reference was a proud allusion to the places of public resort, the
gardens and porticoes laid out with elegance and always open,
to which at his own instance the spoils of Mycale had been
largely devoted, which became a marked characteristic of the
city, and of such popularity that the love of frequenting them
had important influence on the habits of Athenian life, and it
may even be said on the development of Athenian philosophy.

The same fund had supplied the cost of completing the south wall of the acropolis.

Satisfied with his civic victory over his accusers, Cimon was before long again absent from Athens on an expedition of which, as of so many others during this period, no particulars remain. But the party of his opponents had not been idle during his absence, and the success with which they could avail themselves of it goes far to prove that the forbearance of Pericles in the prosecution might be due to consciousness of strength that could afford to be magnanimous. The most ardent and active promoter of change at this time was Ephialtes. Under which of the many influences that dissolve the alliances of politicians he had renounced his former connection with Cimon does not appear; the breach was certainly serious and final. He seems to have been one of the first among Athenian politicians who perceived the advantage of uninterrupted presence at the centre of political action. We [1] read how, at some time after the battle of Mycale, he sailed unmolested beyond the Chelidonian islands with a squadron of thirty ships, as Pericles on another occasion with fifty, but this is the only notice that occurs of his holding a command. He evidently united with an energetic and even passionate character the sagacity to discern at what point an old established system might be assailed not only with success, but with the best promise of a series of successes afterwards.

There is very strong presumption that the great attack of Ephialtes upon the Areopagus dates several years later; but intermediately, though at uncertain dates, very considerable reductions, probably due to his influence and exertions, had been made in the authority of the archons, the council, and other magistracies,—especially through the substitution of appointment by lot instead of by election.

---

[1] Plut. *Cim.* 13.

Plutarch asserts that the great stroke against the Areopagus had been delivered already, as if by one comprehensive change; though this will scarcely stand against counter evidence. But Cimon in any case may have recognised with clearness that unless recent legislation could be turned back upon its course, it must of necessity involve innovations even still more serious, of some of which no doubt there was already notice; and he did not flinch from a resolute attempt to stand in the gap. But it was without avail. The spirit of the time was too strong for him, and such legislation under such circumstances ever proves irreversible.

Foiled, however, in his endeavour to mould constitutional policy, he had a brilliant, though as it proved only a fallacious, gleam of success in foreign, the occasion of which seemed to arrive most opportunely. The Messenian war had now reached its third year, with seven still to come, and was taxing all the resources of the Spartans. Even though we make very considerable deduction on the score of exaggeration from the terms of Lysistrata in [1] Aristophanes, they will still be evidence for the anxiety and urgency with which Sparta appealed to the general allies, among them to Athens, for assistance: 'Know ye not how on a time the Laconian Pericleidas came hither as a suppliant of the Athenians, and sat with sallow face in his scarlet cloak at the altars, begging an army.' Of particular disasters we have but one note, and that undated, doubtless out of many and more serious. It is preserved in an anticipation of history by [2] Herodotus, in order to put on record the fate of Aeimnestus, slayer of Mardonius at Plataea. Leading 300 men in the course of this war in the plain of Stenyclerus, he was set upon by the concentrated Messenian forces and perished with his entire following. At present the difficulty of the Spartans was of a kind that had long been among their greatest. The

---

[1] Aristoph. *Lysis.* 1138.   [2] Herod. ix. 64.

insurgents were established in Ithome, of which the natural strength was aided by fortification, and defied the besiegers, who repeated their past experience of the inefficiency of their military system to cope with enemies defended by works. The fact that time was not patiently relied on to force a surrender by the failure of food, is pretty certain proof that sufficient progress had not been made in the field for the city to be fully invested; but even on account of the difficulty and tediousness of this process, it may have been thought more prudent and promising to risk a blow under whatever disadvantages at the very head of the rebellion in its chief stronghold at once.

Herodotus incidentally alludes to a victory gained by the Spartans, under the auspices of the seer Tisamenus, over the Messenians in the neighbourhood of Ithome; but he only dates it generally, as after two previous victories, over the Tegeans and Argives first, and then over the united Arcadians, and before the open quarrel with Athens and the battle of Tanagra. It is always possible that it was only by these loosely dated victories—if they are to be brought down so low—that Sparta had succeeded in checking the active sympathy with the insurgents of the three states within Peloponnesus which were always most jealous of her power; and that the severe cost of these victories, if not also of that before Ithome, accounts for the urgent supplication for Athenian aid.

The sympathies of the advocates and adversaries of a Laconizing policy at Athens were now declared in all the contrast of an open debate, in which the opposed protagonists again were Cimon and Ephialtes.• The larger confederation of entire Hellas, of Dorians and Ionians conjointly, which had triumphed at Salamis and Plataea, was still formally subsisting, notwithstanding the division of states as grouped under the several headships of Athens and Sparta, but with the cessation of conjoint action against the barbarian had been gradually sinking into ineffectiveness. Athens had had no motive for repudiating it, so long as she was unmolested in the course which it suited her to regard as consistent with it; and at most had only recognised her obligations under it, when in the revulsions of party she was found too willing to co-operate with Sparta in hunting down Themistocles. But a conflict of interests between the two great divisions of the alliance had been gradually ripening, and the time was come when one or the other might hesitate to sacrifice a separate advantage for the sake of securing what was only to be enjoyed in common. Athenians were not only conscious of views as to excluding Sparta more and more from leadership, and as to becoming most decidedly independent of her remonstrances or interference, but were well aware how much their intentions affected the pride and sympathies of Spartans. Unknown as the Thasian intrigue might be—and that it should not have got wind within two years after the surrender is extraordinary—the plain-spoken arguments of Ephialtes would not lack of cogency. 'Why should Athens furnish an army which would simply help to set on its legs again a power that was a natural rival and antagonist to Athens; better allow it to lie prostrate, and learn to abate in pride and pretension by experience of being trampled on.' There is a more generous ring about the reclamations of Cimon, which come to us through Ion of Chios, his contemporary and friend. 'Let us not be indifferent,' he said, 'to seeing Hellas becoming maimed on one side, nor consent that Athens in future should have to draw without her yoke-fellow.' It is intimated that the assembly decided to grant the prayer of Sparta rather out of deference to this sentimental patriotism than from any considerations of policy, though in truth such were not wanting of sufficient force to exert an influence even upon the popular party. To sustain Sparta was for Cimon and his friends to conserve a mainstay of the party throughout Hellas which willingly

held on to old traditions, old institutions, to the authority of
families of lofty claims to descent from mythical heroes, not
to say from demigods, and gods,—to keep up a bulwark
against the ever-advancing inroad of limitless democracy;
but support of the grand confederation was also the best
guarantee for that internal Hellenic harmony which was but
indifferently secured, and which was a condition for the prosecution even on the part of Athens alone, of attacks on the
barbarians as profitable as they were glorious, for which full
opportunities still remained on the coasts of Asia Minor, in
Cyprus and even possibly in Egypt.

Cimon was of all men in the best position to understand
what were the feelings of the allies of Athens as to their
state of semi-dependence, and to be assured that while nothing
would so much confirm the heartiness of their adherence
as the sense which the activity of Athens would convey of
their safety and the extension of their commerce being due
to continued exertions against Persia, there could be no better
check to the intrigues of the seriously discontented than
evidence that Sparta was in such cordial alliance with
Athens that no assistance would come to them from that
quarter. On the other hand, among the usual supporters of
Ephialtes and his party there were those to whom a display
of generosity, tempting enough in itself, was even more so
when, besides the gratification of pride by the exhibition
to all Greece how superior, how indispensable was the
Athenian union of dexterity and skill with courage, an
opportunity was proffered for interference in the internal
politics of Peloponnesus, and a prospect of exerting such
influence upon the course of the war as would tell very
importantly on the terms of its conclusion.

According to Aristophanes, Cimon marched with the large
auxiliary force of 4,000 hoplites; other succours are specified
incidentally of Plataeans, Aeginetans, and the [1] Mantineans.

---

[1] Thuc. i. 102; iii. 54; iv. 57; Xen. *H. G.* v. 2. 3.

who on another occasion, as we have seen, when all Arcadia was banded against Sparta, stood [1] aloof. An anecdote of his march gives welcome information as to some conflicts of parties and states about the Isthmus; his unceremonious passage through Corinthian territory was challenged in the terms, that those who knock at strange doors should not enter without the master's permission. 'Yet you Corinthians,' was the retort, 'not only omitted to knock at the doors of the Cleonaeans and Megarians, but broke them down and forced your way in in arms, considering that all things have to give way to the right of the stronger.' The feelings which are here indicated as already existing between Corinth and Megara had arrived at their state of excitement in disputes about boundaries, and were to have important results before long; the interference with Cleonaeans may have been either the cause or the consequence of assistance rendered by them to the recent aggressions of Argos. There is something unpromising at the outset, for the cordial co-operation of Dorians and Ionians, in the offhand treatment and tone thus assumed by the Athenian towards the firmest allies of those whom he was on his way to assist, if not to rescue.

The consequences in fact of a want of cordiality were soon manifested, and were very serious indeed. 'The chief motive of the Lacedaemonians,' says Thucydides, 'for calling in the Athenians was their reputation for ability in the attack of fortresses, as this was the point in which they were themselves deficient; while from the tedious prolongation of the siege of Ithome, they would fain take it by assault.' They seem to have been quite as incompetent to estimate the difficulty of the task as to execute it, and were disappointed to find that the city did not fall at once; disappointed and alarmed likewise, as they began to recognise what might be

---

[1] Herod. ix. 35.

contingent on the continued presence of such a force for an
indefinite time. The disposition of Cimon was one thing,
but that of Athenians under his command and drawn from
a community upon which he was fast losing his hold might
be and no doubt was something very different. The Lacedaemonians were startled, we are told, and it can easily be
believed, at the daring spirit of innovation which they witnessed for the first time displayed and probably paraded so
near to them, and were even apprehensive lest the mere anti-
Dorian tendencies of aliens might induce them to entertain
proposals from the besieged in Ithome at variance with the
views of those whom they came to assist. Such jealousy
in such a nation as the Spartans might be excited by the
simple ordinary demeanour of such allies as the Athenians;
and any superiority in military dash and brilliancy under
excitement of the occasion, when other allies were looking on,
might reasonably enough be felt by them as impairing their
own dignity and authority, however little it could touch their
established reputation for valour.

Their resolution was taken; Athenian assistance was being
purchased too dearly and desperately, and Cimon was dismissed abruptly enough, though with as handsome acknow-
ledgments as Spartan nature admitted, on the ground that, as
an assault was deferred, the aid of his force was in fact no
longer necessary. But other allies were still retained, and
on the return of the expedition, indignation at Athens recognised a pointed slight and was roused to the highest
pitch; there was indeed no escape from interpreting dismissal
under such circumstances as involving either an imputation of treachery, or—scarcely if at all less galling—of
incompetence for the task which had been undertaken with
such confidence.

This failure completed the reversal of Cimon's long popularity, and one more great Athenian turned upon the track

by which he had contributed to drive out another still greater
before him, and passed into exile under ostracism (401 B.C.),
doomed but for previous recall to be deprived of Athens, as
Athens to be self-deprived of him, for ten years.

END OF VOL. I.